The Social Study of Childhood

D0711756

The Social Study of Childhood

An Introduction

Sally McNamee

 macmillan education palgrave

First published 2016 by
PALGRAVE

Palgrave in the UK is an imprint of Macmillan Publishers Limited, registered in England, company number 785998, of 4 Crinan Street, London, N1 9XW.

Palgrave Macmillan in the US is a division of St Martin's Press LLC, 175 Fifth Avenue, New York, NY 10010.

Palgrave is a global imprint of the above companies and is represented throughout the world.

Palgrave® and Macmillan® are registered trademarks in the United States, the United Kingdom, Europe and other countries.

ISBN 978–0–230–30833–6 hardback
ISBN 978–0–230–30834–3 paperback

A catalogue record for this book is available from the British Library.

A catalog record for this book is available from the Library of Congress.

In memory of my parents, Jim and Dee Railton.

For my children Kate, David and Laura; and for my grandchildren Samuel and Joseph.

Contents

x | Contents

List of illustrations

Tables

Boxes

Acknowledgements

This book is dedicated to my family with thanks for their constant love and support, and to friends, colleagues, and students past and present who have encouraged me in my work. Many thanks to Kate Bacon, Sam Frankel, Alan Pomfret and Patrick Ryan. Special thanks to Brittany Coulter, former student and current friend, who was of invaluable assistance in the early and late stages of this project; and to Kerry Fast for her careful attention to detail in reading and speedy efficiency in editing the later drafts. Thanks also to King's University College at Western University, Canada, for the sabbatical leave and the generous research funding, both of which have contributed greatly to this project. I also wish to thank Lloyd Langman at Palgrave and the anonymous reviewers who have contributed to shaping this text. Julie Seymour and Allison James, you remain my mentors and my inspiration.

Childhood, Children and the Child

This textbook is aimed mainly at university undergraduates who are beginning to engage with the social study of childhood. As such, it provides an overview of the contexts within which children live their everyday lives, an orientation to childhood studies, and an overview of how the discipline developed. It is hoped that students from a variety of backgrounds will find the text useful. Learning to see childhood in a new way can be challenging for students. The dominant paradigms of developmental psychology and traditional socialization theory are so pervasive that it can be difficult to appreciate a different way of seeing what we previously thought we knew. This textbook situates itself firmly in the paradigm of the social study of childhood. It aims to present a simple and clear explanation as to why we study childhood the way that we do, and it explores the social contexts of children's lived realities through a variety of examples and discussions.

The 'new' paradigm of the social study of childhood ('new' because it is no longer quite so new, having been first discussed in the late 1980s and early 1990s) developed out of a rejection of theorizing within the disciplines of developmental psychology and sociology, in which children were nothing more than human becomings. That is to say, children were studied in so far as what they would be when they became adult; children were simply moving from dependent, non-rational childhood to mature, autonomous, rational adulthood. The introduction of the new paradigm of the social study of childhood which was formulated predominantly by British and Scandinavian academics – Allison James, Alan Prout, Chris Jenks, Jens Qvortrup, Berry Mayall, Priscilla Alderson, and Lena Alanen among others and including work by Bill Cosaro and Barrie Thorne in the USA – was at the time a radical move. Children were seen as agents, as meaning makers in their own lives rather than as passive objects of biosocial development. It created a space where children's voices could be heard on the issues that concerned them. It allowed an increasingly interdisciplinary study of the social structures and social institutions of childhood (the legal system, the family, school, and so on), and the way that those structures and institutions acted upon the child.

But further than this, it also allowed scholars to see how the child acted back on those structures and institutions.

Within the social study of childhood, we look at childhood as a concept, at children as a social group, and at the child as a competent social actor. We are interested in the discourses and representations of childhood, both current and historical, and we understand childhood to be a social and historical construction. This textbook reflects the predominance of academic interest in childhood, in that many of the scholars, and thus much of the published work available, is situated in the west, although with notable exceptions, and examples of work on childhood globally are included in the textbook. I have included examples from Canada in particular, and North America in general as the social study of childhood is still gaining ground on this continent, and academic work in this field is only beginning to be done. With the more recent development of children's geographies, many more studies are being carried out that look at childhood from a global, as well as local, perspective.

Structure of the book

Firstly, a note on terminology: the titles of the first five chapters discuss 'childhood' (in history, in theory, in law, in rights, etc.) while Chapters 5 to 10 have 'children' in the title. This reflects firstly a concern with how discourses of child*hood* come to be enacted in and through the various contexts, followed in the later chapters by an exploration of how those discourses shape child*ren*'s experiences in the home, in school, at work, in leisure, and in health, and how the individual child engages and interacts with those institutions as a social actor.

There are many ways of addressing and referring to geographical and social differences and distinctions globally – between, for example, Global North and Global South; the 'Western' and 'Eastern' world; developing world and developed world; First World and Third World. This text demonstrates some slippage between those terms. At times I discuss Western issues, at others I discuss developing world concerns. I note and appreciate the stance taken by some to shift the terminology – for example, Punch and Tisdall (2012) argue that to use the terms 'Majority world' to refer to what is traditionally understood to refer to third world or developing world and 'Minority world' to refer to what is traditionally understood to be the first world/developed world 'acknowledges that the 'majority' of population, poverty, land mass and lifestyles is located in the former, in Africa, Asia, and Latin America, and thus seeks to shift the balance of our world views that frequently privilege 'Western' and 'Northern' populations and issues' (Punch and Tisdall 2012: 241). However, in general throughout this text I am following the terminology used in the studies which I report on. Thus, I may at times use several of these signifiers.

In Chapter 1 we look at childhood over time, and begin to understand the origins of some of the discourses of childhood which are still current today. In this chapter, we begin to see childhood as a historical construction. Chapter 2 provides an overview of the ways that childhood has been studied in social theory. Beginning with a brief consideration of the origins of developmental psychology, the 'new' paradigm of childhood studies is introduced, showing how it rejected 'scientific' knowledge about children and childhood, drawing on cultural explanations of childhood instead. Childhood is described as a social/cultural construction.

Chapter 3 discusses issues in researching childhood. Drawing on the discussions in Chapters 1 and 2, this chapter is positioned to contextualize the following chapters in relation to issues around carrying out research with children. Children's rights, child participation, and the question of citizenship for children are the focus of Chapter 4. Emphasis is placed on the 1989 United Nations Convention on the Rights of the Child and how a childhood studies perspective reveals the tensions and contradictions within that convention. A comparison is made with the African Charter on the Rights and Welfare of the Child (1999). Questions to be considered in this chapter include: can children ever meaningfully participate in matters concerning them, or does the dominant discourse of developmentalism, and a consequent view of childhood as future, prevent that? Are children merely citizens-in-the-making, or can they be holders of citizenship in their present?

In Chapter 5, we look at the role of the state in relation to childhood. It is argued that for the state, childhood is futurity. The chapter contains a consideration of policy measures taken to address child poverty. We introduce a discussion of children's rights, particularly when their parents divorce or separate. A discussion of children in trouble with the law integrates issues of juvenile justice and some of the discourses of childhood introduced in Chapter 1. Here, then, childhood is positioned centrally in thinking about legal and policy issues.

Having contextualized the social study of childhood in the first four chapters, and introduced its main tenets and discussed some of the wider political issues of childhood, we explore children's everyday lives in Chapter 6, focusing on children in the family. Two very touching vignettes open the chapter, illustrating that the family is not a safe place for all children, but also clearly demonstrating the resilience of children in difficult circumstances. We are thus led to consider diversity in children's experiences of family. The chapter contains a discussion of corporal punishment in the home; a look at sibling relationships from the perspective of the child; discussions of power, control, and resistance; and a look forward to future academic work which has the potential to consider children's roles and experiences in family life in a way that prioritizes the child.

Family and school are the two main social institutions of childhood, and have long been considered the 'right' places for children. Having looked at the family in Chapter 6, in Chapter 7 we turn to consider children's experiences of school. The themes of power, control, and resistance, which are present when children describe their experience of being in school, are again discussed. The chapter also focuses on friendships, bullying, cross-cultural childhoods, the concepts of space and time, and how all of these play out in the everyday experience of the child in school.

Child agency in relation to children's work and child labour is discussed in Chapter 8. The inadequacy of the Western view of childhood as a time of freedom and play is discussed, as is the Western denial that child work or child labour does not happen here but only 'somewhere else.' The chapter highlights some of the negative consequences for children when their views are not taken into account in well intentioned efforts to remove children from the world of work. Central to this discussion are the concepts of thin and thick agency, the employment of which allow us to make visible the choices that children make in choosing work.

Chapter 9 explores children at leisure, their engagement with play and their use of electronic media. Play, rather than work, is considered (at least in the West) to be the true province of childhood, and yet it is when children play that they are, possibly more than any other time, subject to adult control. The chapter demonstrates how and why this is so.

The topic of children and health is considered in Chapter 10. Continuing the perspective of the social study of childhood, and childhood as socially constructed, this chapter looks at children's agency and competence through discussions of difference and normality in children's experiences with health and illness. Beginning with a discussion of the origins and development of institutionalized health care for children, we move on to explore children and death, child obesity, and children diagnosed with ADHD.

Chapter 11 focuses on the diversity of childhood. Framed by a discussion of the globalization of childhood and an exploration of global documents and policies for children, this chapter draws on a variety of examples to demonstrate childhood diversity, child soldiers being one example.

Throughout the book there are boxed excerpts from young people and adults about their remembered childhoods. These excerpts were collected from some of my students, colleagues and friends who willingly shared their stories. I have removed any identifying names and each contributor has signed a form which agrees to the excerpts being used in this book.

At the end of this introduction I have provided a short glossary of the key terms used within the book. At the end of each chapter there are suggestions for further reading and reflection points and suggestions for exercises. Taken as a whole, this textbook is designed to encourage students to think about childhood from the perspective of the 'new' social study of childhood: to reflect on their own, and other children's, experiences of being a child; to identify the boundaries around childhood; to acknowledge children's agency and competence; and to begin to deconstruct some of the discourses around childhood and the ways in which those discourses shape the experience of being a child. This textbook leaves little doubt that there is more to being a child than simply progressing through stages of biosocial development. When we adopt the standpoint of a childhood perspective, we begin to see how the world works for all of us – adults and children – and thus are enabled to critique the structures and social institutions of childhood and of wider society.

Glossary of key terms

Advocacy: Using a voice or acting as the voice of another (Wright and Jaffe, 2014: 3).

Agency: The capacity of the individual social actor to make choices and to impose those choices on the world.

Blank slate view: Assumes that children are born without culture. Education from 'good' adults is paramount in shaping the child into what they will become as adults.

Bullying: There are many definitions of bullying. However, the following, reproduced from www.stopbullying.gov, is probably the most commonly used: 'Bullying is unwanted, aggressive behaviour among school aged children that involves a real or perceived power imbalance. The behaviour is repeated, or has the potential to be repeated, over time.' I would qualify this definition, however, by removing the words 'school aged children' as it is clear that bullying can affect people of all ages and social situations.

Child as future: A phrase which refers to a view of the child only in terms of what it will become while ignoring its present.

Child labour: Refers to any work which interferes with the child's education and development.

Child obesity: A medical term which refers to a condition when a child is above the normal weight range and body mass index for their age and height.

Child soldiers: Children who are sometimes – but not always – forcibly recruited to serve in national or rebel armies.

Child work: Usually refers to light work which does not interfere with education or the child's development.

Children and crime: A discussion in Chapter 5 in relation to issues which come to the forefront when children are in opposition to the law. For example, children who kill.

Citizenship: A status that is given to members of a community who share those rights, responsibilities, duties and adopt those social practices that are intrinsic to belonging to and being a responsible member of that community (James and James 2012: 31).

Competence: Simply, the ability to accomplish something.

Control: Being able to influence the behaviour of others by the application or exercise of power.

Corporal Punishment: A form of discipline which includes the use of physical force applied to the body. While illegal in some countries, in others the use of corporal punishment against a child is upheld in law.

Cultural Relativism: An approach which tends to see all cultures and cultural practices as equally valid and therefore neutral in all its aspects.

Difference and normality: This phrase is often used in disability theory. Normal can mean 'average' or 'taken for granted' and in order to avoid insulting words like 'abnormal' in relation to people, the term 'difference' is preferred.

Discipline: Ensuring that the behaviour required of an individual is complied with either by force or other means.

Discourse: A set of ideas which represent a particular view of the world, or an understanding of how the world works. A discourse implies a representation of the social construct in question. Discourses are often shaped by culture, history and dynamics around power.

Disappearance of childhood: This refers to a thesis first put forward by Postman (1982) who argued that the dividing line between childhood and adulthood was being eroded because of the accessibility of TV and other leisure technologies which gave children easy access to adult content. See Chapter 9 for discussion of Postman's thesis.

Diversity: In this text, refers to the understanding that children everywhere are not the same, that is, there is no universal childhood. Alerts us to the idea that we should talk about *childhoods* rather than the singular childhood.

Embodiment: A person or a thing that exactly represents a quality or idea (from www.dictionary.cambridge.org). For example, a child is often represented as the embodiment of our ideals of innocence.

Empowerment: 'Requiring enabling conditions, capability and, above all, belief that one is capable of effecting change' (Shier, 2014: 11). According to Shier (2014), it is not possible to give empowerment to someone; people can only empower themselves.

Ethnography: The study of the way of life of a group of people, usually drawing on participant observation as the main method, over an extended period of time and where the researcher is the main instrument of data collection.

Family law: Refers to judicial proceedings related usually either to the removal of children from their homes or to issues around divorce and separation.

Family practices: 'the idea that family is something that people "do" and in doing create and recreate the idea of family' (Morgan 2011: 177).

Friendship: Being friends, sharing in a reciprocal relationship.

Globalization: The phenomenon that the world economy is on its way to becoming a single integrated system (Prout, 2005).

Informed consent: 'means that research participants have been informed about all aspects of the research: as a minimum the purpose, what is expected of them, the methods, the person or organisation carrying out the research, and how the information will be used and by whom' (Beazley et al. 2009: 373).

Leisure: In opposition to work. Commonly seen as something that adults possess, which children merely 'play.'

'Lost' childhoods: The idea that some children are not experiencing a 'proper' childhood. This notion is problematized in Chapter 10.

Media: Can refer to print, TV, Internet, and so on. Generally, a means of mass communication.

Medical and social model: While the medical model sees impairment or disability as grounded in the individual pathology, and which requires medical intervention to treat, the social model holds that individuals are disabled through the inability of society to – for example – remove barriers to equal access and to promote inclusive policies (see Chapter 10).

Moral panic: A term to refer to the fearful reaction of society when something is considered a threat to societal values and interests. Of importance is the role of the media in over-reporting a particular issue which is of concern.

Participation: 'Now widely used to describe ongoing processes, which include information-sharing and dialogue between children and adults based on mutual respect, and in which children can learn how their views and those of adults are taken into account and shape the outcome of such processes' (Committee on the Rights of the Child, General Comment No. 12).

Play: Often defined as trivial activities, without aim, purely for amusement and is seen as one of the defining characteristics of childhood.

Positivism: The assumption that through the use of the scientific method, 'truth' can be discovered.

Poverty: Absolute poverty means extreme poverty, that is, unable to have the resources for the necessities of life (Brym et al. 2005: 142), while relative poverty means understanding that you are poorer in comparison to others of your social group.

Power: At its simplest, the ability to control others (adult–child or child–child).

Puritan discourse: Not simply subscribed to by 'puritans' but a view which sees children as having the potential for evil. The adult world must therefore discipline the child in order to contain the potential for evil.

Qualitative research: Mostly in-depth, small-scale studies which aim to discover people's experiences and realities. Not looking for any 'truth' or causality.

Quantitative research: That which is concerned with 'quantity,' that is, mostly numerical, statistical analysis – large-scale questionnaire studies, for example, or laboratory experiments which look for causal relationships between variables.

Reflexivity: 'the self critical sympathetic introspection and the self-conscious analytical scrutiny of the self as researcher' (England, 1994: 82, cited in Barker and Weller 2003: 36).

Relativism: A view of different cultural practices which can be said to be 'anti-assimilationist, anti-imperialist, hostile to ethnocentrism' (Freeman 2011: 17). Often used to argue against universalism (see below).

Resistance: Used here mainly in the way that children may reluctantly respond to adult power and control.

Rights: 'Claims that are justifiable on legal or moral ground to have or obtain something, or to act in a certain way' (James and James 2012: 109).

Romantic discourse: A view of childhood as a natural, special and separate time of life. A view of children as inherently innocent, untainted by the adult world. Thus, children are to be protected from adult knowledge and experience, for example.

Siblings: People who share one or more parents. Can refer to either biological or step-siblings.

Socialization: Socialization theory is linked to the concept of the 'blank slate' as discussed in Chapter 1. Here it is assumed that children are simply empty vessels, filled by society through the child observing and modelling the behaviour of the adults around them (e.g. parents, teachers).

Space: A term drawn from geography which can have a variety of meanings – as backdrop to society; as invested with human meaning; as socially constructed. Common uses include domestic space (e.g. the home), public space (e.g. the street) and so on.

Technology: In this text, generally refers to media technology (e.g. computers) but can refer to any practical application of science.

Testing: Measuring performance in a particular area (for example, standardized testing in schools measures the performance of pupils on a standard set of tests in order to compare schools).

Thin and thick agency: Refers to the work of Klocker (2007) who discusses that children's agency can be 'thin' (where there are not many choices of action open to the child) or 'thick' (where the child is able to choose from a range of actions). See Chapter 2 for discussion.

Time: Can be defined as 'the part of existence that is measured in minutes, days, years, etc.' (www.dictionary.cambridge.org).

Universalism: In the context of this text, this refers to the understanding that all children are said to share the same experience of childhood at all times and in all places.

CHAPTER 1

Ways of Understanding Children, Childhood, and the Child Over Time

Keywords: Discourse, romantic discourse, puritan discourse, blank slate view

As Denzin (2010: 192) noted, the basic question to be considered in any analysis of childhood is 'what is a child?' The simple answer to the question is: it depends. It depends on historical, cultural and social context. It also depends on the theoretical perspective of the person who is looking at 'the child.' For example, Ehrenreich and English argue that:

> Today, a four year-old who can tie his or her shoes is impressive. In colonial times, four-year-old girls knitted stockings and mittens and could produce intricate embroidery: at age six they spun wool. A good, industrious little girl was called 'Mrs.' instead of 'Miss' in appreciation of her contribution to the family economy: she was not, strictly speaking, a child. (Ehrenreich and English 1978: 167)

The striking thing about this quotation is just how competent the child described in the quote is, in comparison to what we expect of children currently. The authors of the quotation are comparing the child of Colonial America to a child of the present day, and their statement 'she was not, strictly speaking, a child' reflects that this child's abilities seem to put her outside of our modern conception of childhood. This chapter provides an overview and exploration of central themes in the text, focusing on some of the ways in which children, childhood and the child have been conceptualized over time, across cultures, and in theoretical approaches. What follows from gaining an understanding of different points of view in relation to childhood are a set of understandings about children and the child which in turn affect how we come to situate, treat, deal with, and think about them. Ways of seeing, hearing about, or understanding can be described as 'discourses' (i.e. a set of ideas which represent a particular view of the world, or an understanding of how the world works). Throughout this text we shall explore and discuss the ways in which discourse has effects on the experience of being a child. In order to critically deconstruct a discourse we need to examine the text (or image or representation or what is being said) and identify any taken-for-granted 'truths' about childhood. We need also to look for any relationships between the discourse and power and inequality, and to look for any cultural and/or historical specifics related to the discourse(s). This is important because 'instances of discourse are understood to be potentially revealing about much broader contemporary power relations, social structures and politics (Kraftl et al., 2012: 16). It is important to note here that discourses do not simply reflect some kind of 'reality' but can – and do – frame what can be said or thought about a particular topic. It has been said that 'discourses of childhood are never simply discourses, they are and indeed have to be enacted, given practical realization and material form through the minutiae of the everyday social practices that take place between adults and children' (James and James, 2001: 32). The main discourses which shape and inform perspectives on children, childhood, and the child are introduced in this chapter. Here, then, I begin to demonstrate that childhood has not always taken the same form it does today. Over time, the concept of childhood and the experiences of children have changed. It is important to grasp this idea, as it aids in the critical understanding of childhood as historically constructed (and, as we shall see, also socially and culturally constructed).

Views of childhood in early history

This section takes a broad overview of ideas about childhood from the Classical period (i.e. Greek/Roman society) to medieval times. Prior to that time, the further back in history we go, the less documentary evidence we find which records thoughts about childhood or experiences of being a child, which may reflect the relative unimportance of childhood. It is likely that in pre-history, hunter/gatherer communities found children a burden economically as they could not hunt until older and may have restricted the mobility of the tribe. Once the agricultural-based economy was in place, then birth rates rose as now the survival of the family depended on the labour of all members of the family (Stearns 2005).

It should be borne in mind that most of what we know about childhood at this point in history is taken from the histories of the elite, and of particular note the material presented here draws on a Western history of childhood. There are no examples of histories of, for example, child slaves or servants. What is presented here is therefore a partial glimpse at childhood in history. Family life in Classical times (i.e. Greek/Roman times) was patriarchal; the father was the head of the household which consisted of not just kin but also of slaves and servants. In a hierarchical and patriarchal society, the head of the household had power of life and death over all family members. For example, as the head of the household, a father might decide at birth whether to allow the infant to live or whether to abandon or expose it. If a child was born weak or abnormal, it might be drowned or smothered at birth. Abortion, infanticide, and abandonment were early forms of family planning. Unwanted children would be left out in the open where they might die or be picked up and raised as servants or slaves. Girl infants were more likely to be victims of infanticide or abandonment than boys, although boys were also abandoned or killed if the family already had several sons (Stearns 2005). Girls were a future drain on family wealth whereas boys could contribute as they grew older. Girls, if they were allowed to remain in the household, were less likely to be well nourished or educated, and had less freedom of movement than did boys. I mention the practices of abandonment and infanticide not because they were the overriding way that these societies dealt with children but instead to highlight different ways of seeing – once again, what we expect or find abhorrent today were viewed very differently in other times and other places. Children experienced childhood in Classical society differently depending on social class and on gender – as indeed they do today. However, the experience of being a girl, a boy, a slave or a child servant was very different. Historians have commented that these practices should not be taken to mean that children were not important – children who survived were loved and protected, but it can be argued that this was mainly because of the contribution they would make to future society. This meant strict adherence to norms and roles within the society such as gender roles – 'men were born to rule and women to obey' (Seneca, in Bradley 2013: 21). The prevailing understanding of childhood at this time saw the child as something to be moulded into an adult, who progressed through the stages of infancy, boyhood, and adolescence. Children were, then, inherently impressionable and thus the selection of nurses, slaves, and servants with whom the child was surrounded, was vitally important. Children's play was seen as something natural to childhood as a means of learning and (for boys) of encouraging competition

(Bradley 2013). These views of childhood prefigure later discourses of childhood as will be shown.

Children and childhood in historical religious thought

As we saw in the earlier discussion, the practices of infanticide and abandonment of children were common in Classical times. However, with the advent of religious thought, Islam, Judaism, and Christianity all opposed these practices, with Islamic thought in particular prohibiting them. For example, Gil'Adi comments that infanticide had been widely practised in pre-Islamic Arabia, and that it may well have continued in the first centuries of Islam. While it is assumed that infanticide was more common with female children, it could and did apply to both boys and girls, especially in times of famine when infanticide was used as a form of birth control. As in the Classical period, the person deciding whether children lived or died was the father (Gil'Adi 1992: 107). The Qur'an explicitly prohibited the practice of infanticide and discrimination towards girls.

Similarly, in Christian thinking, infanticide and abandonment were frowned upon and Christianity emphasized the importance of childhood, and that children needed protection because they were the 'future faithful.' Rather than seeing children as being either an asset or a liability in economic terms, or in terms of the future contribution they might make, children had value simply by virtue of being born and raised in the Christian faith. Although Judaism, Christianity, and Islam prohibited infanticide and abandonment, it should not be assumed that it instantly ceased. Neither should it be assumed that children were of no value – documents and archaeological remains demonstrate that people did love their children. What is clear is that we can see the importance of childhood being recognized in these three religions, although that recognition carries with it a degree of ambivalence. Gil'Adi (1992) describes, in his important text on the history of childhood in Islam, the positive and negative conceptions of childhood which were present in Islamic thought – the child as representing purity and innocence but also the notion of the child as evil and full of desires and thus in need of discipline and punishment. These twin discourses of childhood are still common today. In these early concepts of childhood, whether in the Classical period or in the introduction of religious thought, says King (2013), we find 'the foundations for the modern notion of the child as a human individual worth of concern by virtue of being alive' (p 55).

BOX 1.1 Childhood in 12th–15th-century China

A mixture of Confucian thought and the establishment of paediatric medicine brought changes in the lives of children in traditional Chinese society. Confucianism charted moral and social codes of behaviour, emphasizing quietness, respect, and sincerity. Infants were thus taken better care of than previously. The introduction of paediatrics also brought a focus on raising children in healthier conditions and thus the two schools of thought together brought a new consideration of child raising (Hsiung, 2005). While this is not to say that the living conditions of Chinese children of the period were necessarily better than those in the West (again, the experience of childhood varied depending on class and gender), it does illustrate an early interest in childhood as a period of the life cycle which predates the interest demonstrated in it in the West.

Seeing childhood as no different to adulthood: Medieval Europe

What form, then, did childhood take in the Middle Ages? Again, as in the Classical period, that very much depended on class and gender. The Middle Ages was a time of widespread poverty and ill-health for the vast majority of the population. Mortality rates were high, and poor children began work at a young age. Phillippe Ariès (1962) is widely held to have been the first historian to draw our attention to childhood in history, and his work has provided an impetus to the historical, and social, study of childhood. Focusing on medieval French society, Ariès (1962: 36) contended that childhood as a separate time of life did not exist in medieval society. Children were seen as little adults, sharing the same social spaces and clothing as adults. Analysing diaries, documents and paintings of the period, Ariès wrote:

> In medieval society the idea of childhood did not exist; this is not to suggest that children were neglected, forsaken or despised. The idea of childhood is not to be confused with affection for children; it corresponds to an awareness of the particular nature of childhood [...] which distinguishes the child from the adult. (1962: 128)

Thus, once children were no longer in need of care from nurses or mothers, they belonged to adult society. Although influential, Ariès' work has been critiqued by some who have demonstrated that notions of childhood have existed in various historical moments including the medieval period. For

Ariès, however, the *boundaries* of childhood – compared to current conceptions – were fluid and childhood ended early (particularly for poor children). The dimensions of childhood, that is, the differences between children and adults, were less rigid than we currently understand them. Ariès' work not only stimulated the development of the social study of childhood but also inspired an outpouring of other historical work which focused on childhood in different historical periods. This brought attention to childhood as a field of study, and in particular gave rise to the idea that childhood is a *construction*, that is, that the ideas about what childhood is, or what it should be, change over time and for specific reasons. It allows us to see that the boundary between childhood and adulthood which we maintain in contemporary society has been constructed, rather than being something which is somehow natural and which has always existed. Thus, we can use the historical accounts of childhood as a lens through which to explore and critique our current conceptions of childhood.

Common discourses of childhood

We have already encountered some of the discourses of childhood in the above discussion. Here I want to go over the three main historical discourses common in Westernized thinking about childhood and to indicate some of the consequences for children and childhood in holding these views. This narrow focus on Western thought is important because – as shown later and throughout this text – policies and practice with children have developed out of these discourses (e.g. the 1989 UNCRC).

The puritan discourse of childhood

The puritan view of childhood is not necessarily related to the specific group of people called Puritans but has become a kind of shorthand for a discourse which sees children as inherently evil, and thus in need of discipline to keep them away from evil tendencies. Following the reformation in Europe, the radical protestants formed a particular perspective on childhood, as illustrated in the following extract from Menno Simons, who was the leader of the Mennonite faith – one of the branches of Anabaptist thought (that is, those who rejected the concept of the child as born carrying original sin, and thus reserved baptism into the faith until the child was of sufficient age and understanding to become a full member of the religious community):

> Teach, instruct, admonish, threaten, correct and chastise them, as circumstances require. Keep them from naughty, wicked children among whom

they hear and learn nothing but lying, cursing, swearing, fighting and knavery. Have them instructed in reading and writing, bring them up to habits of industry and let them learn such trades as are suitable, expedient and adapted to their age and constitution. (From the writings of Menno Simons 'The Education of Children' 1557, downloaded from http://www .mennosimons.net/ft056-education.html)

The Mennonite and other Anabaptist groups are not Puritans. However, this excerpt shows very clearly the views of the potential for evil in children. The above extract reflects the importance of raising children according to the needs of the society at the time. You should also note Simons' instruction to keep children away from 'wicked' children. The notion of the wicked or evil child draws on the belief that children have the potential for evil if not corrected in the way that Simons asserts. While Simons was a radical Protestant at a time when Europe was predominantly Catholic, the ideas expressed in his thoughts on child raising were largely shared by Christians throughout Europe. A 'godly' household was an essential requirement for order in the church and in the state. Although condemned by the Christian church, the abandonment of children was still widespread, particularly in the case of illegitimate children or those from poor families.

The English philosopher Thomas Hobbes was concerned with power and the nature of social cohesion and the social contract (that is, the legitimacy of the state over the individual) which he outlined in his book, *Leviathan*, published in 1651. Hobbes spoke of the nature of the relationship between parents and children describing it as a contract. In Hobbes's view, the child was subject to the parent (whether father or mother) not because the parent had produced the child but because the parent had let the child live. The child was in relation to the parent as a slave was to the master. Parental dominion over children entitled them to sell, kill, or abandon them as the following quote shows:

Children therefore, whether they be brought up and preserved by the father, or by the mother, or by whomsoever, are in most absolute subjection to him or her, that so bringeth them up, or preserveth them. And they may alienate them, that is, assign his or her dominion, by selling or giving them in adoption or servitude to others; or may pawn them for hostages, kill them for rebellion, or sacrifice them for peace, by the law of nature, when he or she, in his or her conscience, think it to be necessary. (from http://www.thomas-hobbes.com/works/ elements/24.html)

Children, in Hobbes's analysis, lacked reason: Hobbes saw children not necessarily as born with original sin but as beings no more valuable than beasts. Again, this discourse of, or way of seeing, childhood may seem to offend our current sensibilities, but it is important to note that at various points in time and place this version of childhood can reappear. That is, I am not suggesting that there is a progression in thinking about childhood which leads us to a more enlightened time, rather that discourses of childhood shift in and out of focus at various times and for various reasons. For example, the contemporary US TV show 'Beyond Scared Straight' takes teens at risk of – essentially – becoming 'evil' and puts them in prison with hardened inmates in order to scare them into changing their behaviour. There are elements of a puritan view of childhood here in the present (see also the discussion of the James Bulger case in Chapter 5).

Seeing children as blank slates

The Enlightenment of the 17th and 18th centuries was a period when traditional thinking about childhood was challenged. Reason, rather than faith, was promoted. This period saw a decline in the belief of original sin and the view of children as having the potential for corruption from the world and instead a growing interest in childhood as a separate time of life developed in Western philosophical thought. The philosopher Locke was an influential Enlightenment figure in this regard. According to Locke, children were not born in original sin, but children had the *potential* for evil if corrupted by bad educators. Locke's treatise 'Some Thoughts Concerning Education,' written in 1693, was essentially a how-to guide on raising an English gentleman. Locke viewed children as blank slates, or tabula rasa, therefore education (by good educators) was paramount in producing the right kind of adult: 'through education children will become rational, virtuous, contracting members of society, and exercisers of self control. They will not threaten social order' (James, Jenks and Prout 1998: 16). Of course, those children without 'good' education are doomed to become the opposite. It should be noted that at this time in the West only the wealthy, and in particular male children of the wealthy, received an education. In terms of parental approaches to child raising, Locke advised parents to deny their children their 'wants' and only supply them with what was good for them. Throughout his treatise, Locke is concerned that indulging children will negatively affect their adulthood and, more importantly, affect wider society as such children become undisciplined and uneducated adults. Some of the advice Locke provided is remarkably similar to contemporary child rearing advice, which provides an illustration of the longevity of some discourses of childhood.

Seeing the child as inherently innocent: The romantic view of childhood

In contrast to puritan and blank slate theories of children's nature, Rousseau claimed that it was not simply what children would become that was important, it was also important to consider a child *as* a child. According to Rousseau, children were innocent at birth, rather than tainted with original sin as Christian doctrine asserted. Rousseau believed that the world corrupts children, and therefore children should be protected from the world in order to maintain their childish innocence.

The context for this new philosophical interest in childhood can be partially attributed to the child rearing practices in Europe at that time. Over 100,000 babies were abandoned each year in Europe, and 95 per cent of all babies born in France to upper-class mothers were attended by a wet nurse (a woman – usually a poor one – hired to breastfeed another woman's infant). Of the babies sent out to the villages for wet nursing, 90 per cent of them died before their first birthday (Cunningham, 2005). Rousseau challenged the common upper-class childrearing practices of his day such as child abandonment, the practice of wet nursing, and tightly swaddling babies (wrapping them in strips of cloth from head to toe to restrict the movement of arms and legs). He wrote in his work *Emile*:

> These gentle mothers, having gotten rid of their babies, devote themselves gaily to the pleasures of the town. Do they know how their children are being treated in the villages? If the nurse is at all busy, the child is hung up on a nail like a bundle of clothes and is left crucified while the nurse goes leisurely about her business. All those who have been found in this position were purple in the face. Their tightly bandaged chest prevented the circulation of the blood, and it went to the head. The patient was considered very quiet because he had not strength to cry. How long a child might survive under such conditions I do not know, but it could not be long. That, I suppose, is one of the chief advantages of swaddling clothes. (Rousseau, 1979)

Rousseau went on to encourage mothers to fulfil their 'primary duty' (that is, to feed and raise their children themselves). Bearing in mind the high child mortality rate at the time it was likely that many children would not live to adulthood, therefore, said Rousseau, they should enjoy their childhood.

One of Rousseau's main contributions to the Western understanding of childhood is the idea that it is close to nature and is a time of innocence. Rousseau's ideas influenced the Romantic movement, and artists in this period began to depict childhood as a time of innocence and simplicity. Here, for the first time, childhood was clearly marked off from the rest of society as a special and separate social world (Cunningham, 2005).

While the various discourses of childhood which marked children as blank slates, or as innocent, may have been influential among the middle classes, the concept of children as bearing original sin persisted as an important trope. The Evangelical movement continued to assert the innate wickedness of children and to offer remedies for it. Discipline, not protection, was the method recommended to deal with childhood evil. Parents were advised to break the child's will, if necessary by force (Heywood, 2001). The discourse of the evil child was not swept away by Romanticism, but has endured. Indeed, the discourses of childhood that we have discussed thus far still hold sway today, and are sometimes employed concurrently: the child as evil, the child as innocent, the child as a blank slate. Such theories and conceptions of childhood surround us in our daily lives. For example, children who kill can be described as 'born evil' in the same culture that lavishes attention on the 'angelic' child.

Taking the three discourses as described above, it is possible to see consequences of such views in relation to childhood. For example, if you hold a romantic perspective on childhood (child as innocent, as naturally good) your approach is to surround the child with protection from the 'wicked' outside world. A consequence of this view might be to reinforce boundaries between childhood and adulthood in the name of protection but the effect for the child might be exclusion from wider society.

Childhood in Victorian England and in Colonial Canada

Industrialization and urbanization brought several issues to the forefront in relation to childhood. Poor working-class families moving to the growing cities for work suffered from poverty, ill health, and poor housing. In Victorian society, there were very different conceptualizations of childhood in place – childhood was, at the beginning of the Victorian era, quite ambiguous. While childhood was venerated as a time of innocence and children were seen as angelic in some sectors of society, notably by the middle classes, there were children working in cotton mills and being sent up to sweep chimneys, where they frequently got stuck and died. Children starved in the streets of the big cities, whilst other children played in their large homes – one has only to think of the fictional character Oliver Twist to see how class played out in the lives of children in early Victorian London.

Before the advent of public health, poor sanitation and bad diet meant that the mortality rate for children was high. It was expected that many children would die, and thus in the middle classes the focus was often on saving the soul of the child and preparing them for death. Images and representations of children at that time reflected this view; a sentimentality about

BOX 1.2 Childhood in Canadian history

Poverty, industrialization, and poor health and morals among children prompted the rise of many child rescue societies in industrialized nations, particularly the United Kingdom. These societies were founded not only in response to the perceived danger *to* children but also a perceived sense of danger to society *from* children. It is important to note that conflicting conceptualizations of childhood were at play in the movement to save children: the angelic child at risk (with roots in Romanticism) who needed saving and the corrupt child (with roots in Evangelicalism) who needed saving from corruption. According to both views, children needed rescue; either *angelic* childhood needed to be preserved or the vice of unsupervised *evil* children needed to be corrected.

Removing unsupervised and destitute children from the streets of England's cities to the colonies, particularly to Australia and Canada, was one way that child rescue societies addressed the threat children posed. In the late 19th century more than 6,000 British children were living in workhouses and unknown numbers of them were living on the streets of the rapidly growing towns and cities. There was a large demand for cheap labour in the colonies, and children's labour could fill this need (Parker, 2010). Demand was in fact so large that not all applications for children could be met, although large numbers of children did make the journey. Sutherland (1976: 4) reports that between 1869 and 1919, 73,000 children came from the United Kingdom to Canada. These children were 'waifs and strays' rescued from the streets and from the workhouses of England, and who found homes with farming families in the mostly rural, agricultural regions of Ontario, Quebec, and the Maritimes. The children's work made it possible for their foster parents to not merely survive but succeed. Work was also considered to be beneficial to the children themselves. In part it kept them away from idleness which was believed to breed wickedness. The old saying 'the devil makes work for idle hands' was apt in this context.

Thus work was not only necessary but was considered central to a 'good' childhood. This was based on the view that experiences in childhood affected the kind of adult the child would become. There were vestiges of the puritan view of childhood with no clear awareness of children as having an interior, emotional life. It was not until the rise of the social work profession, alongside compulsory education and a renewed middle-class interest in child rearing, that the concept of, and discourses about, childhood began to change in Canada (Sutherland, 1976).

childhood developed. Because of advances in medicine and public health, and the corresponding decline in mortality rates, representations of children shifted from the *angelic* to the *pathetic* child who needed saving (Holland, 2004). It is at this point that child-saving societies grew up which rescued children from the streets and the workplace to be raised in orphanages or sent to the colonies (as seen in the Canadian example on previous page). A whole new set of professional bodies was poised to reshape childhood.

The box on previous page describes the childhood of white settlers in early Canada. The experiences of aboriginal children at this time were quite different, although it could be said that the events which led to the devastating effects of residential schooling were drawing on the very same discourses of childhood – of childhood as blank slate, childhood as future, and so on. Aiming to promote the assimilation of First Nations children into white society, and no doubt prompted by misguided assumptions of the malleable nature of childhood, the residential school system operated from 1849 to 1996 in Canada. Children were forcibly removed from families and communities and placed into residential 'educational' institutions run by Catholic and Protestant orders. Children were not allowed to speak their native languages or visit their communities. Thousands of children were abused physically, sexually, and emotionally. Many of the children never regained contact with their family, and, stripped of their cultural identity, with no understanding of what it meant to be or to raise a child in a first nations community, social welfare problems continue to the present (Sinha, 2013).

The modern institutionalization of childhood: The schoolchild

Tracing the different conceptions of 'the child' through history, Hendrick (1997: 35) states:

> In 1800 the meaning of childhood was ambiguous and not universally in demand. By 1914 the uncertainty had been virtually resolved [...]. A recognizably 'modern' notion of childhood was in place: it was legally, legislatively, socially, medically, psychologically, educationally, and politically institutionalised.

Until the early 20th century, poor children had worked alongside adults from a young age – and in many cultural contexts, of course, they still do. During industrialization, in both Europe and North America, children worked in the new mills and factories. Poverty was extensive, and families had few options available to them for increasing family income other than to have their children in paid employment. Thus, child work was an ordinary, rational solution to the quest for survival – for example, in the late 19th century children contributed almost a third of family income in the United States (Cunningham, 2005: 88; see also Hendrick, 1997: 39). During industrialization, the early spinning machines were designed to be operated by children aged four to ten, thus reducing labour costs (Heywood, 2001). Children were a cheap, and easily replaceable, labour source for the rapidly industrializing nations. They worked long hours – sometimes from dawn until dark – which affected their health and eyesight, especially for children working in textile mills and factories.

Other predominant concerns about child labour during the Industrial Revolution were related to the moral development of child workers. Concerns for the health and morals of children (and, it must be remembered, for the future health of the nation) prompted philanthropists, child saving societies, and others to campaign for the removal of children from factories. Legislation was put in place to reduce the hours that children could work and to raise the age at which children could work; for example, the 1833 Factory Act in the United Kingdom limited the working day to 8 hours (reduced from 12 hours) for children aged 9 to 13, and no child aged under 9 was to work. There was, it should be noted, no intent to completely remove children from the labour force at this point. Their labour was simply indispensable to the manufacturing and agricultural industries and to contributing to the wealth of families and nations.

There were real concerns for the future of society at this time. The future 'stock' of the nation – that is, the working children who would become the adults of the future – was in poor health, and these children were thought to have low moral standards and thus were difficult to control. One solution to the problem was the introduction of compulsory education, which, it was thought, would provide society with a disciplined, literate, and healthy future workforce.

In the United Kingdom, by the end of the 19th century, school attendance became compulsory. The introduction of compulsory schooling was prompted by a concern to ensure that children would develop into the kind of children envisaged by an emerging new idea of childhood, that is, children as a benefit to the future state. For example, placing children in school would remove them from the negative influence of working alongside corrupt adults. The extent to which compulsory schooling influenced ideas about childhood, and childhood became institutionalized in society, cannot be underestimated.

Mass education removed children from the public world of work and the streets and was intended to produce a standard, *national* child (Hendrick, 1997). It acted as a set of disciplinary structures and practices within which the child could be socialized (Wyness, 2011). In tandem with the new sciences, particularly health and psychology, compulsory education was poised to produce the kind of child (and therefore the adult) that society needed (see also Chapter 2).

Western societies were experiencing improvements in all aspects of health care and hygiene, and the child mortality rate was declining. Therefore, the stress on childhood as 'short but holy' and the perceived need to save the soul of the child before death (Holland, 2004) was waning. It was being replaced by a concern about what children would grow up to become, and a need to prepare them appropriately for adulthood. Not only did the changing ideology effectively remove children from the public world of work, it transformed the very experience of being a child. It also meant that parents were now investing in the child, rather than the child contributing to the family economy, as Cunningham (2005) points out, and thus children became an economic liability rather than an asset.

Like Cunningham, Zelizer also discusses at length the ways in which the social value of children changed over time. Because of the implementation of compulsory education, children moved from being economic assets for families to being economically 'worthless to their parents. They [were] also expensive' (1994: 3). However, the transformation of children from economic contributors to children as economic expense paralleled a change in parents' views of children – what Zelizer (1994) calls the 'sacrilization' of children – whereby children became *economically* worthless but *emotionally* sacred to parents.

The introduction of compulsory schooling and the adoption of both romantic and blank slate discourses of childhood means that childhood had become a time of dependence – children were now wholly reliant on parents and the state. At no other point in history has the experience of being a child undergone such transformation (at least, in the industrialized West). Once ambiguous, the conceptualization of childhood now became a clear set of ideals of what childhood should be. Guided by the discourses we have described, childhood was on the brink of its modern institutionalized form.

The work of Hollos (2002) in the Pare tribe of Northern Tanzania allows us to see how a shift in the cultural conceptions of childhood, that as we have noted in this chapter happened historically with industrialization, can be seen contemporarily to be following the same pattern in Tanzania. Traditionally, families farmed their land but with increasing shortages in land available, young men were leaving the farms and moving to the city to find work and to have families. In the traditional family form, children were important in terms of the work that they could do and also in their role in honouring and continuing the lineage of the family. The importance of women in the traditional family was strongly linked to the number of children she had. Hollos found clear differences in how parents in both traditional and conjugal families related to children. In what Hollos (2002) calls the 'conjugal' family form, children were valued, not for the work that they did but as investments. Because in the city children go to school rather than work, children are seen as an expense, and thus the size of the family was limited. Asking mothers about why they had children, mothers in the traditional family form said that children bring them status and help with their work. In the conjugal form, mothers said that children bring happiness and meaning to life. The findings of this study nicely echo those of Zelizer, discussed earlier. It would seem that the shift in conceptions of childhood in Northern Tanzania is paralleling those in the West over 100 years ago.

In this brief overview of the historical construction of childhood, we have encountered discourses of childhood that have dominated in different eras of history and have been subject to historical change.

Conclusion

In this chapter, we have taken a brief look at childhood in history. Over time there have been many different approaches to childhood, but it was not until the 19th and early 20th centuries that childhood took the institutionalized form that is commonly found today in most industrialized societies. Understanding the discourses of childhood (for example, the evil child, the innocent child, child as blank slate), which have been and continue to be employed at different times for different reasons, helps us to deconstruct childhood thus demonstrating the historical construction of childhood. This chapter has demonstrated how childhood moved from the public world of work, and the paid economy, to the more private space of school and home, and thus shows that the current conception of childhood as a period of dependency on adults was created through educational, legal, and health policies which arose out of the prevailing discourses of childhood. What we begin to see is the way that discourses operate in constructing particular experiences of childhood.

Exercise and reflection points

1. Your family history of childhood: Talk to your parent and your grandparent or elderly friend about their childhood experiences. Focus on work done in and around the home, schooling, leisure time away from the home, and how much freedom they had from parental control. Reflecting on what they have told you, draw a chart to show the differences between

your parent's/grandparent's experiences of being a child and your own. Although this exercise will only give a brief and partial look at how childhood has changed over time, it is useful to see the changes that have taken place in only one or two generations – your own personal history of childhood! You will then, as you read through the chapter, perhaps be able to identify some of the discourses of childhood (see below) which we will be focusing on.

2. Look at print and online media news reports, at advertising and TV shows and gather together some contemporary examples of images and discourses of children, childhood, and child raising. Identify any of the discourses discussed in this chapter which might be contained in your examples, and reflect on what consequences of these ways of seeing childhood there might be for children.

3. What were the main issues leading up to the introduction of compulsory schooling in Victorian England and the colonies? In what ways did schooling benefit children? Are there any ways that it did not benefit them?

Further reading

Fass, P. S. (ed.) (2013) *The Routledge history of childhood in the western world*, London and New York: Routledge.

Cunningham, H. (2005) *Children and childhood in western society since 1500*, Harlow: Pearson Educational Limited.

Heywood, C. (2001) *A history of childhood*, Cambridge: Blackwell/Polity.

Ariés, P. (1962) *Centuries of childhood: A social history of family life*, New York: Knopf.

CHAPTER 2

Theories of Childhood

Keywords: Universalism, socialization, agency, competence

In Chapter 1, we saw how childhood has changed throughout history, and noted that discourses of childhood operate to shape, reinforce, reflect, and contribute to the form and experience of childhood for children. This chapter continues the deconstruction of childhood by looking at how childhood has been seen in academic theory. The focus is again on demonstrating that the ways we see, or study, children, childhood and the child have real consequences for and effects on the lived experience of being a child as well as on the social construction of childhood (James 2004). In this chapter I am overemphasizing the dissimilarity between what Wyness (2011) has called 'the dominant paradigm' (i.e. grounded in psychological developmental theory and traditional socialization theory) and the 'new' paradigm of the social study of childhood in order to show the main contrasts and differences between them, and to highlight why a new way of looking at childhood was developed. It should be noted, however, that many working from a psychological perspective are beginning to do work with children in a way that reflects and incorporates many of the ways of seeing children as found in the new paradigm (see Woodhead 1997).

The early science of psychology

Firstly, it is helpful to consider the origins of the psychological/developmental approach to childhood. The growth of academic and popular interest in the natural sciences following the Enlightenment saw the births of other disciplines such as medicine, biology, physics, geology, and chemistry. As the natural world could now be measured and predicted, attention moved to the science of the mind – what James, Jenks, and Prout have called 'the unholy alliance between the human sciences and human nature' (1998: 17). Employing similar methods to the natural sciences (experimental testing, controlled observation etc.), the early science of psychology felt that human behaviour could be predicted and measured. The evolutionist Charles Darwin is acknowledged to have been the first to apply methods of the natural world to a consideration of childhood in his observations of his own child. From his observations, he theorized that children's progress through development and towards maturation mirrored the evolutionary stages of the human species (Burman, 1994). By carefully studying how children developed and matured it was felt that the insights gathered could explain later adulthood, in order to promote progress in wider society. The Darwinian approach to child study led to the flourishing of the child study movement and the beginning of the mass measurement and observation of children and the consequent production of charts demonstrating 'normal' percentiles of child growth and development. The introduction of compulsory schooling (as discussed in Chapter 1) meant that for the first time large groups of children were readily accessible for comparative study and observation by the new science of psychology. Using the methods of the natural sciences, the child study movement positioned childhood firmly within the domain of science (Hendrick, 1997).

In the late 1800s and early 1900s, there was concern about the future stock of the nation (i.e. how children would grow up to become adults) in terms of mental and physical health and the possible effects of racial difference. Francis Galton, an academic and cousin of Darwin, drew on Darwin's work on evolutionary theory (e.g. survival of the fittest) and applied it to the social world. Social Darwinism (or eugenics – 'good breeding') refers to efforts to remove (or breed out) from society characteristics thought to be unwelcome, such as low intelligence, disability, criminality, prostitution and so on. In the belief that such character traits were inherited, the theory proposed that by preventing such afflicted individuals from having children, and passing on those characteristics, society would be healthier. Aided by the new science of mental testing, individuals were given intelligence tests (IQ tests), and these were often used as the basis for measures taken to deal with 'the problem.' In some cases, this was addressed through incarceration and in some cases the compulsory sterilization of those so afflicted, to prevent perceived unwelcome characteristics from being reproduced in a new generation (Burman, 1994). This programme was disproportionately used against people of colour, aboriginals and women.

The reason for including this example and discussion of eugenics is to demonstrate that theories are not simply 'out there' but that they can have very real effects on real children. In the case below, the effect on the child Leilani of a combination of psychological testing and theories of eugenics was devastating. Also, the example demonstrates the centrality of childhood in implementing theories about the future of societies, as does the following discussion.

BOX 2.1 Example: Leilani Muir

In Canada, several provinces ran eugenics programmes. In Alberta, the programme ran from 1928 until 1972, and it was as part of this programme that the 11-year-old child Leilani Muir was subjected to when she was placed into an institution by her abusive mother. While there, she was tested and found to have a very low IQ. She was subsequently sterilized without her knowledge at the age of 14 to prevent her from ever having children and passing on her alleged low IQ. It was not until her adulthood – when further testing revealed that her IQ was in the normal range – that she discovered the reason for her inability to have children. She successfully sued the Alberta government for damages, as did hundreds of other people who had suffered from this programme.

source: http://eugenicsarchive.ca

Using early-20th-century records from the Cleveland, Ohio area, Ryan (2011) describes the compulsory control of the poor through the burgeoning social work profession and the increase in foster care of children. In the early 20th century, Cleveland underwent a shift in the ethnic makeup of its population as immigrants from Eastern Europe and African Americans from the South began to move into the area. Frequently these immigrants and migrants lived in conditions of extensive poverty. Decisions to place a child in foster care were often made on the basis of the family's economic status, but children were also removed from the family if the parents were judged unfit to care for them (if unhygienic conditions were found in the home or if a parent abused alcohol). Ryan also noted some interesting trends in the use of IQ tests in the foster care documents he examined: African American children were often labelled inferior to other children, and it was less important that girls have high IQs than boys because girls were not expected to be in school as they were sent into domestic service. Ryan describes how African American boys were denied access to further education and pointed towards low-status jobs on the basis of their IQ scoring. Techniques such as IQ testing and foster care allowed the surveillance, control, and regulation of the poor, or what was considered the unruly section of society. The early science of psychology can, then, be seen to have been of great importance to the newly industrialized 'mass' society in terms of sorting out the 'right' kinds of people, although we can argue that some of the tools used to implement this were – to say the least – damaging to individuals.

Developmental psychology

Arguably the best-known theorist in relation to developmental psychology is Jean Piaget. Piaget was interested in how children's thinking developed with age. Basing his assertions on detailed experiments, Piaget claimed that it was not until children neared adulthood that they thought as adults. It is not the intention here to rehearse Piagetian theory in detail, as this can be found in numerous textbooks within the discipline of psychology. What is important for the purpose of this discussion is to note that developmentalism describes the child's progress to adulthood as a series of age-related steps. This paradigm posits that the developmental process unfolds naturally, and that all children go through the stages in the same order and at the same age, that is to say, childhood development is universal. Those children that do not develop according to the template are labelled deficient. Simultaneously, developmentalism serves to position children as different from, and lesser than, adults. From this perspective, children become adult by virtue of age-based progression through developmental stages. It is important to see how education became tied to developmentalism, and thus became the dominant way of thinking about childhood (Wyness, 2011). As mentioned in Chapter 1, children's labour was vital in the Industrial Revolution. However, children were part of the masses of the poor, and this extensive poverty resulted in crime and moral degeneration. Compulsory schooling was seen as one of the solutions to these problems. It was felt that children could be taught good habits and moral values through education, which was to be informed by the new scientific perspective on childhood. As Walkerdine (2009: 114) writes, 'the issue then became one of how to produce rational adults out of a mob, mass, or herd, an issue which was at the heart of concerns within a number of emerging branches of psychology.' By applying theories from the new scientific discipline of psychology, educators knew what *stage* a child should be at, and what was 'normal' for that child at different ages. Thus, the 'mass' of children could be trained to become rational adults. Certainly within education, but also outside of education, developmental psychology became the dominant way of thinking about childhood, drawing on and supported by the new child 'experts,' such as nurses, teachers, and social workers (Woodhead, 2009: 18). These new professionals soon became the authoritative voice on children. In this way, the birth of psychology as a discipline was intricately bound up with wider changes in society (Burman, 1994).

Developmental psychology is the discipline that has most often been considered the province of theorizing about childhood, so much so that most of our common-sense thinking about children is (often unconsciously) framed by the discourse of development. With its roots in both the advancement of science as a discipline in the late 19th century and in the beginnings of compulsory education, psychology was particularly well placed to describe how to raise children, and in particular how to raise *the right kind* of child. Methods used in the discipline contribute to the view of the child as different from adults. Based on a paradigm in which the child was an object of study, rather than a human subject acting in the world (Christensen and Prout, 2002), research methods employed in psychology tended to be quantitative and/or experimental, de-contextualizing the child's experience and reporting adults' interpretations of data gathered rather than the child's perspective. The importance of a scientific perspective and the need for objectivity and distance between the researcher and the researched (as reflected in the experimental method) means that we can only ever gain a partial view of the child's reality (see Chapter 3 for further details). As Alderson (2000c) has noted, seeing children as immature and incompetent produces evidence which reinforces notions of incompetence. If childhood is seen as little more than a staged progression to adulthood, children are thus seen as adults in the making, as 'becoming' adult rather than as children in the present. Additionally, the focus on what the child will become (i.e. childhood as future) reveals only part of the story. Psychology can tell us a great deal about how the mind works, but I argue that it cannot tell us everything about childhood, children, and the experience of being a child. What is required (and what follows in this text) is an approach which situates the child centrally as a being in their own right, beginning from a position from which we can see from the child's perspective. We now turn our gaze to how the children, childhood, and the child are conceptualized from the 'new' paradigm perspective.

The 'new' social study of childhood

This way of researching and theorizing childhood arose partly in a rejection of the ideas and methods used in psychological research on children and childhood, but also in a rejection of sociological perspectives. Until comparatively recently, sociology as a discipline had little to say about childhood. Even within the sociology of the family, attention was paid to adults rather than children (James, Jenks and Prout, 1998). Corsaro (2005: 6) notes that children were not only marginalized in social theory but also in society 'because of their subordinate position in societies and in theoretical conceptualisations of childhood and socialization' (see also Alanen, 1988). Children, then, appeared only in sociology as recipients of socialization ('the processes by which children adapt to and internalize society' (Corsaro, 2005: 7) by the adults around them (Turmel, 2008).

In the same way that developmental psychology saw the child as in the process of *becoming*, traditional socialization theory also looks at how the child *becomes* a functioning member of society. The sociological child is envisioned as a blank slate or 'empty vessel' which is then 'filled' by society. Reflecting sociology's early concerns with social order, socialization theory draws on a functionalist sociological perspective to answer the question of how children become the kind of adults society needs. It does this by demonstrating the ways in which 'significant others' in children's lives (parents, the school, the peer group) inculcate children with the norms of and their roles in society. For example, children learn appropriate gender roles in their culture through modelling what their parents do (Denzin 2010), or they learn which employment is appropriate for their socioeconomic status. The idea is that if all children within a society internalize the same norms and roles then society will cohere and be stable. Children who might not adhere to the norms of their society and fulfil the roles expected of them are seen as inadequately socialized, or deviant.

Socialization theory has been critiqued on several fronts. Rather than assisting in the coherence of society, it has been argued that the socialization process maintains existing inequalities and thereby becomes a mechanism of social control in that those with more cultural resources will do better than others (Corsaro, 2005: 8). Also, the socializing process appears to demand no more of children than to internalize or model what they see around them. Children are seen as passive objects of the socialization process, and their own role – or agency – in the process is ignored. To sum up, '[socialization theory] leaves out both what children are doing when others are socializing them, and when others are not. It neglects the worlds that children design by themselves for themselves. It fails to examine children's ideas and activities as their ways of being in the world' (Waksler, 1991: 21).

This gap in understanding childhood that Waksler articulates is filled by work carried out within the social study of childhood, but was certainly foreshadowed by Myra Bluebond-Langner. Bluebond-Langner's (1978) work reveals in sharp detail the part that children themselves play in their socialization. In her ethnographic study of communication and the social order in children with terminal illnesses, she shows that even though adults around the children did not discuss the children's illnesses nor their impending deaths, the children came to know what was happening. In part, they did this by socializing themselves and each other about their illnesses and prognoses. Bluebond-Langner's work stimulated the development of the social study of childhood, both in terms of the methods she used and her findings. Her work clearly shows that children are 'not simply the product of universal biological and social processes, but are active participants in their own social worlds and in those of adults' (James and James, 2004: 24).

Both developmental psychology and traditional socialization theory have positioned children as future – not yet adult, not yet rational, but on the way to adulthood. They are human *becomings* rather than human *beings*. These perspectives show little interest in children's present, but focus on the potential threat children might pose to adult society (because children are seen as inadequately developed and inadequately socialized, and therefore in need of adult guidance and intervention) (Corsaro, 2005). In these perspectives, on the one hand, childhood is nothing more than an age-related progression to adulthood through developmental stages and on the other hand, childhood is nothing more than a period of time in which children learn the appropriate norms of and roles in their society in preparation for adulthood. Also, neither perspective allows for any agency on the part of children in their own development.

The development of the social study of childhood was influenced by developments in social theory, particularly social construction theory, which moves away from seeing society as acting *on* the individual, and instead takes account of how individuals construct society through *interaction*. Rather than society existing 'out there' somewhere, it is theorized that society is built through discourse and through interaction. What appeared once to be natural can be deconstructed, and thus shown to be a social or cultural or historical construction, set in place in relation to what was considered necessary at that time or in that culture. For example, it is now inconceivable in Western societies that women were ever seen as mentally incompetent to be able to vote or to hold property. Constructions of gender which portrayed women as lesser than men, and as incompetent, have been de- and re-constructed over time. Social construction theory invites us to look at such taken-for-grantedness and to deconstruct and critique it. If substituting 'children' for 'women' in this example, what then might be the implications for childhood? In this sense, then, what we 'know' about childhood when examined historically and cross culturally, shows that our ideas, expectations, and assumptions about what 'proper' childhood is, are socially, historically and culturally located. They do not necessarily transfer to other times and settings.

The work of academics in Europe, especially in the United Kingdom and Denmark (Jenks, 1996; James and Prout, 1997; James, Jenks and Prout, 1998; Qvortrup, 1994, among others) and in the United States (Corsaro 2005, Thorne 1994) was seminal in introducing this new way of looking at childhood and at children in society. James and Prout (1997) mapped out what an emerging paradigm of the social study of childhood might look like, and argued that children were worthy of study in their own right, rather than as part of the family as had been the tendency in sociology. The new paradigm of the social study of childhood can be seen as a *paradigm shift* because it is a new way of thinking about childhood (in comparison to developmental psychology or traditional socialization theory which had up until this point dominated).

It:

- rejects a view of children as passive incompetent *becomings*
- highlights the socially constructed nature of childhood
- moves away from a conception of childhood as an age-bound developmental process
- moves away from a view of children as passive recipients of socialization
- moves toward seeing childhood as a time of competence and agency.

While some have argued against the notion of a paradigm shift (e.g. Ryan 2008), what continues to be known as the new paradigm of the social study of childhood has become very influential in the last two decades by: 1) highlighting the historical construction of childhood, noting that what childhood is or is taken to be changes over time; 2) focusing on children's *present* rather than children's *future* roles as adults (that is, children as *being* rather than *becoming*); and 3) documenting the cultural and social and historical construction of childhood. This paradigm provides a critical alternative to what we think we know about childhood (Bacon, 2012). Social construction theory allows us to see that there are multiple constructions and representations of childhood that vary between, but also within, cultures. It is therefore possible to talk about child*hoods* as well as child*hood*; as James, Jenks and Prout (1998: 125) note, use of the former draws attention to social divisions within childhood, while discussion of childhood allows us to consider the commonalities experienced by members of the social group *children*. Childhood can be seen as a social construction (which varies over time and across cultures) but also as a universal characteristic (e.g. as a period of life) (Wells, 2009). It is possible to see childhood as both a social phenomenon and as it is experienced by children (James and James, 2004: 213). The value in this view is that it allows us to see children's contributions to society, as well as how society shapes childhood (Mayall 2013).

Seeing children as possessing agency, or children as social actors

In the social study of childhood, children are conceptualized as competent social actors, or as beings possessing agency. In its simplest, it could be said that agency means the capacity to make choices, and to impose those choices on the world, or 'the capacity of individuals to act independently' (James and James 2012: 3). An interesting distinction between social actors and social agents is addressed by Seymour (2015) in relation to childhood and spatiality. Drawing on the work of Mayall (2002) Seymour describes that the child as actor refers to someone who participates in social life; while the child as agent is someone whose participation makes a difference in social life. Through interactions, children as a generational group (see below) can thus contribute to structural change (Seymour, 2015: 148). The understanding that children are competent social actors is central to the ideas of the social study of childhood, and illustrates the difference in the 'new' way of looking at childhood from the perspectives of developmental psychology and traditional socialization theory. As James and James (2004: 25) write, 'if children were *not* agents and were simply passive beings, at the mercy of some social and developmental trajectory over which they had little control, then the "need" for...forms of ideological control and social intervention would disappear.' As this textbook illustrates, the boundaries visible when social intervention is deemed necessary, and the controls and interventions which children are subject to have not disappeared, indeed they might be said to have been strengthened.

Since the introduction of the social study of childhood more than two decades ago, numerous examples of children acting as social agents in various contexts – home, school, work, the environment – have been generated. More recently scholars have begun to question how far this takes us, and whether we can argue that in fact all children can in all contexts freely exercise their agency. This point is taken up in the following chapters. However by way of prefacing this discussion, some of the more recent qualifications about child agency will be introduced here. Klocker's (2007) discussion of *thin* and *thick* agency is helpful in this regard. Klocker demonstrates that even in situations where children have very little agency in terms of making decisions about their lives, they are still able to exercise agency. It might be *thinned* by structures such as gender and ethnicity, and Klocker highlights that the agency of children is not unfettered (indeed, neither is the agency of adults). But it is still possible for children to demonstrate that they are agentic beings – even though at times their agency might be expressed only thinly, or even negatively, in the form of acts of resistance to adult control. Klocker studied child domestic workers in Tanzania and the context and extent of children's agency in relation to their work. The children she studied were asked to rank themselves among those who made the decisions in their lives. The majority of children positioned themselves at only fourth, fifth, or sixth, with their elders ranking higher, having power over children's decision making.

In Tanzanian society, Klocker informs us, boys are privileged over girls in terms of education. This is evident in that any available money that families have often goes to pay for the education of boys. In this culture, educating girls is seen as pointless as their future husbands will provide for them. Along with the lack of education, there are many factors which structure the young girls' choices, such as gendered social practices (e.g. genital mutilation), poverty, and an absence of opportunities, thus resulting in a 'thinning' of their agency, that is to say, their ability to make choices is extremely limited. In terms of tribal background, Tanzanian employers prefer girls from a particular tribe as they are said to be hardworking and submissive. All that having been said, Klocker notes that the girls *are* making a choice to become child domestic workers and exercising their agency, however thin this agency might be. Klocker (2007: 92) writes, 'this research with Tanzanian child domestic workers has led me to the conclusion that Tanzanian girls do not enter child domestic work (or stay in it) because they are weak or ignorant, they do so because they honestly believe that this decision will produce the best possible outcome for themselves and their families – it is a coping strategy, an active and "rational" response in the face of a crisis of social reproduction which characterizes their life worlds.' Klocker's work is important in the theorizing of children's agency. We can see, by using her concepts of *thin* and *thick* agency, how even those children who are the most constrained are still able to exercise choice and how structural conditions affect the experience of childhood. For example, Solberg (1997: 127) points out that while children may not hold much power within the family compared with the adults, they do not simply passively adapt to what parents say and do, but they can and do negotiate with parents (see Chapter 6; see also Mayall, 2002). Agency is, therefore, contextually mediated and can perhaps best be seen as on a continuum, from no agency to public agency (Robson, Bell and Klocker 2007: 144, see the exercise at the end of this chapter). As Tisdall and Punch (2012) state in relation to children's agency, 'there is still space to consider the limiting contexts where that may not be possible, or the circumstances in which children's agency is perceived as negative, challenging or problematic' (2012: 258). The articulation of thin and thick agency is important in seeing when and where those limiting contexts are situated.

Ways of exploring childhood, children and the child from the perspective of the social study of childhood

Childhood as structure

Qvortrup (1994) bases his perspective on childhood as social structure on three assumptions: that childhood is a particular structural form; that childhood is exposed to the same societal forces as adulthood; and that children themselves are co-constructors of childhood and of society (in James, Jenks and Prout, 1998: 32; Corsaro, 2005). While individual children do not (of course) remain children, but eventually become adults, neither do adults remain in the same state but age and grow old, entering another category of social life. There are an ever-changing number of individual adults, children, or elderly persons making up the categories *adult, child* or *elderly*, but that they age out of a social category does not mean the category itself no longer exists. Therefore, while the people who make up the structural category *child* are always changing, *childhood as a period of life is constant*. In this sense, we can regard *childhood* as a permanent structure in society. As Jenks (2009: 100) states, childhood is 'relatively stable and wholly predictable in its structure but by definition only fleeting in its particular membership.' Of course, Jenks's statement can just as easily be applied to adulthood. Envisioning childhood as structure means that we can move away from a focus on the individual (for example, using personality and behavioural studies in psychology to understand children), and we can remove the focus on the futurity of childhood (children as *becoming*). Instead, we can look at childhood as an ever-present structural form in all societies and can thus look at historical changes, cultural patterns, and differing constructions of it.

Childhood as a generational concept

The concept of generation as a tool in analysing children's position in society was developed by Mayall (2002) and Alanen and Mayall (2001). These authors drew on feminist theory that posits that women's structural positioning in society is a result of patriarchy, or the male domination of society. When it comes to childhood, a generational approach allows us to see children's structural positioning in society as the result of generation, or the adult domination of society. What is useful in this approach is that it does not separate the two categories *child* and *adult*, but sees them as *relational*. The generational approach looks at relations between children and adults in any social setting, enabling us to see the way in which childhood is constructed on four levels: 1) in transactions and interactions between children and adults; 2) in group transactions, for example between teachers and pupils; 3) in the individual relations between people born at different points in history; and 4) in social policies (Mayall 2002: 35).

This allows us to see continuity and change in childhood in terms of generational relations. As Woodhead (2009: 24) states, 'children develop largely through their relationships with adults; they become adults and their status as children is defined in part by reference to largely adult defined expectations of maturity and immaturity.' Thus, we cannot usefully consider childhood without also considering its relationship to adulthood.

Geography and childhood studies

Following the development of the social study of childhood, geographers have joined the critique of developmentalism and socialization theory, and put forward a mass of literature affirming the competence and agency of children in relation to the structures and opportunities of space and place. In particular social geography has contributed to the social study of childhood, and the importance of this subdiscipline is evidenced in the establishment of a new journal, *Children's Geographies*, which published its first volume in 2003, and continues to publish four issues a year. Acknowledging the social study of childhood, and the focus on children as social actors, and drawing on the scholarship within that paradigm, the journal provides a multidisciplinary approach to 'how place and space matter' in children's lives (Matthews, 2003: 4).

Social geography is concerned with how difference and inequality are experienced by individuals, and how they are used globally to organize societies (Del Casino, 2009: 25). Social geography is ideally situated to enhance the existing volume of work because of its focus on non-Western societies. It is able to demonstrate the myriad local constructions and conceptions of childhood that exist, clearly showing that childhood is not a universal concept, but rather, is culturally and historically diverse, while also showing how *global* realities affect childhood (Holloway and Valentine, 2000). For example, geographers have shown how global policies for children play out in the local everyday lives of street children, or children who care for their families. The value of a geographic perspective on children as agents is compelling: as Seymour points out '[...] where some children remain static in the family home well into adulthood and others are in positions of forced migration, a spatial focus provides an appropriate heuristic lens to interrogate [...] the limits of their individual agency' (2015: 159). Social geographers have also been able to mount a critique of development agencies, demonstrating the dominance of Western ideologies of childhood and how they come to be exported to non-Western contexts (see Chapter 11).

Socialization theory reconsidered

Allison James (2013) has recently published a text which re-engages socialization theory (described and critiqued above). What, she asks, can children tell us about being a child and about their experiences of the process of growing up? How should we see children's active participation in the socialization process? To begin to answer this, James draws on newer theorizing about family, in particular the work of Smart (2007) on 'personal lives.' Smart's work focuses on the networks and connections between people rather than seeing family as a *thing* (see also Morgan, 2011b). In the same way, writes James, children are never just children, but they are born into networks of connections (for example, they could be grandchildren, cousins, children of a particular social class, children who share a disability). Thus, they have personal lives, which, as social actors, they can reflect on and incorporate into their own biographies. Children's lives are embodied, and children experience the social structures and institutions of childhood through diverse interactions. Using a child-centred perspective on socialization, we can see it at work in the ordinary, everyday lives of children (James, 2013: 18). By looking at children's involvement in family practices (Smart 2007; Morgan, 2011b; see also Chapter 6), and in a variety of other contexts, we gain a more nuanced understanding of the socialization process – the social context within which children as actors live their lives in interaction with others. This approach has the potential to not just make visible the social lives of children, but also to develop social theory in relation to children and families.

A new wave of childhood studies?

A more recent focus in the social study of childhood is a move away from the extreme social construction position and a cross-fertilization with biological/ neurological studies of children's development. Focusing on childhood as socially constructed, it is felt, ignores that children are also biological. They are not constructed beings but embodied ones, that is to say, they are children with material bodies who interact with the social world (Wells, 2009: 14). As such, childhood cannot be separated from the lived experience of being a child (Jenks, 2009; see also James and James, 2004).

Academics tend to position their disciplinary boundaries along binary dichotomies, which much of the social study of childhood has done (children as *beings* versus children as *becomings*; the social study of childhood versus developmental psychology). This does not advance the field of study (see, for example, Prout, 2005; Uprichard, 2008; Lee and Motzkau, 2011). Uprichard (2008) argues that discourses of the child as either *being* or *becoming* should be seen as complementary, rather than conflicting, discourses. Seeing the child as *becoming*, she says, implies children's lack of competency until they reach rational adulthood. In the same way, seeing the child as *being* also reinforces that children are different from adults. Both children and adults can be competent at some times and incompetent at others, depending on the context.

In his book *The Future of Childhood*, Alan Prout (2005) revisits the social study of childhood that he and Allison James first introduced (James and Prout, 1997). He acknowledges that the paradigm of the new sociology of childhood was constructed in the context of the social theories that were current at the time (notably social construction theory and feminism), and therefore reproduces the then current sociological dichotomies:

nature/culture
structure/agency
individual/society
being/becoming

He claims that the study of childhood is troubled, has to move away from such oppositional dichotomies. He argues that the social construction theory he and James initially envisioned overstated the case, and left scholars unable to deal with childhood as both nature *and* culture. Instead he proposes that childhood is a hybrid of the two.

Lee and Motzkau (2011) reject Prout's (2005) notion of hybridity because it does not provide a useful 'map' by which to carry out research. They contend that it is in the 'multiplicities' of childhoods that the traditional dichotomies which keep the social and the biological separate can be overcome. They illustrate their point with reference to the 'mosquito' device. It emits a high frequency electronic signal only audible to children and young people. This device is commonly used to deter teens from gathering in public spaces, and is installed in such places as outside of a corner store to stop young people 'hanging around.' But as the frequency is inaudible to adults, it does not inconvenience them. As this example shows, *the technical* (the device) intersects with childhood as *biological* (those who employ the device depend on the different developmental stages between children's auditory systems and those of adults) and as *social* (using the high frequency sound to control the behaviour of young people reveals that childhood is seen as a period of potential deviance). The views expressed in this section have been characterized as setting out the foundation of a *new wave* of childhood studies. It remains to be seen how researchers and theorists may go on to develop the arguments of this new wave.

Conclusion

What this chapter has done is to introduce students to a broad picture of how childhood has been studied and to emphasize that the perspective or lens through which we view (and research) it has implications for how we as a society conceptualize childhood and for the way that children experience it. Central themes have emerged: a view of children as *beings* versus *becomings*; children as actors versus children as acted upon by structures; childhood as varied in time and space; childhood as a social construction versus childhood as biologically determined; and childhood as a universal category versus childhoods as diverse. This textbook is situated within the social study of childhood paradigm, with a commitment to take seriously children's voices and experiences, and to analyse how society acts on children and childhood and how children act back on society. These themes will be expanded upon in the following chapters through the use of examples as we continue to explore the social study of childhood. In particular this textbook takes into account the role that children have in shaping their worlds. The following chapter applies some of the issues raised here in relation to research on childhood and with children.

Exercise and reflection points

1. Think of examples in your own childhood which could illustrate each of the degrees of agency in Table 2.1.

Table 2.1 Degrees of agency

Degree of agency	No agency	Little agency	'Secret' agency	'Public' agency
Explanation	Forced to act against one's will; unable to make choices	Acting out of necessity; with little choice	Resistance to adult control	Openly demonstrating agency
Example				

Adapted from Robson, Bell, and Klocker 2007: 144

2. In what ways has developmental psychology been of benefit to children? In what ways might it have been to the detriment of the study of childhood?
3. How might structural, generational and geographic or new wave approaches help us analyse childhood? What can each of them tell us about children's everyday lives?

Further reading

James, A. and Prout, A. (eds.) (1997) *Constructing and reconstructing childhood: Contemporary issues in the sociological study of childhood*, London: Falmer Press.

Qvortrup, J., Corsaro, W. A. and Honig, M. (2011) *The Palgrave handbook of childhood studies*, New York: Palgrave Macmillan.

Jenks, C. (1996) *Childhood*, London: Routledge.

James, A., Jenks, C. and Prout, A. (1998) *Theorizing childhood*, London: Polity.

Montgomery, H. (2009) *An introduction to childhood: Anthropological perspectives on children's lives*, Sussex: Wiley-Blackwell.

CHAPTER 3

Issues in Researching Childhood

Keywords: Qualitative, quantitative, informed consent, ethnography, positivism, reflexivity

Until comparatively recently a focus on children and childhood was lacking in traditional sociology, and research *on* children was primarily carried out in the discipline of psychology, thus, research which produced knowledge about childhood was generally based on a paradigm in which the child was an object of study, rather than a human subject acting in the world (Christensen and Prout, 2002). Methods employed tended to be quantitative and/or experimental, reporting adults' interpretations of data gathered rather than children's interpretations and meanings. Within the psychological paradigm, research often focused on mapping developmental stages by which children progressed via age stages to competent adulthood. Within sociology, research was based in family studies, and tended to focus on parents rather than children. This explains to a large extent why psychological explanations of what childhood is came to dominate. Beginning with the introduction of the social study of childhood, research has taken a different focus: moving from research *on* children to research *with,* and increasingly to an interest in facilitating research *by* children.

In the move away from previous discourses on childhood, and in line with a focus on children as worthy of study in their own right, the development of child-friendly methods to facilitate hearing and representing the voice of the child took place in large part as a move to doing research *with* rather than *on* children. Such methods include drawing, photography, telling stories, keeping diaries, producing vignettes, PRA methods, and observation. These methods are said to 'disregard age as synonymous with children's abilities and aim to be inclusive and to build rapport, trust and confidence with participants' (Barker and Weller, 2003: 36). Further, child-centred or child-friendly methods, contend Barker and Weller (2003), can address power imbalances between adult researchers and child participants as methods used can reflect a child's preferred method of communication. The table below demonstrates the main issues:

Table 3.1 Approaches to childhood

Scientific approach to childhood	'New' approach to childhood studies
Often quantitative in nature (e.g. experiments, structured interviews)	Often qualitative in nature (e.g. ethnographic, child friendly methods)
Research *on* children	Research *with* or *by* children
Children as objects of research	Children as subjects

Children characterized as:
  passive
  incompetent
  becomings
  cultural 'dupes'
	Children characterized as:
	  active
	  competent
	  beings
	  social actors

Childhood is a natural state	Childhood is a social construction

Thus, the social study of childhood is engaged in re-presenting childhood and deconstructing previous discourses about it through research which highlights children's voices, perspectives, and experiences. Drawing on examples from published research reports, this chapter highlights some of the main concerns in researching childhood: method, power, ethics, and voice.

The centrality of children's voices in the social study of childhood

When the social study of childhood was first being used in research with children, 'listening to the voice of the child' was much vaunted. This was linked to the lack of the child's perspective being heard in the dominant (psychological and socialization) models of childhood. In order to do this, research publications tended to incorporate quotations from children as a representation of their authentic voice. Although this was perhaps too simplistic, it was an important first step in the endeavour to theorize childhood. Barker and Weller (2003) note that research *on* children, characterized here as research which is mainly quantitative in nature, gave no opportunity for children to speak for themselves. Placing children's voices at the centre of the research process and renegotiating ways of working with children in research began during the 1990s. One outcome of this renegotiation was the development of child-friendly methods which were employed to enable the voice of the child to be heard (Barker and Weller, 2003). As Lewis (2010) has noted, however, promoting the child's voice has become something of a moral crusade within the research community.

As James (2007: 70) states, 'giving voice to children is not simply or only about letting children speak; it is about exploring the unique contribution to our understanding of and theorizing about the social world that children's perspectives can provide.' *Voice* is not simply about inserting the odd quotation from child participants in a research report when it is suitable, but entails a real commitment to presenting children's experiences and perspectives without the researcher's analytical layer (Grover, 2004). As Komuanen (2007) cautions, we should not use a simplistic notion of *voice* but should reflect on our research process, and ask ourselves whether we are actually representing the voices of our research participants. She uses the example of research carried out with 15 children aged under six, with cognitive and/or physical impairments. In observing professionals communicating with the children, she noted that the professionals assumed that the child had found a voice when they were given a limited choice (for example, did they want a banana or did they want juice?). However, Komuanen could see no evidence that the children were actually making a choice or whether they were getting what they had chosen.

Spyrou (2011) notes that while the goal of hearing children's voices has been at the heart of the work carried out under the 'new' paradigm, scholars have not critically explored issues of representation nor have they been sufficiently self-scrutinizing. The researcher not only needs to provide voice in the way of quotations from the child but also to take into account the research context within which children's voices are produced and represented (see also Hunleth, 2011). It is likely that the setting of the research (whether the home or the school or the playground) will influence the research outcomes. Syprou (2011: 157) states:

> by recognizing how children's voices are multi-layered we can move beyond the often misguided assumption that voice research with children is by definition good, valuable or of high quality. The tendency of researchers to jump in and out of children's worlds in order to quickly 'collect data' which they can also quickly analyse by extracting quotes from children to illustrate their findings may end up caricaturing children more than really offering us meaningful insights into their lives.

It is therefore important to not only attempt to hear the voice of the child, but to recognize that in research one also must consider the context within which the child's voice is heard. The spatial context of research is also important: for example, in Woodhead's early research he found that some children were afraid to enter the room allocated to him for the research by school staff while other children refused to enter at all. He later found out that the room he had been allocated was the 'naughty' room, thus explaining children's reluctance (Woodhead, 2000)!

Qualitative methods became more popular in the 1970s with the emergence of critical sociology where the focus was on producing accounts of experience and perspective, rather than a set of numerical data showing causal relationships between variables. A qualitative approach allows the subjects of research to communicate to the researcher their lived experiences and understandings (Grover, 2004: 84). While both quantitative and qualitative methods have their uses depending on the philosophical and methodological background of the researcher and the kind of material the researcher is hoping to collect, studies carried out in the social study of childhood generally, but not always, use qualitative techniques.

The introduction of the social study of childhood (see Chapter 2) entailed a rejection of and a radical critique of developmental psychological discourse and research on children (James, Jenks and Prout, 1998). As Alderson (2000c) has noted, seeing children as immature and incompetent produces evidence which reinforces notions of incompetence. However, with the introduction of the social study of childhood, and the consequent understanding that children can speak for themselves – that children are actors in the social world, and that their experiences and perspectives are worthy of study in their own right (James and Prout, 1997) – we see children as subjects of research rather than objects of study (Wyness, 2011). Methods advocated in the social study of childhood are heavily based on qualitative techniques, although some research has successfully incorporated questionnaire research with children as young as eight (e.g. McNamee, 1998a).

It is important to remember that researchers are often limited by time, resources, and funding requirements. Research takes place in the real world, and as such is often messy and complicated, and sometimes requires compromise and adjustment of goals and plans. As Lewis (2010: 16) notes, 'researchers are caught between supporting the promotion of authentic "child voice" and a context (e.g. pre-specified agenda, limited development time and minimal opportunities for involving "reluctant" children) which, because of funders' constraints, fails to take into account the painstaking and time consuming underlying requirements.' In this way, the attempts by researchers to present childhood voices can be, and often are, compromised (see Chapter 2 for further discussion). I now want to turn to examining some of the methods and techniques that researchers use when carrying out research in the social study of childhood, focusing on child-friendly methods, and the advantages and disadvantages of these methods.

Child-friendly methods

In the move away from previous discourses on childhood, and in line with a focus on children as worthy of study in their own right, the development of child-friendly methods to facilitate hearing and representing the voice of the child took place in large part as a move to doing research *with* rather than *on* children. Such methods include drawing, photography, telling stories, keeping diaries, producing vignettes, PRA methods, and observation. Child-friendly methods are often used because some researchers may feel that children will see traditional methods (e.g. interviews and questionnaires) as inappropriate and/or boring.

Observation. In their delineation of the tenets of the emergent paradigm of the social study of childhood, James and Prout (1997) argued that ethnography was an especially useful way of carrying out research in childhood. The main tool of ethnography is participant observation. In qualitative research, observation is not impartial or detached from the subjects of the observation; rather the observer takes part in the daily lives of those being studied, sometimes for an extended period of time. There have been several notable studies on childhood using the ethnographic method, including participant observation. For example, Bluebond-Langner's (1978) groundbreaking study of children with a terminal illness used participant observation as a central method, thus uncovering aspects of children's competence previously unsuspected because earlier data had been collected in different ways and from a different stance.

Photography. Using this technique, researchers give children cameras to take photographs of things that are important to them. These can be objects, physical spaces, or people. The images produced are then used as prompts for further discussion. Having used photography in three research projects, Cook and Hess (2007) reported that children enjoyed taking photographs and were engaged in the process. They stated that the use of photographs produced more detail than the use of verbal interviews alone, and provided the adult researcher with unexpected insights. However, they also noted that it was not always clear that the children taking part knew why they were using cameras. Obviously the use of such techniques requires researchers to carefully explain their intentions.

Drawing. While this is a popular technique in research with children, partly because drawing is something children are familiar with in school, there are problems with it. For example, not all children see themselves as being good at drawing and so may not enjoy the process. Hunleth (2011) argues that child-friendly methods such as drawing are problematic in that while this technique is often said to be useful in allowing the child to express complex ideas or to give children time to think over their response, it is in fact often easier for the researcher and not just the child, in that it allows researchers to deal with difficult issues without asking about them directly. Spyrou (2011: 154) reminds us that an image or drawing produced by a child participant cannot in and of itself be an authentic depiction of the child's social reality, because the image or drawing produced is only one of a number of possibilities that *could* have been produced.

Vignettes. Vignettes are a useful technique in research, whether with adults or children. Vignettes provide a hypothetical scenario which the research participant is invited to read and respond to, to tell what they or a hypothetical 'someone' might do in that situation. They can often be used when the research topic is a sensitive or difficult one, and when the interviewee can remove themselves from the situation. In research that explored how professionals constructed childhood in their work with children in family law, multi-level vignettes that described a hypothetical situation allowed respondents to detail what their approach to the problem would be as each vignette outlined a different level of complexity of the hypothetical situation (McNamee, James and James, 2005). In research which examined young people's experiences of violence in UK residential homes, Barter and Renold (2000) gave vignettes to children to read and then asked for their responses to a range of predetermined questions. The drawback with this method is that what people say they will do in a hypothetical situation may not be what they would actually do.

Multi-methods. Very often research studies involve the use of more than one method, sometimes to increase the validity of the research but also to attempt to collect data in a variety of ways. A range of techniques was employed by Punch (2002a) in her study of children and young people's problems, and their use of coping strategies with those problems. She carried out group and individual interviews, as well as using a 'secret box,' into which young people could put their anonymous responses. The researcher read them at a later date. This enabled the young people to write down their most personal concerns, or things that they wouldn't otherwise talk about, without fear. Another technique she found useful was what she called 'stimulus material.' This involved presenting the young people with problem page letters, or excerpts from TV shows, as a springboard to get them to talk about their concerns. She also used techniques such as spider diagrams, ranking, and brainstorming, but found that the young people preferred straightforward interviews (Punch, 2002a: 54). Punch's experience might lead us to question the value of child-friendly or focused methods when children actually prefer just to be talked to and have someone listen.

Participatory Action Research (PAR). PAR is an approach to research which may draw on the multiple methods discussed above, but which is intended to be emancipatory with the intent of bringing about social change. In this approach the researcher facilitates the participants' investigation into a subject which the participants themselves have identified as important. In a sense, and to paraphrase the feminist rallying call, PAR is research by the people, for the people. It is meant to be democratic and empowering. Through the process 'the participants not only transform some conditions related to a practical problem in their lives, but they also educate themselves about their general situation, thereby empowering themselves more generally for future action' (Hart, 1992: 16).

Clark (2004) developed the mosaic approach – based on a multimethod approach which draws on tools used in PAR – in her research with kindergarten children. She claims that use of the approach plays to children's strengths, rather than their weaknesses. The methods used included observation, 'child conferencing' (short structured interviews), child-directed tours of the kindergarten, and map making using children's photographs and drawings. Using these kinds of methods opened up communication between the children and the adult researcher. Further, it was the *process* of using the various methods and not necessarily the data produced by using them that increased her understanding of children's experiences and social lives in the kindergarten context (Clark, 2004: 154).

Questionnaires. Because of the shift in emphasis to qualitative, child-friendly methods, questionnaires have not been extensively used in research with children. Oakley (1994) contends that this reflects a view that children are not competent as research subjects, since they are not able to express themselves, at least not in adult terms (see also Fine and Sandstrom, 1988). To be able to complete a questionnaire, the respondent needs to have a certain level of literacy. In my own research I have successfully carried out self-completion questionnaire studies with children aged as young as eight (McNamee, 1998a). Like any questionnaire-based study, the language used needs to be tailored to the competence of the respondent, whether child or adult. I am arguing, then, that the questionnaire can have a place in research with children. While different data is produced from questionnaires than, say, from participant observation, the methods used in any study depend on the resources available and it may be that for some research questionnaires are the only method which will work.

McNamee and Seymour (2013) carried out a study of more than 300 published accounts of research with children which had been carried out within the social study of childhood. All research articles in the three main 'childhood' academic journals (*Childhood: A Journal of Global Child Research, Children and Society*, and *Children's Geographies*) dating from 1993 (the first date of publication of *Childhood* and arguably the point at which the social study of childhood became prominent) and up until 2010 were investigated. The questions that this research focused around were twofold: who were the children being represented in these research studies, and had childhood studies heeded the calls for research *with* rather than *on* children? Were researchers employing 'special' child-friendly techniques? Firstly, it was found that there was a definite cluster of ages of children represented in the reports, with 10–12-year-olds being the most frequently reported-on age group. Secondly, they found that most researchers used standard methods (e.g. interviews or questionnaires) rather than child-friendly (including observational) methods in research with children, as can be seen in the table below. It would seem therefore that a methodological shift to child-friendly techniques has been slow to happen.

In the below table, *child-friendly methodology* is a collapsed category and includes multiple methods. It was difficult to categorize the child's age in compiling this table as frequently published research reports merely provided an age range or omitted this information altogether. While there has been an upsurge in researchers developing and commenting on innovative and child-friendly methods, this study showed that the majority of published research data was produced using standard methodologies. The assumption that child-friendly strategies in research are superior to standard techniques can arise from the assumption that children are less competent than adults and therefore in need of these special methods. Punch (2002b) notes that the perspective we take on children affects how we carry out research with them. For example, if we see children as having different competencies than adults, then we will use child-focused or child-friendly methods in research. If, however, we see children as essentially the same as adults, then methods used in research with children need not be different (Christensen, 2004). This is an important point because the data collected from research with children feeds

Table 3.2 Methodology used in published research articles by age category

Age	Standard methodology (%)	Child friendly methodology (%)
9–12 only	68	32
Primary school age and younger	79	21
Secondary school age and older	79	21
Wide range of ages	73	27

into what can be said about childhood (see Alderson's, 2000c, point above). Thus, a view of children as different from adults reinforces a view of childhood as a separate and different stage of life. Rather than saying *child friendly*, Punch (2002b: 337) argues, we should say *research friendly*: 'the challenge is to strike a balance between not patronizing children and recognizing their competencies, while maintaining their enjoyment of being involved with the research and facilitating their ability to communicate their view of the world.'

It can be argued that in this sense, research with children should be no different than research with adults. Adult participants in research should not be patronized, and should enjoy their involvement in research too. As pointed out by Thompson (2007), children and adults are both human becomings, and the notion that adults are competent whereas children are not is a myth – all people have different competencies regardless of age. Discussing the similarities and differences between adults and children, Hill (2005) notes that while children can be seen as incompetent and powerless, so too can adults. He contends that the similarities between children and adults are greater than the differences. This then leads us to question whether or not different approaches, researcher roles, and methodological techniques are necessary in researching childhood.

Gaining access to children

Alongside ethical considerations, choice of methods, considerations of age of respondent, and how best to represent their voices, a further complication in researching childhood is gaining access to children. Gaining access can be time consuming and beset with difficulties because the researcher must negotiate with several gatekeepers who can facilitate or block access. For example, researchers may have to get police clearance, and then may have to negotiate with education authorities, head teachers or principals, class teachers, and parents or guardians before they can even begin the process of gaining informed consent from children. When attempting to carry out research with looked-after children (that is, children in state care), this process can be exacerbated, as Heptinstall (2000) has discussed, because the gatekeepers (birth parents, foster parents, social workers, etc.) want to protect the potentially vulnerable children in their care. In Heptinstall's (2000: 872) study, almost 60 per cent of the available children who might have taken part in the research were filtered out by the gatekeeping process: 'gatekeepers ability to block children's participation in research frequently constrains children and young people from deciding for themselves whether or not to cooperate and prevents their voices from being heard.' This can have the effect of preventing some children – who would otherwise like to take part in the research – from taking part, thus demonstrating a conflict between children's rights to express a view and the best interests of children as determined by adults.

The role of the researcher

There is no single researcher role or method which will prove successful in all cases, but rather a variety of positions or techniques is needed as Davis (1998) notes. Mandell (1988) used the *least-adult* role in her participant observation research with children in the United States and Canada. Studying children's social worlds in day care centres, Mandell (1988: 435) described the least-adult role as follows:

> The researcher suspends all adult-like characteristics except physical size. By suspending the ontological terms of 'child' and 'adult' and by participating in the children's social world as a child, the central methodological problem rests essentially on a technical question of the extent to which physical superiority prevents adult researchers from participating in the role of the child.

Both children and day care staff initially found her role confusing. Children would ask her for help and she would refuse on the grounds that she was not a teacher. She would play in the sandpit with the children, swing on the swings, and hide under the porch. Later she adapted her role to include occasionally helping out the teachers. Whether or not it can be said that adults can step far enough out of the adult role to become *least adult* is arguable. Perhaps her role was more that of a noninterfering adult (Mandell, 1988: 450) than *least adult*. Or perhaps that is as far as we can relinquish our adult selves.

Christensen (2004) reflects on her role in a study of Danish children's health-seeking behaviour. Rather than using the *least-adult* role she presented herself as *an unusual type of adult* who was interested in understanding children's perspectives but was not attempting to be a child. In this way, she got to know codes of behaviour and local cultural practices of communication – essentially learning how to behave with the children. In this way the research process became a dialogue between her and the children.

What do children think about taking part in research?

Researchers, whether carrying out research with adults or children, rarely ask participants for their opinions on the research itself. Instead there is an assumption that researchers are the experts, and their methods go largely unchallenged (Hill, 2006; Grover, 2004). Hill (2006) carried out research on what children themselves thought was the best way to get children's perspectives. In this study, many children commented that *not* being chosen to be a research participant was unfair, although some felt that invitations to take part could be unwelcome. Hill (2006) noted that children's stances in relation to taking part in (adult-led) research ranged from engaged and enthusiastic to detached, where children provided minimalistic responses, to being subversive, where children provided false or joking responses. In my doctoral research most of the children and young people who took part were engaged and enthusiastic, but there was a significant minority who took the subversive stance (see box below).

BOX 3.1 Resistance to the research process?

My research (McNamee, 1998a) focused on children's ownership and use of computer and video games. While initially I envisioned the research as a small-scale qualitative study, in the process of negotiating access with schools it became apparent that what suited the schools better was a questionnaire survey which would be administered to the whole school in one 20-minute session on the same day. The survey was delivered to 1600 children aged 8–18 in two secondary schools, one in an urban location and one in a rural setting. Getting consent from children was not something the schools were well-disposed to, but the head teachers in both schools agreed that I could present the research to the children during assembly. In my presentation I informed the children that they did not have to take part in the research and if that was their choice, they would experience no repercussion. Because of the size of the study, I was personally unable to deliver the questionnaire myself and thus relied on schools and teachers to do so. However, teachers did not give the children the option to decline to take part and it seemed that children expressed their resistance to 'having' to take part by spoiling the questionnaire form, or by drawing what might be seen as inappropriate images. For example, in response to the drawing exercise 'please write or draw anything you like to do when you're not at school' some drew male or female genitalia or dismembered body parts. Others wrote antagonistic or nonsensical statements. However, on the whole most of the children completed the questionnaire appropriately, and the use of the questionnaire as a research tool provided previously uncollected data on children's ownership and use of computer and video games.

Including children in research

'To involve all children more directly in research can... rescue them from silence and exclusion, and from being represented, by default, as passive objects, while respect for their informed and voluntary consent helps to protect them from covert, invasive, exploitative or abusive research' (Alderson, 2000c: 243).

Researchers who involve children in research detail many advantages of doing so (Kellet et al., 2004). For example, including children as researchers can help facilitate access to children's perspectives in a way that adult researchers could not. It may also resolve some of the issues that arise from the differential power relations between adults and children (Coad and Evans, 2008). It is important to remember, however, that it is not necessary to include children as researchers for epistemological reasons, that is, that knowledge about children and childhood does not have to be produced by children themselves (Bluebond-Langner, 2008). Grover (2004) claims that research participants have inherent rights to contribute their unique perspectives on, for example, the formulation of research questions and their experiences of research and secondly to be able to challenge any misrepresentations of their contribution brought about during the interpretation of data by the researcher. Researchers must therefore, where possible, build up a relationship with the research participant based on trust. As indicated in the boxed example above, however, this is not possible when carrying out quantitative research where the research subject may not ever meet the researcher.

One study which built up this kind of relationship is Bluebond-Langner's (2008). Employing eight teens as peer researchers in a project looking at child health, she trained the teenagers in anthropological methods, and developed an open-ended interview guide for them to use in their interviews with 8–12-year-olds. However, some of the teenagers did not want to interview children, but did feel that they benefited from and wanted to continue their methods training and the discussion sessions with the adult researchers. The focus of the research therefore shifted to a more reflexive project on the teenagers' own health-seeking behaviour.

While the outcome of Bluebond-Langner's project was beneficial for both the young people and the researchers, sometimes engaging peer researchers has negative consequences: 'there is a danger that researchers will over-identify with interviewees and assume they understand too much....[Y]et shared knowledge can be an advantage' (Alderson. 2001: 140). Engaging children as peer researchers can therefore be a balancing act.

Coad and Evans (2008) note that while there has been a growth in research which involves children as peer or co-researchers, less has been said about children's role in the data analysis process, although it should be noted that generally adult research subjects are not generally involved in this process either. Coad and Evans suggest a framework to facilitate the involvement of children in data analysis, and to reduce power imbalances between adult researchers and children:

Least power for children	Adults plan the research, collect data, and do the analysis without children's involvement.
	Adults plan the research and analyse the data, but children collect the data using participatory methods. Children verify researcher's interpretation.
	Adults train children to act as an advisory group to guide the research process and interpret findings.
	Adults train children as peer or co-researchers to work alongside adults at every stage.
Most power for children	Children and young people lead the research team and adults facilitate.

The balance of power between adults and children thus shifts along this continuum from adults holding all the power, to children leading the process and sharing power with adults. However, even at the most equal stage, the authors note, 'a major dilemma for the adult researcher/facilitators was the fact that the children did not always initiate all the ideas and sometimes needed adults to prompt them or to enforce rules' (Coad and Evans, 2008: 48). This then acts to limit child leadership, and negatively affects the balance of power.

Many scholars who involve children in research do so as part of a commitment to children's rights to participation, following the United Nations Convention on the Rights of the Child. Drawing on articles 12, 13, 33, and 36 of the Convention, Beazley et al. (2009) have produced a list of requirements for rights-based research.

(1) Children's perspectives and opinions must be integral to the research
(2) Methods need to be used which will help children to express their perspectives and opinions freely
(3) Children must not be harmed or exploited through taking part

(4) Research carried out must conform to the highest possible scientific standards

(5) Researchers must be carefully recruited and supervised.

Abebe (2009) has pointed out that child participation in research is very much based on Western conceptions of childhood and that this can put child participants in a difficult situation as was the case in her research in rural Ethiopia. Researchers may want children to participate so that their voices can be heard. But in Ethiopia 'if they are "participating" and "vocal" it sits at odds with the diligent, respectful "good" child traditionally valued by parents and communities' (2009: 455). Children in Abede's study took some time to become the kind of child the researcher wanted, rather than the kind of child their society approved of.

The differences in constructions of childhood between the developed and developing world and the effects that has on research has also been noted by Czymoniewicz-Klippel (2009). According to her, Cambodian children are seen as cognitively immature, which, she argued, justified the control of children, which at times took the form of beatings and/or emotional and psychological abuse. This had real implications for those carrying out research with children in her project: children would not consent to take part in the research until their parents had agreed that they could. In addition, it could be dangerous for children to participate in the way that researchers might have wanted them to because it would have been culturally inappropriate, indeed danger-ous for some children. Demonstrating participation and engagement with researchers would be interpreted by parents and other adults as defiant behav-iour, and therefore the child may be punished. As Czymoniewicz-Klippel (2009: 20) concluded, 'for researchers to expect Cambodian children to dem-onstrate overt agency in research is not only unreasonable, but potentially dangerous, and therefore arguably unethical.' Here we have clear examples of the potential dangers of ignoring cultural context.

The Children's Research Centre (CRC) at the Open University in the United Kingdom has, since 2004, facilitated children's own research. Children who take part are selected by teaching staff, and receive training in research methods, analysis, and the dissemination of research. The research produced by the children is clearly grounded in their own experiences and concerns. Furthermore, the quality of the work produced by the children is impressive. The CRC claims that child-led research provides a genuine child perspective, and that child researchers are able to get responses from their peers that adults could not because of power/generation issues. It is also empowering for those children who take part (Kellet et al., 2004; Kellet, 2005). However, as Hill (2006) noted, and as discussed above, children who are not selected to take part in research activities may feel anything but empowered and indeed may experience non-selection as unfair and unjust. Also, it should not be forgotten that relations between children are also characterized by power relations – not all children would be able to get responses from peers (see, for example, Abebe, 2009). Nonetheless, the work of the CRC is an innovative and worthwhile attempt to give children the opportunity to have their voices heard in a way which is meaningful to them.

Ethical issues

Academic institutions have particular sets of ethical guidelines which researchers are obligated to follow. In Canada academic research is governed by the Tri-Council Policy Statement which reads:

> Many individuals who lack legal capacity to make decisions may still be able to express their wishes in a meaningful way, even if such expression may not fulfil all of the requirements for consent. Prospective participants may be capable of verbally or physically assenting to, or dissenting from, participation in research. Those who may be capable of assent or dissent include:
>
> (a) those whose capacity is in the process of development, such as children whose capacity for judgment and self-direction is maturing
> (b) those who once were capable of making an autonomous decision regarding consent but whose capacity is diminishing or fluctuating
> (c) those whose capacity remains only partially developed, such as those living with permanent cognitive impairment.
>
> While their assent would not be sufficient to permit them to participate in the absence of consent by an authorized third party, their expression of dissent or signs suggesting they do not wish to participate must be respected. (Tri-Council Policy Statement, 2010)

Here we can see that children are perceived as lacking the ability to make decisions.

In the United Kingdom, the British Sociological Association statement of ethical practice states:

> Research involving children requires particular care. The consent of the child should be sought in addition to that of the parent. Researchers should use their skills to provide information that could be understood by the child, and their judgment to decide on the child's capacity to

understand what is being proposed. Specialist advice and expertise should be sought where relevant. Researchers should have regard for issues of child protection and make provision for the potential disclosure of abuse (Statement of Ethical Practice, 2002).

The legal and professional guidelines for ethical conduct with children rests on several assumptions: that children are incompetent to give consent; that children are in the process of developing and thus not rational; and that children are in need of protection. As has already been discussed in this chapter, however, ethical approaches to the child need not be different than ethical practice in research with adults (Christensen and Prout, 2002).

Hill (2005: 69) argues that children should give positive consent, rather than merely not expressing dissent. He argues that in the process of gaining consent, adults should ensure that children are informed of the goals of the research; the length of time and depth of commitment required; who will get to know the results of the research; whether the child will get feedback following research participation; and whether or not what they say in the research context will be confidential. The very definition of informed consent (see above) requires the person consenting to have some degree of competence – they must be able to understand, and respond to, the information presented.

Whether carrying out research with adults or with children, informed consent is vital in the ethical process. However, gaining informed consent can be difficult. Often adult gatekeepers do not see that there is a need to inform children. For example, in my doctoral study one head teacher said 'oh, you don't ask children what they want to do; they'll only say no.' Reflecting on the process of gaining informed consent from children in the school setting, David et al. (2001) realised that they could not escape the dominant educational/developmental approach to childhood even when ostensibly trying not to take that role. The information leaflets they developed for children fed into the assumption of children's age-bound progression to competence. They used bright colours and simple text for the youngest children, progressing to more muted colours with a more adult style of text for older children. Even though the researchers were trying to engage with children in a participatory manner, they found themselves presenting information as if they were teachers. They argue that this has implications for children's ability to give meaningful consent, because the power relations between adults and children make it is hard for children to opt out of doing research, as the teaching model compels or requires children to take part (David et al., 2001: 351; Wyness, 2011).

It can also be difficult to gain informed consent from children when they cannot speak or lack cognitive ability. Cocks (2006) introduced the notion of *assent* rather than *consent*, which grew out of her research with children with disabilities. The social study of childhood has focused on competence and agency, and therefore disabled children, Cocks (2006: 255) argued, have been left out of the discussion. There is, she states 'a need to incorporate incompetence, dependence and immaturity in such a way that they are not portrayed negatively or misunderstood and thus left open to misuse.' Unable to get informed consent from the disabled children she studied, she developed the notion of assent. Assent, rather than consent, does not require understanding of the research but is illustrated when the child displays trust and acceptance of the researcher's presence. Further, assent must be ongoing throughout the research process – if acceptance of the researcher is not present, then the researcher must not continue.

In the same way that we have argued in this chapter that methods used with children need not be different from those used with adults, Christensen and Prout (2002: 482) contend that ethical issues need not be different either:

> We suggest that the understanding of children as social actors and participants is best founded on an a priori assumption of what we term 'ethical symmetry' between adults and children. By this we mean that the researcher takes as his or her *starting* point the view that the ethical relationship between researcher and informant is the same whether he or she conducts research with adults or with children. (emphasis in original)

The consequence of seeing children as competent social actors and participants means that we should treat children as such in research with them. Employing special methods and approaches may give rise to the assumption that there is something different – and deficient – about the nature of childhood when contrasted with adulthood.

Protection from harm

As mentioned above, the legal and professional ethical codes for researchers require that adult researchers protect children from harm. Writing about research in urban and rural Ethiopia, Abebe (2009) reflected on the challenge of applying ethical issues in the context of research with street children, where many of the children were involved in illegal activities. She made the decision not to report such illegal activities in order to maintain the trust she had developed with the children: 'I found myself treading a fine line between encouraging the children to tell me their stories and yet protecting them from either disclosing something they may not have wished to, or damaging their fragile coping mechanisms' (Abebe, 2009: 457–8). As mentioned earlier in the discussion of research with children in Cambodia, the potential danger for children who participate in research is real when research expectations conflict with expectations of children's behaviour (Czymoniewicz-Klippel, 2009). Any abuse uncovered as part of the research process should be reported to the relevant authorities, and this must be made clear to the child, but it also compromises confidentiality. The protection of the child is therefore paramount in research with children.

This chapter has presented some of the issues arising from research with children. But what of future directions? Having, over the past two decades, made room for children's voices, experiences, and perspectives, and engaged with deconstructing discourses of childhood, what might be next for scholars? Uprichard (2010: 3) argues that we need to move outside of children's social worlds:

> Although, in theory, children are conceptualised as active agents in their social world, the type of research that children are typically involved in implies that children are competent, knowledgeable and agentic only in terms of their own lives, their own spaces, their own childhoods. The notion of children as agents of the *wider* social world tends not to be empirically explored. (emphasis original).

Thus, not soliciting children's perspectives on the wider world, Uprichard states, limits and undermines their agency and competence. We therefore have to involve children, she argues, in research that goes beyond childhood, but which moves away from the adult–child boundary.

Exercise and reflection points

1. Imagine that you are carrying out some research with children on the topic of children's friendship. How would you go about doing this? What methods would you choose?
2. How can we be sure that we are gaining the voice of the child in our research?

Further reading

Christensen, P. and James, A. (ed.) (2000) *Research with children: Perspectives and practices*, London: Falmer.

Greene, S. and Hogan, D. (2005) *Researching children's experiences: Approaches and methods*, London: Sage Publications.

Lewis, V. Kellet, M., Robinson C., Fraser, S. and Ding, S. (ed.) (2004) *The reality of research with children and young people*, London: Sage/Open University Press.

Punch, S. (2002b) 'Research with children: The same or different from research with adults?' *Childhood: A Journal of Global Child Research*, vol. 9(3), 321–334.

CHAPTER 4

Childhood, Rights and Citizenship

Keywords: Rights, participation, citizenship, advocacy, empowerment, universalism

Having introduced the social study of childhood in previous chapters, and having begun to problematize 'childhood' as a concept, and introduced the importance of deconstructing discourses of childhood, in this chapter we turn to children's rights and citizenship. While other chapters will continue the discussion of children's rights, here we begin to see how ideas of the child and concepts of childhood play into the formulation of international conventions on children. First, the chapter introduces the 1989 United Nations Convention on the Rights of the Child (UNCRC), and discusses the tension inherent in this document between rights and protection of children. The chapter then explores children's status as citizens by outlining how traditional notions of citizenship position children as *citizens in the making* rather than as *citizens in the present*. It utilizes research conducted with children and young people to demonstrate to what extent they are active in shaping their communities and voicing their opinions about matters affecting their lives. Throughout the chapter we examine the obstacles to children's participation in decisions which concern them, and discussions of children's citizenship which coalesce around issues of adult power and control.

The United Nations Convention on the Rights of the Child

The Declaration of the Rights of the Child was drafted in 1924 by Eglantyne Jebb, who founded the Save the Children charity in the United Kingdom. Sister societies were soon established in Canada and Australia and then

> The text of the United Nations Convention on the Rights of the Child can be found at http://www.ohchr.org/en/professionalinterest/pages/crc.aspx

throughout the world (Gnareig and MacCormack, 1999). The impetus to start the organization was Jebb's concern for children who were suffering in the aftermath of the First World War. 'For better or worse, the world can be revolutionised in one generation according to how we deal with the children,' Jebb wrote (in Holland, 2004: 102). Jebb went on to draft the first version of 'The Rights of the Child' in 1923, adopted by the League of Nations in 1924. Although the United Nations produced a new Declaration of the Rights of the Child in 1959, it was not until 1989 that the Convention, which is the most recent document, was formally drawn up. The Convention has now been ratified by most of the countries in the world (Holland, 2004). Until very recently there were only two countries who had not signed up – Somalia and the United States. Somalia ratified the convention in 2015. The US still has not, and although it was instrumental in drafting the Convention, it has not been ratified by any United States government. Earls (2011) argues that the United States does not ratify the document because it is concerned that the rights outlined in the UNCRC may interfere with other rights, such as the rights of parents over children. The consequence of non-ratification and the lack of awareness of the UNCRC in the United States has, Cahill and Hart (2007) note, resulted in a lack of participatory initiatives (initiatives that include children in decision making in matters that concern them) in that country. However, as we will see, other countries also fail to implement participatory initiatives, and even when governments do, not all efforts are successful.

According to the Convention, a child is defined as a person below the age of 18 (unless the age of majority is obtained earlier). It contains more than 50 articles specifying the rights of the child and details how the Convention is to be implemented, as well as two optional protocols which may be signed and ratified by States Parties – optional protocol 1 deals with child soldiers and optional protocol 2 deals with the sale of children and child prostitution and pornography. The UNCRC is a legally binding international document which subjects ratifying nation states to inspection by the UN Committee on the Rights of the Child. This committee expects reports from every ratifying nation detailing how it has implemented the articles of the Convention (Howe 2007; UNCRC, Article 44). Latterly, Optional Protocol 3 for communications sets out an international complaints process for any violations of children's rights (http://www.childrightsconnect.org/connect-with-the-un-2/op3-crc/).

The Convention is said to incorporate the 'three Ps' of children's rights: rights to provision (such as food and shelter), to protection (for example, from abuse) and to participation (in matters concerning the child) (Alderson, 2000b). As will be shown, there is an obvious tension in the Convention between the rights of protection and the rights of participation, and the Convention has been criticized in this regard.

A further criticism of the Convention centres on its universalistic approach to childhood. There is an implicit assumption running through the document that all children are the same and that childhood is defined by Westernized notions of developmentalism and protectionism. Nieuwenhuys (2008: 7) calls this 'abstract universalism,' by which she means that it ignores the cultural context within which a child lives, and also denies children agency. She states, 'in the name of children's right to an abstract good called childhood, abstract universalism actually reduces children to mere victims in need of expert scrutiny and guidance.' However, she also cautions against employing cultural relativity, that is, the assumption that all cultures are neutral and equal and therefore cannot be judged nor compared. Both positions are, she claims, essentialist. For cultural relativists, culture is an enduring phenomenon and for abstract universalists, childhood is. Both are problematic when addressing children's rights. Taking an extreme cultural-relativist position would mean opposing any interventions in local cultural practices, while uncritical adherence to abstract universalism would see taking no action as immoral, thus the focus would be on taking every action possible. What is needed, she argues, is a rejection of both positions in favour of a focus on children's perspectives and children's agency (Nieuwenhuys, 2008: 6–7).

Participation rights and practices

While the UNCRC is often seen as a convention that provides participation rights to children, this chapter will show that the rights to participation enshrined in the document grow out of a Westernized, paternalistic view of childhood informed by a romantic developmental perspective. This can be clearly seen in the preamble to the Convention which enshrines children as immature and as a *special* and vulnerable category of person in need of protection: 'Bearing in mind that, as indicated in the Declaration of the Rights of the Child, the child, by reason of his physical and mental immaturity, needs special safeguards and care, including appropriate legal protection, before as well as after birth.' Such a view of childhood is further entrenched in Article 3, which makes very clear that the best interests of the child as defined by adults underpin all other rights of the child (Freeman 2007).

The tension between protection and rights is starkly highlighted by considering Article 12 in relation to Article 3. Article 12 is one of the articles of the Convention which should hold most promise for children's participation rights. However, in it we can see three distinct conditions that govern when a child can and cannot exercise that right: 1) the child has to be seen

---

BOX 4.1   UNCRC Article 3 and 12.1

UNCRC Article 3
In all actions concerning children, whether undertaken by public or private social welfare institutions, courts of law, administrative authorities or legislative bodies, the best interests of the child shall be a primary consideration.

UNCRC Article 12.1
States Parties shall assure to the child who is capable of forming his or her own views the right to express those views freely in all matters affecting the child, the views of the child being given due weight in accordance with the age and maturity of the child.

---

as *competent* by adults to hold a view; 2) the child has to be considered old enough *or mature enough* to have a view; and 3) if the adult judges that these two conditions are met, only then is the child's view considered. It should be noted that nowhere does the Article state that children have the right to make decisions; they only have the right to a view. The onus is on adults to decide whether a child's view will count. Ryan (2010) has also pointed out that under the UNCRC children 'are not cast as social subject with rights to negotiate and participate in a moral and spiritual world. They are to be protected and well-nurtured children' (2010: 30).

Article 12 can be overridden by Article 3. Even if the child is deemed mature enough to have formed and expressed a view, if that view is not in the child's best interest according to the adult, then under Article 3, the child's view need not be taken into account. The right of the child to participation, then, is qualified by developmental notions of age and competence as determined by adults. This shows that the constructions of childhood employed in the Convention, and the clear boundaries between childhood and adulthood that it establishes, have a direct bearing on how children's rights are implemented (Aitken, 2001). However, more recently, some of these concerns have been addressed. The General Comments on the Convention with regard to Article 12 and Article 3 are dealt with in General Comment No. 12 (2009) and General Comment No. 14 (2013). These two documents spell out in detail exactly how the Articles are to be interpreted and implemented. Reinforcing that the best interests of the child should be taken as a primary (or in some cases, paramount) consideration, General Comment No. 14 (http://www2.ohchr.org/English/bodies/

crc/docs/GC/CRC_C_GC_14_ENG.pdf) nonetheless states that Article 12 and Article 3 are to be taken as complementary rather than in tension with each other, noting that there can be 'no correct application of Article 3 if the components of Article 12 are not respected' (see also Lansdown et al., 2014: 5). The question remains, however, exactly how these articles may be used in practice.

The African Charter on the Rights and Welfare of the Child has been seen as the most progressive treaty on children's rights in the world (Viviers and Lombard, 2012) and one which deals with the problems between the universal view of the child reflected in the UNCRC and the African understandings of the responsibilities of children (Tisdall and Punch 2012). Although some of the wording and articles of the Charter closely follow that of the UNCRC, other articles reveal interesting differences. Article 4.1 of the African Charter (see box below for the text of Article 4) is, in some ways, very similar to the UNCRC when it comes to the best interests of the child, but the African Charter intriguingly sets a revision of Article 12 of the UNCRC alongside the best interest clause:

The requirement to hear the child's views (although qualified by the child's competence not unlike Article 12 of the UNCRC) makes it clear that it is in the child's interest to be able communicate their view. The tension previously discussed between Article 3 and Article 12 of the UNCRC is, in this formulation, less apparent.

The Charter is progressive in that it rejects the universalism of the UNCRC and takes into account the context of the African continent This is most clearly addressed in Article 31 (see Box 4.3) which articulates the rights and responsibilities of the child.

BOX 4.2 ACRWC Article 4: Best Interests of the Child

1. In all actions concerning the child undertaken by any person or authority the best interests of the child shall be the primary consideration.
2. In all judicial or administrative proceedings affecting a child who is capable of communicating his/her own views, an opportunity shall be provided for the views of the child to be heard either directly or through an impartial representative as a party to the proceedings, and those views shall be taken into consideration by the relevant authority in accordance with the provisions of appropriate law.

BOX 4.3 ACRWC Article 31: Responsibility of the Child

Every child shall have responsibilities towards his family and society, the State and other legally recognized communities and the international community. The child, subject to his age and ability, and such limitations as may be contained in the present Charter, shall have the duty:

(a) to work for the cohesion of the family, to respect his parents, superiors and elders at all times and to assist them in case of need

(b) to serve his national community by placing his physical and intellectual abilities at its service

(c) to preserve and strengthen social and national solidarity

(d) to preserve and strengthen African cultural values in his relations with other members of the society, in the spirit of tolerance, dialogue and consultation and to contribute to the moral wellbeing of society

(e) to preserve and strengthen the independence and the integrity of his country

(f) to contribute to the best of his abilities, at all times and at all levels, to the promotion and achievement of African Unity.

While the articles of the UNCRC focus on provision, participation, and protection, Article 31 acknowledges the role that the child plays in his or her community and culture. Although the Article could be criticized because of the inherent conflict between the principles of participation and the requirement to respect 'parents, superiors and elders' at all times, the Article does recognize children's competence in work in their local and national context (which of course remains subject to age and ability).

In South Africa, one of the countries to ratify the Charter (not all African states have ratified the Charter), three additional pieces of legislation regarding children's participation in decision making in health and schools have been implemented (Viviers and Lombard, 2012). One of them, the South African School's Act (1996), obliges schools to ensure that children participate in governance of schools at all levels. Although charters and documents about children's rights promote participation, Viviers and Lombard (2012: 11) remind us that 'freedom to participate...is influenced by power, status and relationships between adults and children.'

It has been said that children's participation in matters concerning them is important in several ways: to fulfil the requirements of the UNCRC, to improve services to children, and to empower children (Sinclair, 2004; Lansdown et al., 2014). Often, however, participation is at best nothing more than consultation with children and tokenism at worst. Hart (1992) uses the image of a ladder to illustrate the broad range of children's participation, but it is also representative of the implicit power relations between adults and children. The 'rungs' on the ladder progress as follows:

Rung 1: Children are manipulated.
Rung 2: Children are decorated.
Rung 3: Children are tokenized.
Rung 4: Children are assigned and informed.
Rung 5: Children are consulted and informed.
Rung 6: Adults initiate participation but share decisions with children.
Rung 7: Children initiate and direct action.
Rung 8: Children initiate and share decision making with adults.

By way of an example of tokenism and non-participation, some research conducted on a government funding scheme set up to address poverty and social exclusion in England (Craig et al., 2005) uncovered some of the challenges of children's participation as it relates to Hart's ladder. Although this was a national scheme, the funding was delivered locally through community groups. Funding was dependent on children and young people sitting on the local funding committees and thereby contributing to decisions about where funding should be allocated. Yet one local funding committee consistently had a problem getting young people to sit on the committee. The experience of the youth representative on the funding panel in one of the areas studied, a young woman aged 15, provided quite a different perspective. According to her the meetings had all been scheduled during school time so she had only been able to attend one meeting. She also revealed that she had felt out of place and was talked down to by adult committee members during the one meeting she had attended. This made her uncomfortable and hesitant to attend another meeting. Little wonder that such 'inclusion' of young people in decision making failed. On paper, participation of and consultation with children can be documented, but in reality, children are tokenized and marginalized. In order to make children's participation meaningful, Sinclair (2004) contends, attitudinal barriers on the part of both young people and adults need to be addressed (see also Lansdown, 2011).

Research in the United Kingdom that explored the implementation of the Children's Fund by The Children's Society (Craig, McNamee and Wilkinson, 2004) revealed further barriers to children's participation. An expectation of the Children's Fund was that children and young people were supposed to participate in the partnership boards. It was in relation to such participation that Children's Society staff, when interviewed, expressed concern about child participation:

> [sigh] Any barriers? I think there's a lot of misunderstanding still... about what participation means, how it should develop. I think it's been reduced, to some extent, to a kind of output thing, you know? In other words, we need one or two children/young people on certain committees etcetera, rather than them being engaged in the kind of everyday operation and running of the Fund, you know. (Craig et al., 2004)

Child participation is often reliant on adult facilitation and recognition that children are *able* to participate. The child's voice is thus weakened when adults fail to fully address participation rights in practice. Children themselves understand this to be the case as Hill et al. (2003) demonstrated in their Scotland-based study of children's views of consultation. Children, they found, wanted to be consulted if it was done properly, if the issues directly concerned them, and if there were likely to be results which would benefit them and other young people. That is, children wanted genuine and meaningful participation in the consultation process, but were often disappointed when they felt that their views were not taken seriously (Hill et al., 2003: 372). Even when children are invited to contribute and participate at the highest levels their views are not necessarily taken seriously as Ennew (2008) notes. Researching children's contributions to United Nations meetings and reports, she found that children's views were filtered and manipulated by adults to be more in line with adult views. In relation to Hart's ladder then, even the United Nations can be guilty of fostering un-meaningful participation.

West (2007) conducted research on children's participation in projects carried out by the Children's Society in Southeast Asia. He noted that when adults resisted children's participation they described their resistance as concern about the quality of and reason for child participation. Primarily, though, adults resisted child participation, West (2007: 126) argued, because it challenged the status quo, and disrupted adults' established working patterns. What is needed, West noted, is for children's participation to be recognized by adults as benefiting not only children themselves, but society and organizations working with children as well.

In order to assist adults in their efforts to facilitate children's participation, Shier (2001) developed five levels of children's participation. Not intended to replace Hart's ladder (discussed above), Shier's model entails five levels and incorporates, at every level, *openings* and *opportunities* for adults to promote child participation. It also takes into account the policy or legal obligations of the adult when a child participates. At level 1, the starting point, where the outcome is to listen to young people, the *opening* adults are offered is the question, 'Are you ready to listen to young people?' The *opportunity* they are given is the question, 'Do you work in a way that enables you to listen to young people?' These questions assist the adults in reflecting on their personal and professional capacity to listen to children. At each level, the adult is asked, 'Is it a policy requirement that young people must be listened to?' This ensures that at every stage the adult considers legal and policy requirements. It is not until Level 3 (the *opening* question being, 'Are you ready to take young people's views into account?') that the requirements of the UNCRC are met. Shier's pathway model would seem to be an invaluable tool for adults to reflect on and promote children's meaningful participation.

In the preceding section we discussed the tension between protection and participation. This can also be expressed as a tension between rights and welfare. Hanson (2012) usefully lays out the discussion of children's rights and welfare as four typological approaches: paternalism, welfare, liberation, and emancipation. In the paternalistic approach, children are *becomings* in need of protection, dependent, and incompetent. In the welfare approach, children are both *becoming* and *being* in that children are mainly considered incompetent but could be considered competent if proof of such was

---

BOX 4.4 Example: Children's participation rights in schools

Although Article 42 of the Convention states that: 'States Parties undertake to make the principles and provisions of the Convention widely known, by appropriate and active means, to adults and children alike,' in the Canadian context it is exceedingly rare that schoolchildren know anything about the UNCRC or the rights that they hold. This may be because in practice schools are more concerned with maintaining social stability than encouraging children's participatory action. Exploring participation rights in English schools, Wyse (2001: 111) found that children's opportunities to express their opinions were limited despite the fact that pupils sat on school councils. Children felt that teachers didn't listen to them even when they expressed a view. In other cultural contexts, however, children's rights to participation have been taken up at a national level. For example, kindergarten children in Norway have daily meetings to choose their activities for the day, and children's participation rights are enshrined in many pieces of legislation (Kjorholt, 2011).

demonstrated. Liberationists see children as independent citizens who are competent and have rights to autonomy and full participation in society. The emancipatory typology characterizes children as both *being* and *becoming*, but starts at the opposite end from welfarists – children are competent unless it can be shown that they are not (Hanson, 2012: 73–8). While Hanson proposes this typology as a road map for research, we can use it as a frame of reference in order to deconstruct what is being said about children and childhood.

Children's rights in health

Article 24 is a provision right of the child. It does not speak to the competence of children to make decisions about their health care, although Article 12 should provide for this. Many children do want to take part in decisions about their health care. They can feel angry and upset when not included and conversely feel valued and less anxious when they are included (see Alderson, 1992). Children, particularly those with chronic illnesses, are often quite knowledgeable about their illnesses. Children as young as two have been found to know the names of their cancer drugs and why they have been prescribed them (Alderson, 2007). Bluebond-Langner's (1979) study of children with leukaemia clearly demonstrates the competence of children in understanding their illness even when adults do not discuss it with them (see Chapter 10). Yet often such knowledge does not always translate into children being considered competent to be included in or to make decisions about their health care. Moore and Kirk (2010), in their review of literature about children's participation in their health care, found that children's right to have a say in their health care was not respected in nursing practice. While not all children wanted to

---

BOX 4.5   Article 24 of the UNCRC

States Parties recognize the right of the child to the enjoyment of the highest attainable standard of health and to facilities for the treatment of illness and rehabilitation of health. States Parties shall strive to ensure that no child is deprived of his or her right of access to such health care services as set forth in the present Convention and in other international human rights or humanitarian instruments to which the said States are Parties.

make decisions and would prefer to be supported by the adults around them, other children felt excluded by and ignored in their interactions with health staff. Other obstacles to children's participation in their health care included children worrying that their parent might feel excluded from the decision-making process and so deciding not to participate, and children worrying that their parents might interrupt and block the child's interaction with medical staff. Nursing staff found it difficult to act in the best interests of the child and also respect children's right to have a view. Ultimately, however, they gave priority to ensuring that the children's best interests were attended to: 'when children protest against treatment, nurses report that they try to elicit cooperation but if this fails they will proceed anyway' (Moore and Kirk, 2010: 2221).

Factors which enable children's participation in healthcare decisions include familiarity with and knowledge about their condition, parental encouragement, and being treated by doctors who are experienced in talking to children. Usually, however, children's views are considered to be less important than adult interpretations of what is in their best interest, that is, a protectionist stance. It should also not be overlooked, as Alderson (2007: 2277) points out, that efforts to protect children from having to decide about healthcare research and treatment may protect adult power as much as children's interests.

BOX 4.6 Examples: Children refusing cancer treatment

In one court judgement in Connecticut, United States, a 17-year-old was denied the right to refuse treatment for her cancer. Child protection officers removed her from the care of her mother, and she was forced to undergo treatment (although she ran away from the hospital after two days)(http://time.com/3660088/connecticut-cancer-chemotherapy-cassandra/). In two other cases, this time in Canada, two First Nations children refused chemotherapy and the courts upheld their decision (www.cbcnews.ca). In the United Kingdom, a girl who had already almost completed three rounds of treatment begged not to be given any more. Her father promised that her wishes would be honoured. In that case the hospital threatened to call in child protection services. She had to finish her treatment, and her father reported that she no longer trusted him (http://www.dailymail.co.uk/health/article-441889/Whose-life-The-cancer-girl-whos-treatment.html) (see the exercise at the end of this chapter).

Are children seen as citizens?

'In one way, children acquire the status of citizenship by virtue of being born in a state [but] they are not fully citizens until they are old enough to vote, serve in the military, or hold public office' (Earls, 2011: 8). Children have traditionally been seen as citizens in the making (Lister, 2007) rather than in the present, again reflecting the view of children as future, or *becomings*, rather than *beings*. Although the UNCRC does not mention citizenship for children, it 'follows an uncompromising path along which citizenship, with its rights and obligations, can be envisioned' (Earls, 2011: 6). Alongside the theorizing of childhood that is carried out in the social study of childhood and the recognition of children as social actors, the participation provision of the UNCRC 'opens up possibilities for the recognition of children as active citizens in a way that a construction of them as passive objects of adult policies and practices did not' (Lister, 2007: 697). It would seem, then, that there is potential for children to be recognized as full citizens in society, and yet, as will be shown, this is not happening.

Because children are conceptualized in discourse and in practice as different than adults, the possibility that children will be viewed as citizens is compromised, argues James (2011). She focuses on the notion of children's lived citizenship, that is, drawing attention to children's agency. James highlights one of the barriers to children being citizens in the present, rather than in their (adult) future: the dominant view that conceptualizes childhood as a time of immaturity and potential irresponsibility. Despite documents such as the UNCRC, children's rights depend on adults *bestowing* those rights on children. It will not be until children's real and meaningful participation is facilitated in society that children will be recognized as political and social actors (Lister, 2007).

In a paper focusing on children's participation in Nicaragua, Shier and Méndez (2014, see also Shier 2010) suggest that the rhetoric of taking children's opinions seriously has not often successfully been implemented in practice, particularly in terms of children's ability to influence policy that concerns them. They identify *adultism* as one of the main obstacles to children's participation; in other words, it is believed that adults are superior to children, and children are viewed as objects of adult intervention (based on their best interests) and the property of parents. However, the authors also provide suggestions as to how children's participation in policymaking can be improved, including: beginning with the interests of children and allowing children a leadership role to reduce children's dependence on adults; ensuring that there is support for young people's participation from parents, schools, local decision makers, and NGOs; and ensuring that children and young people have their own spaces to participate, which includes training, mentoring, and support. What is also needed is access to adult-dominated decision-making spaces, which are often inaccessible to children and young people. Importantly, children need to feel empowered. This does not means that someone should empower them, but that they empower themselves through their participatory actions. According to Shier and Méndez, there needs to be accountability and follow up. When young people's participation in policymaking is not given its rightful due or the decisions they make are not implemented, any feeling of empowerment is removed and children's citizenship is countered.

What is needed is respect for and recognition of children. Yet children *do* participate as citizens in their communities, and many adults committed to fostering participation and citizenship *do* work with children. Perhaps what is needed is action on a wider level. Cockburn (2005b) has argued that civic culture which marginalizes or ignores children and young people's attempts to be involved in the political arena needs to change. Actions taken by young people to express political views, such as protest or resistance, are seen as illegitimate, and yet there are no other channels for action available to them. By way of example, in the United Kingdom during the protests against the war in Iraq in 2003 many children joined student movements, organized protests and school strikes throughout the country, and joined the worldwide movement against the war. Student anti-war protests were surely a display of active citizenship, and yet some children and young people were arrested, and some schools claimed that participation in the protests was nothing more than truancy (Cunningham and Lavallette, 2004).

Some blamed the compulsory citizenship classes that were introduced into elementary and secondary schools in 2000 and 2002, respectively (Fortin, 2008; Wyness, 2006), for encouraging this kind of political protest. The goal of the citizenship classes was to change the political culture of England through educational initiatives, and to encourage children and young people to think of themselves as active citizens able to engage in community and political affairs. However, as Cunningham and Lavallette (2004) point out, in actuality the content of citizenship classes had become more about moral obligations and responsibility than political action and they give little credence to the criticism that the classes fostered civil discontent among children.

In 2011 the National Citizen Service was introduced in England and Northern Ireland. This was set up to encourage young people – 16–17-year-olds – to become active citizens in their local communities. Service involves a short residential course away from home where the young people engage in team-building activities. Young people then spend one week in their home communities where they learn new skills through serving groups in their community. Participants also design a social action project, and then implement it with the intention to improve or contribute to some aspect of their local community. Examples of projects include fundraising for charities and anti-bullying campaigns. Carrying out a discourse analysis of the documents that introduced the service, Bacon, Frankel, and Faulks (2013) argue that the service does not truly consider young people to be citizens, although it gives lip service to their citizenship. Rather, it is adult directed and the documents assume young people lack the skills, attitudes, and values of citizenship prior to their participation in the service. Thus, the service ignores the skills that children and young people already possess. Bacon, Frankel, and Faulks argue that the discourse about the National Citizen Service is defined by an adult understanding of citizenship which is informed by a view that young people are citizens-in-the-making rather than citizens in the present. This reflects the dominant view that childhood is preparation for the future.

Can children be citizens then, bearing in mind the barriers to rights and participation described in this chapter? Leibel (2012) argues that they already are. Using the concept of *citizenship from below*, he points out that children participate in society through work or in the community or in the family. While recognizing the differences between children (in terms of power, socioeconomic status, gender, etcetera) and between children and adults, Leibel contends that citizenship from below can be realized when children become aware of their common interests and work together to do something about them. '[T]he necessity to do something in order to survive leads many children to take part in the spontaneous formation of groups whose self-help is frequently denigrated and criminalized as an early or concealed form of delinquency,' Leibel (2012: 187) writes. While Leibel is referring to working children's movements, we can clearly see how his assessment also pertains to the above example of schoolchildren's action against the Iraq war. Others agree with Leibel that children can be identified as citizens now rather than as citizens-in-the-making. This is because children are meaning makers, part of the everyday running of society, and have a role in defining and working with the norms and values of the social context within which they live (Bacon, Frankel, and Faulks, 2013). They are able to move within and between the hierarchies and boundaries of their everyday lives (James and Prout, 1995), with what Bacon and Frankel (2013) call 'strategic flexibility.' Rather than employing binaries of citizenship/non-citizenship, they contend that we could more usefully employ the notion of 'variable citizenship' where at different times and in different contexts children may be able to employ stronger or weaker strategies and performances of citizenship. This has resonances with Klocker's (2007) notion of thin and thick agency, and would seem to be a valuable approach to the question of children's citizenship.

Leibel (2012) asserts that citizenship for children can only become citizenship in practice if children have the opportunity to participate, which is best facilitated through education aimed at empowering children. This, however, leaves us with a question: to what extent can adults set aside their vested interests of power and control? Children may therefore remain marginalized from citizenship, as were other groups (people of colour, the poor, women) before them.

Conclusion

Children's rights and children's welfare are presently inextricably at odds with each other. Participation rights under the relevant articles of the UNCRC are difficult to ensure when enjoyment of them is so dependent on adult will.

For example, one important requirement of the UNCRC is that States Parties should appoint a child ombudsman, or advocate, to represent the interests of children to government. In Canada this has not been done, and there are particular problems in this context: the governments of Canada comprise provincial-level and federal-level governments responsible for different jurisdictions. Some provinces have appointed child advocates, while others and the federal government have not. Those provinces that do have child advocates do not all speak to the same mandate, so there is no cohesion in the Canadian approach. Canada's piecemeal approach and lack of federal commitment to an ombudsman is another example of an inadequate commitment to children. Canada has routinely been criticized by the Committee on the Rights of the Child for its failure to appoint a federal ombudsman and thus to truly work towards the participation aspects of the UNCRC.

This chapter has briefly considered what it means for children to be considered rights bearers and whether or not we can move beyond this to a conception of children as citizens in society. It would seem, despite the work of many adults who are committed to improving the lot of the world's children, that this is something which is not likely to happen any time soon. It has taken almost a hundred years for advocacy for children's rights to develop from the first draft of the Declaration to the present UNCRC when almost every nation in the world has ratified and implemented the UNCRC. It should not surprise us that progress is slow. This is no reason not to continue to raise the issues, and following Eglantyne Jebb, to attempt to revolutionize how we deal with children. Returning to the quotation with which this chapter opened, it may be that until we stop seeing children as *becomings* and begin to see them as *beings*, children's rights will never be fully met and policymakers will continue to ignore the rights that children have in the present and prioritize the need to protect the adult that they will become in the future.

Exercise and reflection points

1. Imagine that you are chairing a committee which is planning community events. How could you include children on the planning committee? What steps would you take to ensure that any child participation would be real and meaningful? Draft out a plan of action for doing this.

2. Follow up the newspaper articles mentioned in this chapter in relation to children making decisions about their health care (http://time.com/3660088/connecticut-cancer-chemotherapy-cassandra/, and http://www.dailymail.co.uk/health/article-441889/Whose-life-The-cancer-girl-whos-treatment.html). Consider how these cases are discussed in the articles. What view of the child is being represented? What is being said? Do you think that there are any circumstances when children should not make decisions about their health care?

3. Citizenship has been defined as 'a status that is given to members of a community who share those rights, responsibilities, duties and adopt those social practices that are intrinsic to belonging to and being a responsible member of that community' (James and James, 2012: 31). In your opinion, do children in your country have status as citizens? If not, is it something that they should have? Are there any reasons why children should not be seen as citizens? What do you think the consequences for society might be in seeing children as citizens?

Further reading

Bacon, K, Frankel, S. and Faulks, K. (2013) 'Building the "Big Society": Exploring representations of children and citizenship in the national citizen service,' *International Journal of Children's Rights*, vol. 21(3), pp. 488–509.

Lansdown, G. (2011) *Every child's right to be heard: A resource guide on the UN Committee on the rights of the child General Comment No. 12*, Save the Children Fund.

Percy-Smith, B. and Thomas, N. (eds.) (2010) *A handbook of children and young people's participation: Perspectives from theory and practice*, London: Routledge.

Shier, H. and Méndez, M. H. (2014) 'How children and young people influence policy makers: lessons from Nicaragua' *Children and Society*, vol. 28, pp. 1–14.

CHAPTER 5

Childhood and the State: Children, Social Policy, and Law

Keywords: Moral panic, poverty, family law, children and crime

Thus far the text has noted that childhood is a historical, social, and cultural construction. It has also been discussed how childhood came to be institutionalized in the family and in the school. This happened not through unfocused social progression, but was a determined effort carried out through the development and implementation of law and policy. In this chapter we want to show how and why childhood takes the form that it does with an emphasis on childhood in the developed world. In this chapter I again demonstrate that the discourses of childhood affect the experience of being a child and reciprocally, that the experience of being a child affects the discourses of childhood. To do this we will examine a variety of substantive topics: parental separation and divorce, children in need of welfare and protection, and children in trouble with the law. Following on from the discussion of children, rights, and citizenship, this chapter questions whether the state's interest in childhood is about protection of children, or whether it is about protection of the state. The chapter also helps us to see how law and social policy have effects on childhood as an ever-present structural form in society (Qvortrup 1994, see previous chapter).

The rise of the social

The French sociologist Jacques Donzelot (1979) is well known for charting the rise of the *social*. He posited that distinct social sectors developed in which diverse problems were grouped together and which comprised specific institutions with qualified staff. For example, school became the avenue through which education, social work, and medicine became intertwined in terms of access to children and families. The aim of this social organization was twofold: to ensure that everything that was a part of the state served the state, and at the same time served the public welfare.

In charting the rise of the social, Donzelot (1979) described how *government changed from a* government of families to government *through* the family. During the ancien régime, French society functioned by a system of obligations and protections involving patriarchal heads of families and the state. If heads of families kept their families in order, then they had the support of the state (Barrett and McIntosh, 1982). This system of obligations and protections crumbled in the French Revolution. The patriarchal control of the family disintegrated for many reasons, one of which was that certain segments of the population were without adequate state or familial control as evinced by the abandonment of illegitimate babies, the old, and sick to save expense. In order for the state to control the population (and for the purposes of this discussion, have control over children as future citizens) and to prevent future revolution, the state used the *tutelary complex* (Donzelot, 1979), or welfare through advice, to create the 'family' home. This enabled the state to intervene in the family. Laws were created to grant the state access to families who were suspected of improper child rearing.

Beginning at this time – not only in France but throughout the Western world – parents (and particularly mothers) were given power over the family, but this was conditional on them following the advice of the new professions (health, medicine, education, social work, etc.). As Wyness (2011: 97) states, 'a range of economic, political and moral forces converged on mothers and their children to produce childhood as a period of prolonged seclusion from the adult world of politics, employment and responsibility.' The family thus became privatized and yet at the same time susceptible to state intervention.

In a parallel fashion, in North America, the state promoted scientific child rearing. The emphasis on scientific child rearing became pronounced at the end of the 19th century and was, describes Dowdeswell (2013), associated with several societal shifts: the move to industrialization and urbanization the medicalization of childbirth; and the growing popularity of bottle feeding promoted by paediatricians. Essentially, the move to scientific mothering and child rearing removed the power of knowledge from women midwives and put it in the hands of doctors and other specialists. Doctors were also motivated to promote bottle feeding rather than breast feeding because they stood to gain financially. An example of the impact of scientific child raising is discussed on Box 5.1 on next page.

The interest of the state in childhood and in children is not simply about the protection and welfare of the child, but is also related to the interests of the state in producing future citizens required by and for the state. There is a tension here, however, While it would be true to say that many governments

---

BOX 5.1   Reshaping childhood and parenting: The Dionne quintuplets as an example of state intervention in family life

The Dionne quintuplets were born to a family in rural Ontario, Canada, in 1936 and were the first known case of quintuplets surviving. For the first few months of their lives they were in the care of their family, but the Ontario government removed the babies from their (poor, working-class) parents, ostensibly to care for the still vulnerable children. They were made wards of the state, and were raised in a hospital in their home-town built especially to house them, known as Quintland. When they were nine years old, their parents won custody of them. In Quintland, the girls were raised according to the latest scientific knowledge with a focus on cleanliness and regularity of feeding times and sleep. In this arrangement, the medical profession controlled the knowledge about raising children. Quintland was a bigger tourist attraction than Niagara Falls, with visitors lining up to observe the children at set times during the day.

We can see in this example the way in which the tutelary complex worked in Canada; the state directly intervened in family life. The Ontario government used the case of the quintuplets to promote the new scientific child raising (Strong-Boag, 1982). While the state argued that it was acting in the best interests of the children, Quintland also served the interests of the state. Publicity about the quintuplets and the scientific way in which they were being raised, 'encouraged' families to bring their children up in a more scientific manner as well, thus ensuring a healthier population for the future.

(see www.quintland.com for further information)

---

invest in childhood, and that what drives such investment is a need for the future adult to be adequately socialized, healthy and educated, some groups of children remain marginalized, as the following example shows.

Example: Child poverty in Canada

Child poverty is often seen as a problem for the developing world, but in fact it is endemic even in some of the richest countries of the world. In this section, Canada will be used as an example of how rich countries address child poverty. Much of the debate on child poverty centres on the definition of poverty and whether *absolute poverty* (that is, having nothing) should be the measure of it or whether *relative poverty* should be. (UNICEF defines relative poverty as 'living in a household in which disposable income, when adjusted for family size and composition, is less than 50 per cent of the national median income' (Measuring Child Poverty, 2012).) In its 2012 report, 'Measuring Child Poverty,' UNICEF created a league table showing child poverty rates in rich countries using relative poverty as the measure. The report places Canada and the United Kingdom in the middle of the table. In Canada, 13.3 per cent of children under age 18 live in poverty. In the United Kingdom, 12.1 per cent do. The United States has one of the highest rates of child poverty in the developed world with 23.1 per cent of its children living in relative poverty. In comparison, Iceland has only 4.3 per cent of children living in poverty. However, figures vary depending on the measurement used, as mentioned above. Another recent study shows that 37 per cent of British children are currently living in relative poverty (Adams et al., 2012). The poverty rate of children in immigrant or racialized groups within each country mentioned above is significantly higher than the UNICEF figures. The rate also varies depending on geographical location – inner city children generally fare the worst (Maxwell, 2009).

In Canada, investing in children with the intent of eliminating poverty among children by the year 2000 was a key objective in the 1997 Throne Speech. In fact, child poverty has increased annually, rather than it being eliminated. A recent policy in the province of Ontario, Canada, has been the Ontario Anti-Poverty Legislation enacted in February 2009. It seeks to reduce child poverty by 25 per cent. It would seem that the goal of completely eradicating child poverty is no longer at the forefront of policy, instead reducing the level of poverty is now the goal. UNICEF reported in the 2012 report:

> It is now more than 20 years... since the Government of Canada announced that it would 'seek to eliminate child poverty by the year 2000.' Yet Canada's child poverty rate is higher today than when that target was first announced. In part this is because the commitment was not backed by a compelling political and public consensus or by any firm agreement on how child poverty should be defined and monitored. Targets can only be a first step. (Measuring child poverty, 2012)

Article 27 of the Convention puts the responsibility on states parties to ensure the right of every child to an adequate standard of living (UNCRC, 1989). An adequate standard of living is, however, not available for many Canadian children, and indeed for even more children around the world. Despite local, national, and global measures that highlight child poverty, the problem has increased worldwide. Yet there is a contradiction here – in this chapter we have seen that policies about childhood are frequently created by the state with the intention to protect the future of the state, while at the same time the state presents itself as being concerned about child welfare. But by not adequately addressing child poverty, the state is jeopardizing its future citizens. For example, children living in poverty are more likely to be disabled and less likely to have access to medical and community support than other children. Aboriginal children are also more likely to experience poverty. For those children living off-reserve, the 2006 Canadian Census found that 49 per cent of first nations children aged under six were in low income families compared to 18 per cent of non-aboriginal children (see www.best start.org). The seeming reluctance of Canada to adequately deal with child poverty – especially for those most affected by it – structures the form that childhood takes in those communities. Food scarcity, inadequate housing, unemployment and poverty combine to make the experience of being an aboriginal child very different than that of other Canadian children. This might lead us to pose the question – who counts as a future citizen? Who doesn't? And why not?

Children, family, and family law

One of the main ways in which the state involves itself in childhood is when children are, for one reason or another, removed from the family. This section questions the role of the state as parent in troubled children's lives. The best place for children is said to be within the family, and this is reflected in several articles in the 1989 UNCRC as can be seen in the boxes below.

BOX 5.2 The UNCRC and relevant articles

From the Preamble: Recognizing that the child, for the full and harmonious development of his or her personality, should grow up in a family environment, in an atmosphere of happiness, love and understanding.

Article 9

1. States Parties shall ensure that a child shall not be separated from his or her parents against their will, except when competent authorities subject to judicial review determine, in accordance with applicable law and procedures, that such separation is necessary for the best

---

> **BOX 5.2 (Continued)**
>
> interests of the child. Such determination may be necessary in a particular case such as one involving abuse or neglect of the child by the parents, or one where the parents are living separately and a decision must be made as to the child's place of residence.
> 2. In any proceedings pursuant to paragraph 1 of the present article, all interested parties shall be given an opportunity to participate in the proceedings and make their views known.
>
> **Article 20**
>
> 1. A child temporarily or permanently deprived of his or her family environment, or in whose own best interests cannot be allowed to remain in that environment, shall be entitled to special protection and assistance provided by the State.
> 2. States Parties shall in accordance with their national laws ensure alternative care for such a child.
> 3. Such care could include, inter alia, foster placement, *kafalah* of Islamic law, adoption or if necessary placement in suitable institutions for the care of children. When considering solutions, due regard shall be paid to the desirability of continuity in a child's upbringing and to the child's ethnic, religious, cultural and linguistic background.

In these articles, the state is positioned quite clearly in the role of providing for and protecting children, as well as ensuring that the child – as an interested party – has the opportunity to make his or her views known. Here we focus specifically on how that tension plays itself out when children's family life is subject to state intervention.

Children's voices in parental separation and divorce

Scholarship of children and parental separation and divorce has grown over the last decade. Influenced by the social study of childhood as well as the corresponding focus on highlighting children's voices and experiences, scholars from a variety of disciplines have reported on what children feel and think when their parents separate or divorce. Birnbaum and Saini (2013) carried out a broad-based study in which they reviewed 44 published research studies that involved 1525 children from 13 countries. They found that the majority of children were surprised that their parents were separating because this had not been communicated to them previously. They found that most children were sad that their parents were separating, although a few felt relieved. Children worried about being caught between their parents, and many felt that they wanted some say in their post-separation residence. It should be stressed that the children did not want to choose one parent over another; they just wanted to be heard. Children also wanted to be fair to both parents, and to share their time equally between parents. The vast majority of children wanted to be better informed at all stages of the process. Many also valued having someone to talk to, such as someone appointed by the court (Birnbaum and Saini, 2013). However, not all children wanted to talk to strangers about their parents' divorce.

Children actually have little say in where they will live following parental separation or divorce even if they do express a preference. The allocation of residence to children post-divorce is a decision made by the court and is based on what is in the best interest of the child. In arriving at a decision, the judge will hear from practitioners (social workers, guardians, court-appointed persons) working with children to ascertain their wishes. According to Article 12 of the UNCRC, children have a right to have a view in all matters concerning them. However, Article 3 puts the best interests of the child (as defined by adults) as a primary or sometimes paramount consideration (see Chapter 4). In this way the competence and agency of the child (which is only partial under the Convention, as discussed in Chapter 2) is secondary (or at least, complementary) to what adults decide is best for the child. The law therefore disables children by determining how and when they have a say in matters that affect them. Not until the passage of time, that is, until they are adults, are children considered competent to make decisions for themselves (McNamee et al., 2005: 234).

Hemrica and Heyting (2004) note that judges and practitioners – social workers or other advisors to the court – involved in cases of children affected by parental separation and divorce are working with a similar set of assumptions and adhere to similar discourses of childhood. Thus, even when there is disagreement about whether the child or the judge should decide on residence, the justification for each argument is heavily based on the future outcome for the child.

The construction of childhood employed by those working with children affected by parental separation draws heavily on developmental psychology (see Chapter 2). Because children are considered incompetent and the property of parents, their need for protection overrides their status as rights-bearing individuals. The right of the child to have a view is thus often deferred, as practitioners work to protect the child's future relationship with each parent (James, James, and McNamee, 2004). It is deferred until the child is considered of an age to have a view, showing the dominance of the psychological discourse of aged-based development. We can see that constructions of childhood *and* constructions of adulthood are brought into play in court decision making about children. Thus, adult-perceived best interests and protection of the child override the rights of the child.

In a study that explored how constructions of childhood influenced practitioners working on cases of parental divorce or removing children from the family, James, James, and McNamee (2004) found that the practitioners filtered children's wishes and feelings, and in so doing, marginalized children's voices. In one of the families of the research project, the divorcing parents disagreed over the children's future residence. During the research observation, the middle child made it clear that he wanted very much to live either with or close to his father. He was obviously distressed throughout the interview, and was in tears at times when he talked about his mother moving the family away from the father. However, the court report prepared by the practitioner and presented to the judge provided no hint of the distress that the child was under, but merely stated that the child would like to continue contact with the father as the non-resident parent. Practitioners write children's feelings and emotions out of the court reports in order to protect both the child and the parent for the child's future relationship with both parents. 'Until there is a willingness to consult children in ways which go beyond the token and to publish their views whether they be critical or not, we will continue to marginalize and exclude children at the same time that we ostensibly protect their welfare' (Day Sclater and Piper, 2001: 429).

When asked what they considered to be the best and the worst things about being a child, practitioners reported that the best thing about childhood was innocence and lack of responsibility – 'the fact that you can go out and play and not feel guilty.' The worst thing, they said, was being powerless and not being respected for your views. Powerlessness is the experience of not having responsibility, so the best thing about being a child is intimately related to the worst thing: 'This suggests that those childish pleasures associated with the "freedom from responsibility" can easily be transformed into darker feelings of "powerlessness," which are, however, precisely those feelings, according to practitioners, that make childhood a less than happy experience' (McNamee, James and James, 2005: 229)! This short discussion of children's voices in cases of parental separation and divorce has revealed tensions between the discourse of the best interests of the child and the discourse of children's rights to a view and to be heard. In sum, 'the law works to restrict children's agency through the reliance on adult interpretations of children's needs' (McNamee et al., 2005: 242). It should be noted that more recently courts in Canada and in the United Kingdom are moving towards judicial interviews, whereby judges speak directly to the child. It has been said, however, that judges need to know and understand the social study of childhood and the view of the child as having understanding irrespective of developmental age because in practice they still tend to equate chronological age with understanding, thus they are still not listening to the child's wishes and feelings in all matters affecting them (Henaghan 2012).

Children in the care of the state

A historical example of state intervention in childhood can be seen in the examples of the Australian 'Stolen Generations' (Ivec et al., 2012) and the Canadian 'Sixties Scoop.' Aboriginal children were forcibly removed from their families and placed with white families for the purposes of assimilation into white culture. In Canada, between 1960 and 1980, about 20,000 children were taken, many of whom were emotionally and/or sexually abused by the families who adopted them (Narine, 2012). These kinds of policies of forced assimilation have since been described as genocide (Van Krieken, 1999). While these policies are no longer in effect, there are still disproportionately higher numbers of indigenous children in the care system that non-indigenous children in Australia (Ivec, 2012) and in Canada, where in some provinces almost 80 per cent of children in care are indigenous children – even though they make up only 5 per cent of the population of Canadian children as a whole. Similarly, in the United States, the number of Native American and African American children in care is three times higher than it is for Caucasian children (Trocmé et al., 2004).

On the face of it, these figures might seem to be reflecting racist approaches to child welfare and child protection, but as Trocmé and colleagues point out, there is a more complex explanation. First, there are more risk factors among the aboriginal population (for example, poor housing, high rates of single-parent families) which child protection officers take account of. Second, the experiences of abuse suffered in residential schools might affect parenting of future generations (Trocmé et al., 2004). The echoes of forced assimilation of children through state removal into care or residential homes continue to reverberate in the experiences of children today.

Children who have been in state care – 'looked-after children' as they are commonly known – usually fare worse when it comes to education and future employment than non-looked-after children. Many looked-after children have physical, mental, and emotional health difficulties in later life, which can be exacerbated by the transition from care to independence (Dixon, 2008). Looked-after children become independent at an earlier age than children who are not in care, who may continue to live with parents into their twenties and even beyond. In Canada, children 'age out' of state care at 18, and child welfare agency support stops at the age of 21. In a report on care leavers by the Ontario Association of Children's Aid Societies (CAS), social workers commented that children in care deserve to be treated by CAS 'as a good parent would' treat their own child. Cutting off all state support to children and young people at a comparatively young age in comparison to children who have not been in the care system leaves care leavers with no emotional, financial, or physical support. The report states

BOX 5.3 Wanting to move into foster care, contributed by 'Laura,' a student reflecting on her childhood

At the age of twelve, I was placed into foster care after I demanded that my mother call the children's aid on herself because her mental illness was affecting her ability to parent. This was made worse by her abusive boyfriend who had also moved in. I knew at twelve what I was doing when I said I wanted out. As much as it may have hurt to tell others that my mother was physically and emotionally abusive, I knew that it was what I needed to do to have a better life for myself. When I entered foster care it was difficult to understand why I had a different set of rules then other children my age. It felt unfair and I fought back. I stood up and expressed that as a child my age it was normal to go for sleepovers, to go to movies late and to have friends over. I constantly had to fight for not only what I wanted but what I needed. As I approached the age of sixteen I expressed that I wanted to live on my own. I did not see this as a problem because I had been paying my own cellphone bill since I was fourteen, had a part time job at the age of thirteen and by the time I was sixteen I had two part time jobs. I worked twenty to twenty five hours a week while I attended high school and maintained a high average. As a young adult I enjoy sharing my story because I like to demonstrate that children can be their own advocate and show their agency in many ways that are often ignored. What children want most is to be listened to and have their interests and desires acknowledged. As a child in foster care I often felt alone and unheard, and although it took a lot of gusto, patience and reliance on my social worker my hard work paid off. Some people look at me after I share my story with pity and sadness and express that they are sorry for the childhood I had. However, although I experienced many adversities I would not change my experiences. These experiences allowed me to see my strength and to demonstrate to others the knowledge and power a child can have if they are heard and the happiness it can bring a child to know that not only are they being listened to but their opinion matters in terms of their own life and where it is going. In a nutshell, it is important that when we consider a child's best interest we focus on the child's needs and desires and reasoning behind those as opposed to forcing our own opinion on a child. All children have a voice, and they need to be heard.

that young people leaving care have two additional challenges that other young people do not:

(1) they have to manage the emotional and other impacts upon them of early disruptions in their familial life, often including serious forms of abuse and neglect and (2) the system which provided for their care during the necessary childhood separation from birth families, requires that these youth leave care in an arbitrary fashion unrelated to the readiness or capacities of the youth. (OACAS, 2006: 18)

When the state acts as a parent, then, it is not acting as a 'good parent' but is failing 'its' child.

In several Canadian provinces, 16 is the upper age limit for children to receive protection (even though the UNCRC defines *child* as anyone under the age of 18). This leaves many children, defined thus by the UNCRC, in difficult situations. Ironically, by ending the funding and support of children at age 16, the state assumes that children have a high degree of agency and competence (which elsewhere is denied them) even if they have not been responsible for making decisions about themselves. Although advocacy on behalf of children in care takes place at the provincial level, it may be that the lack of a federal ombudsman or advocate for children limits the efficacy of provincial advocacy work, and as a result the situation of children in and leaving care has not improved. When looking at the role of the state in relation to childhood it is clear that it is failing as a parent to children in state care. We now move on to consider conceptualizations and discourses of childhood which come into play when children are in conflict with the law.

Children in trouble with the law

In order to contextualize society's response to children who commit crimes, it is firstly helpful to consider the concept of the 'moral panic.' The term *moral panic* is drawn from the seminal work of Cohen (1980, third edition 2002; see also Goode and Ben-Yehuda, 2009). It refers to the public's heightened fear of crime or other social ill that is often caused by over-reporting of the media. The over-reporting of a particular crime results in the general public having a skewed perception of the extent of the crime or problem and, in its fear, to call for increased police attention. Increases in prosecutions and sentencing lead to further news reporting, fuelling a panic among the general public that the matter is out of control. This leads to further calls for more policing, and so the cycle continues. This process ends only when the news media moves on to some other issue. The following discussion exemplifies the construction of a moral panic when childhood itself was seen as a threat to societal values.

About 20 years ago, two-year-old James Bulger was abducted from a shopping mall in Liverpool, England. The boys who took him walked around the city for several hours before killing him and abandoning his body on railroad tracks. They were seen by many people but no one intervened. The murder of James by two ten-year-olds inflamed public opinion, no doubt promoted by a collective sense of guilt, to the extent that any details about the boys continue to provoke violent responses in many people even today. This was not the first case of children killing children by any means, so the question arises, why did this case cause so much outcry? In part, because the death of one particular child appeared to signify the death of childhood (James and Jenks, 1996). The romantic illusion that childhood is a state of innocence and purity could no longer be defended after the Bulger murder. The murder proved our worst fears, that children had the capacity to knowingly commit violent crime (James and Jenks, 1996: 320). The young killers stood outside of the category *child* by virtue of their crime, and they were vilified in the media and in popular opinion. Newspaper headlines of the time called them 'evil freaks,' 'the spawn of Satan,' and 'little devils' (Jenks, 1996: 128). Further, it was not just the two boys who began to be classified in this way, but constructions of childhood in general began to be questioned. Was childhood a time of innocence, or were children actually born with original sin?

At the time of the Bulger killers' trial, English law presumed that children aged 10 to 14 were too young to knowingly be responsible for their crimes (the legal concept of *doli incapax*). During the trial, the prosecution drew on evidence, primarily from psychiatrists and welfare workers, to show that the boys did know what they were doing and therefore were criminally responsible for their actions. They were tried in adult court rather than in youth court, and thus denied the status of *child* in law.

Following the Bulger case, and the resulting moral panic, childhood was no longer believed to be a state of innocence but a time of evil. Many stores instigated a 'truancy watch' in the wake of the murder, whereby any children seen in shopping malls or stores during normal school hours without an accompanying adult were reported to police. Thus the surveillance of children in public space increased as a result of the changing perceptions of childhood (Frankel 2012).

Comparing this case with another child murder a year later proves illuminating. In Norway, a five-year-old girl was beaten, stripped, and left to die in the snow by two six-year-old school friends. This case did not see any of the publicity and outrage that the Bulger case did. The murdered child's mother had no hate for the children who killed her daughter. 'They were punished enough by what they did,' she said (Hattenstone, 2000). In contrast to the Bulger killers, the two Norwegian boys were never named, were not prosecuted, but were given ongoing therapy and assisted in their transition back into school. There was no publicity, and no moral panic emerged in relation to childhood. They were seen as too young to have known what they were doing (James and James, 2004). The age of criminal responsibility in the England is ten, and eight in Scotland. In Norway, the age of responsibility is 14 (James and James, 2004). The Bulger killers could not have been tried as adults in Norway.

Although the next example involved teens rather than younger children, it also shows how one set of constructions of childhood and youth can falter and be re-constructed in the face of violent crime committed by children. The Public Broadcasting Service (PBS) TV documentary, 'When Kids Get Life,' documents the cases of five teenagers who were sentenced to life without parole in the state of Colorado.

Following a media-orchestrated moral panic over the so-called 'summer of violence' – media reporting of violent crimes by young people far exceeded *actual* crime – a special session of the legislature was called and juvenile justice laws in Colorado were redrafted to include heavily punitive legislation (Dorfman and Schiraldi, 2001). Fifty young people who had committed serious violent offenses including murder while under the age of 18 where imprisoned for life. (This legislation has since been struck down, although many who were imprisoned before the change in the law remain in prison for life and have not had their sentences reassessed.) The PBS documentary shows adults in the justice system talking about some of the teens featured in ways that echo the media discussion of the Bulger killers. The young people were said to have 'holes in their souls,' to be in effect less than human – and certainly not 'children.' With regard to child imprisonment, under the 1989 UNCRC all states who sign on to the Convention are in agreement with Article 37 which holds that no child should be imprisoned for life without the possibility of release for offences committed before the age of 18. The laws enacted by the state of Colorado clearly breach this Article, but of course the United States has not ratified the Convention.

The demonization of children through media reporting and in public opinion can lead, as we have seen in these examples, to a range of responses which includes harsh punishment for those who violate the category of *child*. As Goldson (2001) demonstrates, the symbolic demonization of children becomes an institutional demonization through the implementation of law. The individual child offender's background is ignored and instead morality and responsibility are emphasized. Children as young as ten years old – an age at which, in other arenas, children are considered far too young to take on responsibility – are made to take on adult responsibility for their actions. The examples presented here show how shifting constructions of childhood can have very real effects on the lives of children and young people: 'Constructions of innocence and vulnerability necessitating protection contrast sharply with conceptualizations of a threatening and dangerous childhood demanding correction' (Goldson, 2001: 41). State responses to children in trouble with the law move away from a protectionist and welfare-driven approach to one of punishment and removal of the offender from the category *child*.

Conclusion

In this chapter, we have considered the state's interest and involvement in children and childhood in relation to social policy on poverty and law in the developed world, and have argued that the state's interest in childhood lies in its concern with the future of the state. While ostensibly developing social policy for children to protect them and ensure their wellbeing, frequently the overriding concern is the future wellbeing of the state. When in trouble with the law, children are placed outside the social category of *child*. When the state began to demonstrate an interest in child-rearing through the promotion of 'scientific' methods, as shown in the example of the Dionne quintuplets, it became involved directly in parenting. However, when the state acts as parent to the children it apprehends, it appears, from the evidence discussed here, to be failing. What this chapter shows is that childhood is structured by society in various ways, and that discourses of childhood continue to shape the way that childhood is experienced, whether for the structural group 'children' or for individual children.

Exercise and reflection points

1. Try and think about any moral panics in relation to children and young people in your country. Gather news or media reports and critically examine them to see what discourses of childhood are being employed in the discussion.
2. What do you think might be the consequences of *properly* hearing children's voices in family law? For the parents? For the child(ren)?
3. Can you identify any policies in relation to child poverty in your country? How well do you think these are working? What could be done better?

Further reading

Bala, N. (2004) 'Child welfare in Canada: An introduction,' in Bala, N., Zapf M. K., Williams, J., Vogl, R., and Hornick J. P. (ed.) *Canadian child welfare law: Children, families and the state*, Toronto: Thompson Educational Publishing Inc.

Barrett, M. and McIntosh, M. (1982) *The anti-social family*, London: Verso.

Frankel, S. (2012) *Children, morality and society* London: Routledge (especially Chapter 3).

Jenks, C. (1996) *Childhood*, London: Routledge.

CHAPTER 6

Children and Family

Keywords: siblings, corporal punishment, power and control, family practices

We have seen in earlier chapters that childhood became firmly institutionalized in the school and in the family. While these are the two main structural institutions of childhood in that they act to shape the form that childhood takes in society, they are also arenas of action for children, that is to say, where children can exercise agency. Drawing on existing research, this chapter provides examples of the lived experience of being a child in a family setting. While the family is often seen as the best – even the 'right' – place for children, it is true that many children do not have happy family lives. In fact, the family is often not the wholesome place for children that we would wish it to be. Many children for one reason or another are removed from or choose to leave their families, abuse and neglect being two of the many reasons this happens. The following example, written by university student 'Angelina' reflecting on her childhood, clearly demonstrates this.

BOX 6.1 Angelina

It was not my age that made me vulnerable; it was the law and the societal perception of childhood which stopped me from being able to escape from the abuse perpetrated by my parents. I knew exactly what I needed: to get away from them. As a child in a society which does not acknowledge that it is ever best for a child to be away from his or her parents, my only options were to run away or to harm myself, both of which I did several times. These attempts – thoroughly logical and well thought out given my circumstances – were perceived as mental illness and rebellion. This allowed me to be further victimized and isolated and made it impossible for me to seek the help that I needed.

This example, and the one following, do not reflect the innocent and free childhood as constructed in Western society. What they do show very clearly – and without wanting to dismiss or underestimate the difficult childhoods these women experienced growing up in North America – is children's agency, competence, and resilience.

BOX 6.2 Veronica

Speaking about her reflections on growing up, Veronica said:

I thought we should let him die. My father was normally brown, the colour of coffee when only a drop or two of milk is added, but on that night he looked purple. I was called down from my bedroom by my mother late that night (or early that morning) to evaluate the situation. His breathing was shallow and his pulse was weak. I had the most formal medical knowledge in my family because I was attending a high school whose focus was on health professions. I was at this school because when I was twelve I had forged my mother's signature on the permission slip that allowed me to apply for admittance. I understood, at the age of twelve, that I would have to gain some type of marketable skill if I wanted to live on my own. And I definitely wanted to live on my own. I was certain of that. I wanted to leave home as soon as it was legally possible to do so because even though I had no evidence of it, I believed that I could create a life for myself that did not include violence, rape and drug use which were all rampant in my home life. That life would be possible when I turned eighteen, and so I needed to prepare for that date. My parents were not planners, they were negligent. In fact, the reason dad was purple that night was because he had done some combination of drugs that did not mix well. And the reason I thought we should just let him die was because that would fix a lot of our problems. It was a solution to the nightly beatings my mother endured, and the constant fear we felt. If he died, things could start getting better. I hinted at this thought to my mother but she was horrified. We held vigil that night and dad pulled through. As the morning dawned his breathing improved, his pulse returned to normal and his colour went back to his normal shade. Mom was relieved. Dad was oblivious. I was disappointed.

These two accounts show that when we focus on how children experience their family, their stories frequently fall outside of the common-sense 'cornflakes packet' understanding of childhood – the nuclear family with 2.5 happy smiling children. While the study of the family has a long history within sociology, children's *experiences* of family and children's *voices* within the family have received significantly less attention, with the main focus being on the socialization of children (see Chapter 2, and below). Within psychology, the study of children has been decontextualized from the family; the emphasis has been on what the child will become rather than on what the child is presently experiencing. It has been pointed out that the social study of childhood has not demonstrated much interest in families either (Wells, 2009). This has in part been due to the desire to study children's lives in their own right. Conceptually removing children from the family has allowed scholars to prioritize children's voices and perspectives (McNamee and Seymour, 2013). However, scholars grounded in the social study of childhood are beginning to address this lacuna, and some of these studies will be reported on in this chapter.

We will first turn to an examination of children's relationships with parents and siblings before going on to address issues of power, control, agency, and resistance in relation to time and space in family life. Children may be the primary focus of the family; however, they often experience family life from a position of powerlessness, although there are opportunities for agency and resistance in everyday family life, as we shall see. As Solberg (1997: 126) has argued, 'it is in the organisation of daily life, the dividing up of tasks between family members and the laying down of rules of conduct that implicitly determines what it means to be a child.' Given this, the context in which childhood plays itself out emerges as parents and children interact. This chapter therefore encapsulates a discussion of children's lived experiences in the family.

Children and family in non-Western contexts

Not all of the world's children live within a Westernized, nuclear family structure, consisting of parent(s) and dependent children. For example, in those parts of Africa that have been affected most seriously by the AIDS epidemic, many children have taken on the role of household head, either because their parents have died or because their parents are too sick to manage the household. Usually concern about child-headed households (CHH) positions children as *too* responsible (in other words, children are meant to be dependent, not responsible), and thus as vulnerable victims in need of social intervention. However, children in CHHs are positive about the responsibilities that they have and the challenges they face, and they are proud that they can contribute to their family's wellbeing. It can be difficult when they lose their position as head of family. One young woman had cared for family members since the age of 12 and generated the income in her CHH because her mother was an alcoholic (Payne, 2012). She was competent, and happy and proud, to do so. She found it difficult to give up her responsibilities as head of the household on those occasions when her mother was able to resume her place as head of the family. In other words, she found it difficult to return to being 'a child.' Children in CHHs see their responsibilities as part of their everyday lives, not as anything special, nor do they feel that it makes them vulnerable.

All too frequently childhood and children's everyday lives are viewed from the perspective of Western conceptualizations of childhood. This does children in non-Western cultures a disservice because they are seen as different and therefore deficient. Payne (2012: 407) states that seeing children in CHHs as competent social actors rather than as victims 'give[s] due respect to the agency exercised by children and young people *as they are*' (my emphasis) rather than trying to 'fix' them to fit the Westernized conception of the vulnerable child in need of adult protection. Payne's perspective clearly reveals children's competencies. In the West parents leaving a child unaccompanied for a comparatively short period of time may cause outrage, but when we consider the diversity of childhoods throughout the world we can see that children unaccompanied by adults actually have the ability to sustain and lead families.

There is still much work to do in relation to researching children's views and experiences of family life in non-Western (and indeed in Western) contexts. While there may be very good descriptions of family life in other cultures (e.g. Lancy, 2008), research that positions the child centrally in the analysis is scarce. It is for this reason that this chapter now focuses on children and families in the West – but the reader should be conscious of the diversity of experiences cross-culturally.

What is a family?

To begin, it is useful to consider what parenting and family mean to children. Reviewing and reporting on a range of studies, Pryor and Emery (2004) found agreement in the various findings in children's views on family. For example, children's views of family composition – who makes up a family – matters less to children than an atmosphere of love, caring, and support. Further, being loved and cared for takes precedence over blood ties, co-residence, or legal status in children's views of family. Children have been asked about their views on family life during family transitions such as parental separation and divorce. While family changes such as these are often out of children's control, they do feel that they should have a say in family decisions. They feel that family life should be focused on the children in the family rather than the adults. Following parental separation or divorce, it is important to children that they continue to be loved and cared for; this is more important to them than the form their family takes (Pryor and Emery, 2004).

But the question remains, how do children define family? Children reject the concept of a 'proper' family, holding a much more fluid and pragmatic view of family, although they felt that to be a 'proper family' there had to be children (Brannen and Heptinstall, 2001; see also Wade and Smart, 2002). At a time when blended families have become more common and children experience multiple family forms they are able to draw on a much wider experience of family than merely their own to define family. Wade and Smart (2002) carried out a study that looked at the strategies and resources children employed during times of family change, particularly when their parents separated. In particular, they were interested in the type of support that children had, or that they needed.

Wade and Smart categorized the families of the children in their study into four types:

Aggregated families – families that have seen several complex changes, and where there are several parents attached to various children within the family.

Divorced families – this family structure is straightforward in comparison to aggregated families. It is characterized by small family size, and cooperation between parents post-separation.

Meshed families – a family where the extended family is important and children in these families are 'emotionally literate' as emotions are not suppressed.

Diasporic families – a family where a parent has returned to the home country or where the extended family is dispersed.

There was no one family form or set of experiences of childhood that could be made to fit all the children/families, thus Wade and Smart (2002) contend that we have to see the complexities of children's lived realities in terms of family. This study found that what matters most to children is the quality of the relationships that they have rather than the biological connections within whatever family form they live in.

Children in this study used two main coping strategies at times of family change: diversion and emotional expression. Children who used diversion described just wanting to forget about what was happening. Often they wanted to sleep because they knew they would feel better when they woke up. Those who employed 'emotional expression' tended to show emotions such as anger. Some talked to their friends, but others didn't trust other children to keep their family matters private. Children said that they didn't want to talk to teachers, because they felt that teachers didn't listen. Children wanted kindness and a choice as to whether or not they would speak with the professionals working with the separating family.

Children's views of being parented

While there is a large body of academic and popular literature related to parenting – in particular related to how to be a 'good' parent – most of this does not come from the perspective of the child. However, there are some studies in which children have been asked about their views on parenting. We turn to them now in order to demonstrate how children and parents view parenting differently. In a British study children said that they wanted to be loved and cared for, listened to, and taken seriously by their parents. However, according to one study, only 71 per cent of eleven-year-olds actually *felt* loved and cared for by their parents, and this declined with age – the older the children got, the less likely they were to report feeling loved and supported. In respect to being listened to and taken seriously, only 41 per cent of adults felt that listening to children was important while 75 per cent of children said that this was important – clearly a dissonance between what children think and what adults think (Madge and Willmott, 2007).

Studies carried out in Switzerland (Montandon, 2001) and Finland (Böök and Perälä-Littunen, 2008) found that children in those countries also expected similar qualities from their parents. In the Finnish study, children said that they thought that parents should be responsible, that parents should teach children by example, and further, that parents' responsibility to children should be lifelong. In a Serbian study, only about one-third of children said that parents asked them for their opinion in making family decisions, while parents said that they did not think children needed to routinely take part in decision making (Tomanovic, 2003). The right of the child under Article 12 of the UNCRC (see Chapter 4) – to be able to have a view on all matters affecting the child – is clearly not always upheld in the private space of the home. In children's views of parenting, then, children expect parents to listen, love, provide support, and to be responsible. However, as has been discussed, many children do not feel that their parents demonstrate these qualities.

Family time, parental control and punishment

Policymakers often assume that families are spending an inadequate amount of quality time together, and blame this for any problems within the family – family time is under threat. This concern is evident in the recent establishment of Family Day in the province of Ontario in Canada. This holiday was intended to give families the opportunity to spend more quality time together. Christensen (2002) addresses the issue of 'quality' family time from a child's perspective. She found that children did not feel they needed *quality* time, but instead, *ordinary* time with parents – eating meals and watching TV together – was important to them.

In everyday family life, there are struggles over resources, and time is one of the resources which is controlled, contested, and resisted.

BOX 6.3 Mary

My parents divorced when I was 2 years old and my father left my older brother, older sister and myself with my mother. As I didn't remember him or when they split up my life really wasn't any different because I didn't know anything different. It wasn't until I met my stepfather that I understood my childhood wasn't average. Shortly after my stepfather married my mom my father came back into our lives and we began to see him. He lived about an hour and a half away so we would go to his house every other weekend which was not always fun because we would hate the drive and we would only stay for two days and we couldn't hang out with all our friends in our home town. It was always tough when there was a birthday party or sleepover that we couldn't attend because we were out of town at our father's. Not long after, my stepfather and mom had two children, which definitely shifted how we were treated, and the attention we got. I felt as though my childhood got cut short because once my younger brother was born I was responsible for myself and also helping with him. I was in charge of getting my school work done, doing my laundry, babysitting, etc. and having that responsibility has really shaped me into who I am now. Once my stepfather and my mother divorced there was even more responsibility put on to myself and my older sister to take over co-parenting and help my mother through her legal battle with my stepdad. At the end of the day my fondest memories are still running around hanging out with all my friends on the street and being with my older brother and sister. We felt like we could do anything and had so much fun escaping into our own world for a few hours a day.

Within the family, children's time is subject to control. Parents decide what chores children do and when they do them, what time children get up and go to bed, when children can play outside with friends and when they have to come home, when children do their homework. In addition, children's play or leisure time is also subject to adult control as parents have the power to interrupt the child's play at any point with requests and demands. In response to this sometimes overbearing control of their time, the children of Christensen's (2002) study demonstrated strategies of resistance by not doing immediately what parents asked – most children said that they would comply with parental demands 'after a few minutes.' Similarly, Montandon (2001) found that children employed a range of strategies to resist parental control: circumvention of parental dictates, 'wearing down' parents, and negotiating, which included arguing and bargaining. Montandon found that, although subject to parents' demands, children did not see themselves as 'defeated' by parents, rather they saw themselves as full participants – or actors – in the family setting.

It is not only children's time that parents control, but their use of indoor and outdoor space can also be controlled and policed by parents and siblings (McNamee, 1998a). This section shows how children as agents encounter spatial restrictions within the family. One of the factors that keeps children inside during leisure time is increasing parental fear of 'stranger danger.' This limits and controls children's access to outdoor space. As Halden (2003) has noted, there is a tension between the belief that the outdoors is the perfect space for children and parental fear for children's safety. Children, however, while aware of potential dangers in public space, see themselves as experts in their own lives, and feel that their personal safety is not the responsibility of their parent, but their own (Valentine, 1997b: 78). One strategy that children use to negotiate their access to public space is not telling parents about risky situations they have been in so as not to worry them and have their freedom curtailed. Children do not simply passively accept parental restrictions, but see themselves as competent to deal with the dangers of their neighbourhoods. More recently research findings appear to confirm that the 'stranger-danger' fear amongst parents is limiting children's outdoor play (Holt et al., 2015) and that girls' outdoor mobility is more restricted than that of boys (Foster et al., 2014).

Children who disobey parental restrictions or instructions may in some cases be punished. This is one reason why some children choose to obey or comply with parental demands. In Christensen et al.'s (2001) study, children were often grounded. This means that children were confined to the home, or perhaps even to their bedroom, for a specified period of time, depending on what the child had done. Punishment, which often was gendered, also included the curtailing of children's activities – boys were most often punished by parental restriction of their indoor activities (notably the removal of computer and video games) while girls were most often punished by making them stay home (rather than being allowed to go out with friends). It is interesting that when children refused to spend time with family members (for example, refusing to visit grandparents) they were seen as problematic, and yet at the same time the practices of grounding children or excluding them from family events was seen as punishment (Christensen et al., 2001: 150).

The punishment of children has thankfully changed over time. To take a historical perspective, Albanese (2009: 201) reports that in the Massachusetts Bay Colony in the 17th century, a 'stubborn or rebellious son of sufficient years and understanding' could be brought before the courts and put to death. Grounding and the restriction of favourite activities is positively kind compared to this! It has to be noted, however, that corporal punishment in the home is still a regular reality for some children. There are class and gender dimensions to this however – fathers are more likely to use physical force than mothers when disciplining children, and lower-class families more likely than middle-class families to use force (Valentine, 1997a: 56).

Even in countries that have banned corporal punishment in schools and other institutions, banning it in the home has proved more difficult. Article 19 of the United Nations Convention on the Rights of the Child requires states to protect children from 'all forms of physical or mental violence' while in the care of parents or others.

BOX 6.4   UNCRC Article 19

1. States Parties shall take all appropriate legislative, administrative, social and educational measures to protect the child from all forms of physical or mental violence, injury or abuse, neglect or negligent treatment, maltreatment or exploitation, including sexual abuse, while in the care of parent(s), legal guardian(s) or any other person who has the care of the child.
2. Such protective measures should, as appropriate, include effective procedures for the establishment of social programmes to provide necessary support for the child and for those who have the care of the child, as well as for other forms of prevention and for identification, reporting, referral, investigation, treatment and follow-up of instances of child maltreatment described heretofore, and, as appropriate, for judicial involvement.

The Committee on the Rights of the Child has consistently interpreted the Convention as requiring states to protect children from all corporal punishment and has recommended that prohibition should be accompanied by public education to promote positive discipline. Many countries follow the guidelines of the Convention, and some have implemented anti-corporal punishment laws (for example, Sweden implemented such laws in the 1970s). However, it is still legal in many parts of the world. No American states have banned corporal punishment in the home, nor is it banned in the United Kingdom. In Canada, corporal punishment is allowed in the home for children over the age of 2 and under the age of 12. Some European states have outlawed the practice, but overall the progress towards ending corporal punishment in the home has been less readily adopted than the move towards ending it in schools and other institutions. Very little research has attended to the child's views on this issue (but see the excellent and growing research documented at the website endcorporalpunishment.org). The charity Save the Children did, however, do some research specifically about children's views of discipline and corporal punishment in Scotland. Ninety-three per cent of children thought there were other ways parents could punish, and 76 per cent felt it was wrong to hit a child. In a study conducted in Northern Ireland in 2002, 94 per cent of children said they would not hit their children when they had them (Rustemier, 2004: 6), tellingly displaying children's views on corporal punishment.

Sibling relations

Exploration and analysis of sibling relationships have largely been the province of psychology. The focus there has been the role of sibling relationships in the development of the child and the effects of age and gender on sibling interaction (Bacon, 2012; Punch, 2008). While psychological studies of siblings can reveal useful information, psychology cannot help us to see all of the experiences of the sibling relationships (Edwards et al., 2006: 119). Until comparatively recently, the social study of childhood has not systematically explored sibling relations either, although there has been some notable work done in this area since the late 1990s (Bacon 2010, 2012; Edwards et al., 2006; McNamee, 1998a, 1999; Punch, 2005, 2008) and the following section will focus on such studies.

Social geographer Samantha Punch has made a valuable contribution to the study of children's perspectives on family relationships, particularly in looking at sibling relations. In several publications she has shown how children, as competent social actors, negotiate and interact in the sibling relationship. She shows how the sibling relationship can be explained in terms of generational practices, rather than simply as developmental outcomes (2005); how time and space in the family affect sibling relationships (2008); and the strategies siblings use to 'bribe' or 'barter' with each other (Punch and McIntosh, 2009).

Running throughout Punch's work on siblings we have considerations of age, power, and negotiation. Children in her study felt that their siblings were 'always there.' This made them difficult to get away from, but also meant that they didn't have to expend as much effort in the relationship as they had to with friends. Punch (2008: 337) details many aspects of child siblings' negative interactions with each other, stating, 'the children themselves suggested reasons for their antagonistic behaviour towards siblings which included their shared history, the permanence of the sibling bond, their lack of privacy and control of space in the home and the obligation of living together.'

Physical proximity does not always relate to feelings of closeness among siblings, as another study on twins noted. Although from the outside the twin sibling relationship seems to be the very epitome of closeness, many twins used strategies to put distance between themselves and their twin (for example, dressing differently, preferring different music). The feeling of a sibling being 'always there' can be more intense in the twin relationship. For example, same sex twins may have to share a bedroom, toys, and even clothes, and sometimes the only way they can feel alone is by locking themselves in the bathroom (Bacon, 2012). However, other studies have shown that even though siblings may dislike each other, they will often protect their sibling when they are being bullied at school, as Hadfield et al. discovered. At the same time, older siblings reported wanting to be separate from their younger brother or sister at school (Hadfield et al., 2006: 69).

As mentioned above, birth order of siblings is important in their relationships from the psychological perspective. However, Punch and McIntosh (2009) demonstrated that birth order was not experienced as a fixed, static hierarchy but played itself out in a much more fluid way. Drawing on the perspectives of the social study of childhood, and exploring strategic interaction between siblings in exchange and bartering practices, the authors showed that children commonly used bribery and made deals with each other in order to get their siblings to do things for them. Some siblings were more successful than others in these deals and this can be linked to birth order. Younger siblings had a less developed range of tactics than did older ones. Thus, there were advantages to being the older sibling, but younger siblings also capitalized on their positions, for example youngest children might elicit special treatment because of their 'smallness.' Punch and McIntosh's (2009) work allows us to see that the social structure of age and birth order is not fixed, but is dynamic and fluid, and that children – as competent social actors – negotiate and redefine their relations with siblings.

BOX 6.5   Jean

Mama wakes us up by saying 'wakey wakey.' We have sliced bread (with no crust) with Nutella and sometimes jam when the Nutella finishes too fast for breakfast. We have hot chocolate or sometimes cold milk. We have to hurry, because the school bus comes to pick us up at 8:20. School starts at 8:50.

We live in the French countryside so the school system is very different from the towns and cities. There are three schools spread out amongst five villages. Each school is a class and each teacher is also a head mistress. In the morning, my sisters take two buses and I take three. The infant school is in our village. The next two schools are juniors from 6–9 and 10–11. My sisters are in the same class and they get on each other's nerves. There are only about 25 children per class.

Each school has a kitchen and a lady who cooks delicious meals for us. On the TV they say we have to eat five fruits and vegetables a day – Yuk. She's very kind and bakes a cake for our birthdays. Our teacher is also very nice, even though she tells us off when we don't listen. Our class has an interactive white board and we use the computers a lot. We also talk with other schools in our district. During the year we go on school trips together. The teacher says it's good for us to meet other children who aren't our family and neighbours. The mayor is also one of our bus drivers, he's a nice man.

School finishes at 4:30 pm and we get the buses home. Most of the time mama is already home and we have tea time. We love tea time. Mama makes cakes, crepes, or waffles and we're allowed to have juice or milk. Most days after school we have sports: football, basketball, tennis, karate, roller hockey. And on the weekends we have all the matches. We also get homework from school for the week, but we do it all on Sunday mornings. We don't go to school on Wednesdays, I don't really know why. The President decides that.

I love wakeboarding, Pokemon cards, watching One Piece and playing on my DS and the Wii. My sisters like all the girly things like Barbie and Hello Kitty and playing mama and papa. When I play with them, I'm the dog!

Another example of tension or difference in sibling relations can be found when looking at Mennonite families. Interviewing adults about their childhoods growing up in Mennonite families, it was common that women would talk about the differences in their experiences of family compared to those of their brothers. Many of the women I spoke to had as many as 12 siblings. Mennonite girls are expected to take part in cooking, cleaning and child care from a very early age – mothers of such large families rely on the work of their daughters to help. Many of the women described cooking their first family meal at the age of seven, and caring for babies also at around that age. Boys also do work for the family, but their work is outdoors. Boys would work on the family farm or work on neighbours' farms, although in summer girls worked in the fields too, in addition to their household chores. One woman recalled how her brothers received very different treatment than she and her sisters, which was clarified for her when one day they sneaked into the boys' bedroom and found that they had a TV. The girls had never had the opportunity to watch television, never mind have one in their rooms. Girls served their brothers and parents meals before they ate themselves, and were subject to stricter control in terms of what they could do and where they could go. One woman told me that she felt that her childhood had ended when she was nine. This was how old she was when her mother gave birth to a sickly baby and suffered from depression, which meant that the girl had to take over the household responsibilities. Poignantly, one woman when describing her resentment that her brothers got a weekly allowance whereas the girls in the family didn't, explained that girls were simply not seen in her family and not heard either. This experience was not uncommon. While the Mennonite example may be seen as atypical, it was not experienced that way for the women describing their childhoods. Feelings of difference within the family and in the community were compounded by understanding that not all children experienced life in that way. What this example does is to highlight gender differences in the experiences of childhood.

Children *doing* family: A way forward in research of children and family?

A recent turn in sociological studies of the family has been influenced by the work of David Morgan (1996, 2011a, 2011b) and his notion of family practices. Morgan advocates looking at what a family *does* instead of what a family *is*. According to him, family is a quality rather than a thing. This understanding shifts us towards an understanding of family as a set of activities or practices which can take on different meanings at different points in time. The potential of this new theorizing of family for the social study of childhood is that it includes children in the analysis. Traditional sociological work on families mainly focused on parents, leaving children strangely absent from the family in sociological analysis unless they were being socialized. As stated earlier, the development of the social study of childhood involved conceptually removing children from the family in order to explore their experiences. As a corrective, a focus on family practices as Morgan advocates enables the conceptual repositioning of children within the family so that children's accounts of how they *do* family can be heard; the perspectives of all family members, children included, are taken into consideration. As Seymour (2007: 1098) notes, the concept of family practices 'allows for the recognition that family life is being both created and reproduced in the process....[This is] achieved through the activities and interactions of family members.' Thus, the activities of children creating and reproducing family through interaction can be taken into account.

We do not only *do* family in the private space of the home. For example, Seymour (2005, 2007) has looked at family practices in family-run hotels and guesthouses demonstrating the ways in which people *do* family in the combined location of home and workplace. Dorrer et al. (2010) drew on the work of Seymour (2005, 2007) in developing their research of food practices in residential care homes for children in Scotland. In this work, Dorrer et al. examined the strategies of residential workers who tried to create an environment for children that was like family and home, and these efforts were frequently focused on food and meal times. In the attempt to make living in the care home more like home, staff gave children menu options, encouraged children to participate in food preparation, and put in place more informal 'take-away' meals around the TV during weekends. For the children, however, it was more about the feelings and relationships present while preparing and consuming food that made the home feel like home, and less about participating in food preparation as differences existed between the home's kitchen and the kitchen at home. For example, the kitchen in the family home would not be locked outside of meal times, while in the care home it would frequently be locked.

Children, family and socialization theory revisited

A recent publication has bravely re-engaged socialization theory, the critique of which has been at the core of the work carried out within the social study of childhood. Allison James's (2013) text takes another look at socialization theory, but attempts to see the socialization process through the child's perspective and experience. She aims to see *how* socialization happens, and to see the active part that children play in the socialization process. In so doing she shifts the emphasis away from seeing the process as something done *to* children to something which children are actively engaged in. Drawing on the work of Smart (2007) James posits that:

(1) Like adults, children have personal lives and are able to reflect on them
(2) Children's lives are lived in interaction with others
(3) Children's life experiences are embodied and emotional
(4) Children experience the structures and institutions of the world through diverse interactions
(5) Children's personal lives are biographical.

(James, 2013: 17)

James structures her text around these five points, showing through examples from research with children that the socialization process is at work in their ordinary, everyday lives. There is not scope in this textbook to discuss more fully this potentially important new text in detail here (see also the discussion in Chapter 2), but what James does is to reposition childhood as central in theorizing about children in the family. As she states in her conclusion, childhood studies should speak to more than just childish concerns, but also to social theory.

Conclusion

This discussion has shown that children's agency is generally *thinned* by parental authority, but also that it can be *thickened* by the child's strategies of resistance (Klocker 2007). Katz (1994, in Seymour and McNamee, 2012) has discussed 'spaces of betweenness.' In the gaps between parental and child power, children may employ strategies of resistance. Children can be seen, then, to have relatively little autonomy over their daily lives; at school their time is controlled by adults, and at home it is controlled by parents and some-times by siblings. Even the calls for increased family time can have an unfore-seen negative effect – more family time may in fact lead to increased power struggles within the home over children's use of time. However, as Solberg (1997: 127) states: 'although in many ways children's position is a weak one, they do not passively adapt themselves to what their elders say and do.' In other words, children are, and indeed see themselves, as agents in the family relationships. While children's everyday social lives are structured by parental supervision and control, children can, and do, exert agency within the fam-ily. While this may often be in the form of resistance to control rather than unfettered agency, we can see children as competent agents within the fam-ily setting. We have discussed children's ideas of what a family is, explored children's views on being parented, sibling relations, the control of children's

time and space, and pointed to newer possibilities for researching childhood through the use of the concept *family practices*.

Exercise and reflection points

1. Why is there a difference between what children expect of parents and what parents think? Can you remember a time in your childhood when you disagreed with your parents but were given no choice in the matter? How did this make you feel? Now that you are an adult, do you assess the situation any differently than when you were a child?
2. Should corporal punishment in the home be allowed? Under what circumstances? Why do you think that some countries are reluctant to abolish it?
3. Exercise: Collect some images of children and families in diverse contexts. What is being portrayed in the images? What assumptions are you making about the child in the family? Is there a particular discourse of childhood being represented in the images?

Further reading

Bacon, K. (2010) *Twins in society: Parents, bodies, space and talk,* Hants: Palgrave Macmillan.

Dermott, E. and Seymour, J. (ed.) (2012) *Displaying families: A new concept for the sociology of family life,* Hants: Palgrave Macmillan.

James, A. (2013) *Socialising Children,* London: Palgrave.

Punch, S. (2005) 'The generationing of power: A comparison of child-parent and sibling relations in Scotland,' in Bass, L. (ed.) *Sociological studies of children and youth,* vol. 10, pp. 169–188.

CHAPTER 7

Children in School

Keywords: Friendship, bullying, space, time, testing, discipline, agency, power

The view of the child as *becoming* is central to educational approaches to children, and schooling is thus necessary to turn the incomplete child into a finished adult. Children spend a large amount of their time in school. Indeed school (along with the family) could be said to be where children best 'belong.' It is surprising, then, that children's views about school are not often elicited nor incorporated into educational policy. On the face of it, schools seem to be run by adults for the adults within them for the purpose of educating students. However, rather than focusing on the purpose of schooling from the educationalist's perspective, in this chapter we highlight issues of power, control, resistance, and agency in children's experience of school. In relying on the perspective of the child rather than the adult educator, this chapter will provide examples of how children experience school: how peer relations play out in friendship and in bullying; how gender, race, and ethnicity shape children's experiences of school; and how time, space, and physically being in the school affect children.

In Chapter 1 we discussed how the introduction of compulsory schooling in the developed world was an important turning point in constructions of childhood. Children were moved from the economic world of public space into the controlled spaces of home and school (see Wyness, 2011; Hendrick, 1997). During industrialization in the West, children came to be seen as a potential problem, and the solution to the problem was compulsory schooling whereby children could be taught moral, mental, and physical discipline. This would also ensure that the next generation of adults would be socialized into the social and cultural norms of society. The purpose of education for the masses was thus not simply about learning, but about providing a specific form of education and effectively containing children in the educational institutions. This was done, in part, by envisioning children as ignorant becomings rather than experienced actors, whose ignorance could only be remedied by age-related progression. As Wyness (2011: 144) notes, 'through the ordering of the curriculum, children were to become relatively less ignorant as they moved in incremental fashion towards a state of full social membership.' Bolstered by advances in psychological testing and theory (discussed in Chapter 2), the new compulsory school system positioned children as becomings (Albanese, 2009: 88), inferior to adults, and as deficient in competence, thought, and understanding. This was not, it should be stressed, merely an accident or a by-product of a system that was there to protect and help children, but a deliberate shift in the construction of childhood; children were not to be seen as people with competencies and agency but as 'others' who needed to be reshaped to fit the requirements of society (Heydon and Iannacci, 2008: 3).

Currently, there are global attempts to remove children in the Global South from the world of work and instead to place them in schools. For example, one of the UN's Millennium Development Goals is to achieve universal primary education, whereby all children should – by 2015 – be able to complete a full course of elementary education (http://www.un.org/ millenniumgoals/education.shtml). The shift to universal education will place particular demands on children and families in developing societies in terms of balancing schooling with work (see next chapter). It will be interesting for childhood scholars to see if the changes in the construction of childhood that happened historically in the West are echoed in the developing world (see Chapter 2 and Hollos, 2002) as the movement towards universal education continues. Without doubt, many inequalities exist in relation to access to education due to poverty and gender in particular.

BOX 7.1 Equality of access to education: Malala

Malala Yousafzi was, in 2014 and at the age of 17, the youngest person ever to be awarded a Nobel Prize. This was in recognition of the work that she has done in promoting education for girls. Shot in the head by the Taliban in Pakistan in 2012 in an attempt to permanently silence her outspoken views on education, she subsequently recovered and has continued her campaign. July 12th (her birthday) has been nominated 'Malala Day' by the United Nations. She has famously said 'one child, one teacher, one book and one pen can change the world' and working with the hashtag #booksnotbullets she points out that if spending on arms was stopped worldwide for just eight days, it would provide enough money to put every child in free education for 12 years (www.malala.org).

Frequently, children living in poverty work to support their education, by the money they earn going to pay for school fees, books and so on. A true commitment to universal education requires careful thinking about the consequences of simply abolishing child work.

Power, control, and discipline in schools

Discipline through the control of space

The spatial arrangement of the school serves to clearly define child spaces and adult spaces. Teachers and administrators use space as a form of control. Classrooms are set up to emphasize the hierarchical system within the school institution (Devine, 2002: 311). Children's desks are often set out in disciplined rows so that children can see the teacher, but more importantly so that the teacher can easily see all of the children. The movement of children through school space is ordered and regulated by adults, and while this may ostensibly be to protect children, it also ensures that children are subject to the gaze of adults. Devine (2003: 114) writes, 'space as symbolic of the power relations between adults and children in school is reflected in the children's lack of ownership over the school itself...when they say that the school belongs to the principal; the classroom to the teacher.' Children, then, do not see their school as 'theirs' – it is a place *for* children, rather than a children's place (Rasmussen, 2004).

Discipline through the control of the child's body

When children first start school, they move from their homes, where they have been under the influence of their parents, into a new environment in which their wishes and routines no longer count to the same extent as they did at home. Teachers see their job as training children to fit in with school expectations of what a pupil is. On one hand, this requires pupils to be independent but, on the other hand, this independence means conforming to the rules and norms of the school. This, Mayall (1994: 75) argues, sends a mixed message to students. For example, when children begin school, they are expected to be independent enough to take care of their own bodily needs and yet because they are required to conform to the norms of the school they have to wait for permission from the teacher before using the washroom. As Christensen et al. (2001: 213) point out, teachers tend to see children as mature when they demonstrate their acceptance of the rules of the school – when they conform.

Much of the discipline imposed on children in the school setting is about controlling their bodies. Children are at one and the same time seen as *at* risk (from other children and from adults) and *as* risks. Both of these views justify adult perceptions of when and how to control children and childhood (Caputo, 2007: 180). It was pointed out in Chapter 2 that children are not simply the product of discourse, but are real, embodied beings. As such, a child's body is both a site of adult control and a tool in children's resistance to that control. Children may also be subject to bodily discipline in the form of corporal punishment in school in some countries. The Global Initiative to End All Corporal Punishment of Children (www.endcorporal-punishment.org) tracks the progress of eliminating all forms of corporal punishment of children country by country. Only 33 nation states have imposed a complete ban on the practice – whether at home or in school, and the United Kingdom, Canada, the United States and Australia do not appear on this list.

Children are moved through the school day by means of the timetable; they are physically instructed in how to move between classes, in the proper comportment of the body, and when to move or be still. Simpson (2000: 72), in her ethnographic study of schoolchildren in England, argues that because control is gained by way of the child's body, children demonstrate the greatest amount of resistance to that control through the same medium, that is, through small acts of defiance using their bodies, bodily functions, and bodily waste. In Simpson's study boys belched, broke wind, spit, and generally made noises with their bodies. Girls tended to express their resistance by flaunting the rules of the dress code. During a boring lesson the girls swapped shoes under their desks until each girl was wearing an unmatched pair of shoes. A more worrying manifestation of 'distraction' was the boy who, in order to get out of a music lesson, deliberately stabbed himself with a pencil and drew blood, thereby necessitating a visit to the school nurse (Simpson, 2000: 73–76). Children's agency and resistance, as Simpson points out, is often carried out in direct opposition to the very controls imposed on them.

Discipline through the control of time

Time in school is tightly controlled both for students and for staff. The timetable, aurally enforced by the ringing of the bell, structures daily life in school. The timetable lets children know where they are expected to be at all times, and also makes sure that children who are *not* where they are supposed to be are visible to the disciplinary gaze. Adults in school control all aspects of children's daily experience of time passing in school, and can punish children by further controlling time, for example, depriving them of playtimes – perhaps the only time within the child's day which is at least theoretically free from adult control (Christensen and James, 2001: 204). The control of children's time by the school extends to the space of the home, as seen in the requirement that students complete homework. In this way, control is passed from the teacher to the parent to ensure that work is completed (Smith, 2000).

The study carried out by Christensen and colleagues described above drew on ethnographic material collected from English schoolchildren transitioning from primary (elementary) school to high school (middle school) at ages ten and eleven. As part of this project children were asked whether they felt time passed quickly or slowly at school when presented with various scenarios. Children felt time passed quickly when they were interested in the lesson, when they could work with their friends, and when they liked the teacher delivering the lesson. When none of these features were present, children felt that time dragged. Lunchtime (which in the schools of the study was for an hour, and included time for eating and play) was seen as 'a rest from work' and 'a time to be with friends.' Indeed, being with friends was one of the things that children liked best about school, whereas they found the process of being educated 'boring' (Christensen and James, 2001: 84). Children in this study were aware that they had very little control over how their time was spent, who they could sit with, what they could wear, where and when they could eat, what they were supposed to work on, and so on. Children therefore saw themselves as powerless in school (Christensen and James, 2001: 79–81).

Children in the Asian continent often spend more time at school, or in private tutoring, than their parents spend at work. Children characteristically rise early in the morning and attend school until 4:30 in the afternoon, followed by homework, test preparation, and perhaps individual tutoring in school subjects. On the weekends they have 'enrichment' classes such as piano lessons or sports practice. The time that they have available for play and rest is thus severely restricted. Play is seen by adults as potentially harmful, and is discouraged in that it may encourage unruliness. Chinese mothers interviewed by Naftali (2010) felt that the child's main duty in life was to study in order to enhance their future careers and to repay parents' investment in the child. Drawing on the comments of one of the adults interviewed in the study, Naftali describes Chinese children as 'caged golden canaries,' cooped up in school and then in the home, their time controlled throughout their childhood.

Schooling: Difference and exclusion

Children's experience of being at school is also structured by culture, race, and ethnicity. This section provides examples from different cultures of how this plays itself out in children's lives.

BOX 7.2 A Chinese student recalls her childhood experiences at home and at school

I was born into a middle-class family in a middle-sized city in China. My father is a businessman and my mother is a scientist. I think that most of the Chinese parents value their children's school performance a lot, and it is pretty common for parents to hit their children for getting a poor grade, but my parents never did so. However they did hit me for other reasons, usually for disobeying their orders. I did not know that in some countries hitting children is illegal, so I did not have bad feelings back then.

In Chinese middle schools, at 7:40 a.m. we start the morning reading and then the first two classes which are both 45 minutes long and have a 10-minute break in between. After that, we have to do some 'morning exercise.' After that are two other classes. We have a longer lunch break which is from 12:00 to 2:00 or 2:30 (one for winter, the other for summer). In the afternoon, we have four 45-minute classes with a 10-minute break in between each. Then, in my high school, we go home, but almost all other high schools have a night self-study time.

Some teachers do not finish their class so they would keep teaching during the breaks, and we hated those teachers. But when I look back, those are things I can actually remember and the moments are like little icons of my high school life so they become kind of precious to me.

I did skip class several times in high school. I started to do it because it was intense and exciting. Plus, some of my teachers really suck at teaching. After the first few times, I just did it because I did not want to go to the classes and I found that I did not really have to. I rarely went out of the school when skipping the classes because that was more dangerous and I do not really have things to do outside of school. It was more like a challenge to the school rules. I usually stayed at the sports ground because it is a place full of students so I would not be so suspicious.

Tremlett (2005) explored the history of the segregation experienced by Roma children in the Hungarian education system and why Roma children so often fail in school. The Roma are an ethnic group of travelling peoples. Despite very clear guidelines in Hungary about racial discrimination, Roma children are marginalized within Hungarian state education. Many of them are placed in 'special' schools for children with learning difficulties where

BOX 7.3 Bailey

Preschool in Ecuador, contributed by Bailey, a student volunteer who spent a summer working in a preschool

The preschool was run by the most wonderful, caring, intelligent women – that having been said, the preschool was not at all run 'properly' by Western standards. The children had full reign of the goings-on during the day and within the space. They had a choice as to their participation in every educational session – when supplies allowed for one. Most importantly, the children were only physically constricted from leaving the premises – how they got there, how they got home, and where/when/how they went within the preschool grounds was entirely up to them to decide. Specifically, one of the children was four, and about to start kindergarten – it was her responsibility to walk her younger sister aged two to and from the preschool every day. In this scenario, children were not only allotted the freedom to make their own choices within the walls of the institution, but were in fact expected to live up to what others might claim to be 'adult-like responsibility.' Despite the fact that these children are in fact children, supposedly advancing through the same developmental stages, it is clear the cultural reality did not adhere to Westernized romantic views of childhood.

they receive lesser quality education. Tremlett (2005) contends that over 40 per cent of children in special schools in Hungary are Roma. Though there has been an increase in the number of Roma students attending school since 1971, a gap remains between educational attainments of Roma and non-Roma students in Hungary. Additionally, unequal funding distribution to educational facilities, lack of professional training for teachers, and improper report monitoring have contributed to Roma children being denied proper education (Tremlett, 2005: 160). To further explain the discrimination against Roma children, Tremlett provides an extract from an interview that she carried out with a teacher who is apparently pleased that she doesn't teach Roma children: 'I teach only the best children,' she states. 'I don't really like [the Roma children]... they are very different' (Tremlett, 2005: 153). The children in this study knew that they were treated differently, and while some had strategies to deal with this, many children felt the segregation keenly.

In another example of ethnic exclusion, First Nations and aboriginal children in Canada, the United States, and Australia have received a very different kind of schooling than non-aboriginal children. The history of residential

---

BOX 7.4 Martha: A First Nations person

For some people, being a First Nations person doesn't mean anything. Either you are lazy or greedy by taking welfare or not paying taxes. No one ever wants to look at the positives, to see the humble lives that First Nations want to live. I mean, who wouldn't be angry or frustrated when people are confined onto a piece of land called reserves and racial comments are being thrown every which way when they leave? I left the reserve when I was ten years old, but I still consider myself as a First Nations person despite the harsh misgivings. I want to be a teacher so no-one, especially First Nations children, will ever feel like the lesser human. We are human. Just like everyone else.

---

schools in Canada will be explored here as an example, but what happened in Canada also happened in the United States and Australia. Residential schools were designed to assimilate First Nations children into white society (Albanese, 2009). Children were – often forcibly – removed from their homes on reserves and placed in institutions run by churches and religious orders. There they were prohibited from speaking their own languages, brothers and sisters were separated, and the physical, emotional, and sexual abuse of children was common. Generations of children were removed from their families, and grew up without any understanding of what it meant to be a member of their traditional community, or of belonging to a family. The consequence of this for First Nations people has been devastating.

The level and quality of education of aboriginal children in Canada is still far from equal to that enjoyed by non-aboriginal children. Less than one-third of aboriginal children have a high school education (Centre for Social Justice, 2007). Education in Canada is still very Euro-centric, with little attention paid to providing aboriginal content in schools off reserves. Overall the situation is improving slowly, with many reserves now operating their own schools.

While not a racialized group, Low German-speaking Mennonites will be explored next in relation to children's experiences of school. Children living in the colonies in Mexico attend school until they are needed for work within the home or on the farm – generally around age 12. Additionally, the school year is built around the agricultural calendar so that their education does not conflict with when they are needed in the fields. Sometimes attending one-room schools, children may still write on slates, and their learning may be focused on the catechism and other religious texts. Many

Mennonite families migrate between the Mexican colonies and Canada, either for seasonal work, or more permanently. When Mennonite children arrive in Canada to live permanently, they encounter a school very different than what they are used to. They may not be able to understand English (Low German is the cultural language of the Mennonite population) and will dress, look, and feel very different from the other children in school. As one in a series of interviews carried out with adults reflecting back on their child-hood experiences, a Mennonite woman described to the author her experi-ence of school in Canada as being 'a nightmare' because of the difference between her very traditional clothing style and the contemporary style of her peers. She felt that everything about her life was wrong. The traditional dress referred to consists of a dress which comes past the knee and fastens up to the neck with elbow length sleeves and which may sometimes be worn with a long apron covering it. When entering the public school system in Canada, Mennonite girls' clothing immediately marks them off as different. What also made this interviewee different was the attitude of her parents to education – homework was 'a waste of time' and she was not to be seen with school books when she was supposed to be working in the home. In fact her brothers would burn any school books that they found her with. She was taken out of school at age 12 to help at home.

This example makes clear that not all children experience school in the same way – for this interviewee her faith and culture meant that childhood for her was not only different from many of the other children at school, but that she experienced it as much *more* difficult. Several of the Mennonite adults I spoke to experienced feelings of difference from other children, which may or may not have resulted in being bullied at school. It is not, of course, only Mennonite children who are or who feel different at school, but this example illustrates how aspects of cultural and religious identity can shape children's experiences of childhood.

Many researchers have pointed out gender inequality in the classroom. It has been noted that boys have more classroom talk with teachers and speak out more than girls. Girls are often encouraged to resist traditional roles, but boys are rarely ever encouraged to do the same, and elementary schools are still seen to reinforce hegemonic masculinity (that is, the dominant cultural form of masculinity in a society) (Albanese, 2009: 87), as evident in the fol-lowing example. In a study of gender socialization of kindergarten children in Hong Kong, it was found that teachers treated boys and girls differently. The researchers visited four kindergartens on 105 occasions. In many observed episodes, there appeared to be a 'boys first' rule, which was imposed by teach-ers and not questioned or resisted by girls. Indeed, girls were expected to take second place in terms of gaining attention from teachers, and the researchers contend that the schools have a male-centred hidden curriculum which reflects the traditional Chinese value of male privilege (Chen and Rao, 2011).

An issue not often discussed by scholars researching children and school is that of sexual harassment and violence among children. (This hesitancy reflects, in part, a refusal to see children as anything other than innocent.) Research which has focused on this, however, shows that it is an everyday occurrence in the experience of schoolchildren. In a study of gendered sexual harassment in elementary schools, Reynold (2002) describes how boys use sexual language to intimidate girls, objectifying them and displaying misogynistic attitudes towards them in ways that confirm their masculinity. Physical sexual violence was also reported by the girls in her study which this took the form of boys pulling the girls' underclothes or punching them in the breast area. Reynold (2002: 420) argues that 'physical sexual violence seemed to be another means of reasserting and reproducing boys as powerful in social circumstances which often rendered them powerless or [which were] out of their control.' Boys also used homophobic language to tease other boys who did not fit normative masculinity, although this was less common than heterosexual harassment. Similar findings are discussed by Pascoe (2007) in the context of American high schools. She describes groups of boys talking about girls as sex objects, including talking about the rape and brutalizing of girls and women in ways that drew on and reinforced particular masculine identities. Thus, the everyday school experience of girls may be marked by feelings of powerlessness at the hands of both teachers and boys in school.

Friendship and bullying at school

There are many studies to show that peer pressure has a large impact on young people's decision making (Frankel 2012, Albanese, 2009). In searching only for *effects*, academic research can and does miss the importance of what friendship *means* for children and young people. Looking at the meaning which friendship has for children, rather than effects, allows us to view children as competent beings rather than potential becomings (cf. James, 1993). For children, school is not simply a place of education, but also a social space where friendship can be performed. Children often report that they enjoy being at school, but it is usually in describing their friendships that they talk about their enjoyment rather than when they describe their learning (Bendelow and Mayall, 2002: 297). This section explores some of the academic literature pertaining to children's friendships in school, and also discusses the antithesis of friendship – bullying.

Friendships can be circumscribed by the organization of the school and by the restrictions on children and young people's free time. For example, the young people in one study (Amit-Talai, 1995) spent an average of 50 hours a week either at school, in part-time jobs, or in extra-curricular activities, and this time does not take into account hours spent on homework or domestic chores. Thus, the young people had little time to spend with their friends outside of school in the form of simply hanging out with them. It was at school, therefore, that the young people were able to be with friends. However, even in school children found it difficult to find time and space to spend with friends. This meant that the time they did have for interaction with friends was intensified – and school staff often intervened in this inter-action. As Amit-Talai (1995: 151) states, '[l]unch time presented an ongoing contest between the determination of students to cluster and the equal deter-mination of staff to disperse them.' Consequently, students had to find other spaces, often marginal school spaces, for friendship encounters – girls used the washroom. This example shows that despite the attempts of adults to control children's time and space in school, children demonstrate *thin* agency (Klocker, 2007) through resistance – in this case, by using marginal spaces in which to perform friendship.

In contrast to many studies of girls' friendships (mostly psychological) that have characterized them as dyadic (that is, between two people), Browne and George (1999) looked at friendship groups. These groups consisted of a leader, the 'inner circle' and a wider periphery of girls. The leader of the group was often chosen because she was the person most of the other girls would like to have as their best friend. In this kind of group, the leader generated feelings of insecurity among other group members as a way to maintain control of the group. All girls other than the leader demonstrated some form of anxiety over the possibility of exclusion (Browne and George, 1999: 294–295). This anxiety within the group sometimes had negative effects on the girls' school-work in that they would spend more time worrying about their friendships than focusing on school. In this way, while the friendship group could func-tion as a support mechanism for the girls, it could also be destructive in the way that group tensions played out. This also shows how power in children's relationships can be exerted by children themselves, not always by adults, as the following discussion shows.

Devine (2003) studied schoolchildren in Northern Ireland. While friend-ship was not the main focus of the study, her work revealed some interesting findings. First, 72 per cent of the sample of schoolchildren identified other children, rather than adults, as having the most power in school (see also Frankel 2012). This finding may run counter to some of the arguments out-lined above, which emphasize the power that adults have over children in school. What it reveals is that when children are directly asked about these issues, a different understanding emerges – children see other children as having the power to include and exclude (see also James, 1993). Second, in the pressurized atmosphere of a school, with the educational emphasis on testing, children require friendship for support. Indeed, in Devine's study, 53 per cent of children said that the most important trait in a friend is that they are supportive.

In terms of friendship traits, Dutch schoolchildren said that the main characteristic they looked for in friends was trustworthiness, unlike the previous example in which children wanted friends to be supportive. This study also highlighted some of the gendered dimensions of friendship. When a friend betrayed trust, girls, as opposed to boys, tended to hide their feelings and to confide in a mother, female teacher, or another supportive friend. Girls were also more likely to confront the individual who had betrayed them, either verbally or physically, than boys. Girls also seemed to be more emotionally affected by betrayal than were boys (Singer and Doornenbal, 2006).

What of those children who are unpopular and cannot attain status in school and through friendships? Albanese (2009: 92) argues that children who are bullied at school are those more likely to have low attainment levels, to be from marginalized groups and have attributes (related to appearance, race, socioeconomic status, or gender) which are negatively perceived by other children. Much of the research carried out on bullying in schools is grounded in the discipline of psychology, with, perhaps surprisingly, very little work coming from the social study of childhood. Psychological research provides statistics of bullying rates and the gendered nature of bullying, and focuses on the effects of being bullied on children. While it is important to know and understand how widespread and pervasive bullying is in school, what should not be forgotten is that it does not only take place in school, but also in wider society. Without wanting to underplay the often devastating results of being bullied, it is interesting here to look at the context of bullying in school.

In an educational climate of conformity and competition, and where issues of power are at play between adults and children, and among children, it is perhaps not surprising that bullying in school is so prevalent. Bullying is not, however, exclusively situated in childhood and school, but is endemic in society. The work of Leonard (2006) clearly shows how conflict in wider society plays out in children's experiences of school. As she states, 'the inequalities that exist outside the school gates often get replayed within the school setting' (Leonard, 2006: 443). Writing of schoolchildren in an area of Belfast, Northern Ireland, which for decades had been marked by sectarian violence between Catholic and Protestant populations, Leonard interviewed schoolchildren who had to travel across sectarian lines to school. Only 4 per cent of children in the area attended schools which were integrated, while all other children attended either Catholic schools or state-run Protestant schools. During the period when she was carrying out her research, some of the schools she was working in experienced violent episodes including smashing of teachers' cars, bomb threats, and sectarian attacks on children and adults. Although children travelled to school in specially provided buses, the buses were often attacked by adults of the other religious group throwing stones and debris. The violence in that society curtailed children's movement, as no children were allowed to walk to and from school. Indeed, some girls talked about the school playground as a 'no-go' area because of the risk of being pelted with stones if they played there. However, the children were resilient even in this dangerous atmosphere. They developed strategies to cope with threat and risk, for example, they removed their school uniforms so that they couldn't be identified as belonging to one side or the other. For children, it was important that the adults around them gave them full information rather than protect them by withholding information about the conflicts. With full information the children could further develop strategies to cope, and increase and demonstrate their resilience and agency, thus demonstrating children's competence.

Standardization and testing

The provision and enforcement of education for children is not separate from wider social, political, and economic issues. Education policy is not developed in a vacuum; discourses of childhood and dominant ideas about what kind of children a society needs influence it significantly. In Western societies, education has become a consumer product where the consumer is not the child but the parent. Policies that promote standardized testing of students to produce league tables enable parents to choose the 'better' school based on performance ranking. While the objective of the tests is to measure student skills relative to the curriculum and within and between school districts, the public sees it as an assessment of school performance. Thus, teachers are 'teaching to the test,' that is, training the students to take the test (Volante, 2004). This comes at the expense of the student's experience, as classes in subjects not being tested are dropped in favour of test practice sessions. In their study of schoolchildren's experiences in the North of England, Christensen and James found that some schools tried to retain activities such as sport, art, and drama, but scheduled them during the children's own time (lunch playtime or after school). Some schools even extended the length of the school day so that these extra activities could be maintained (Christensen and James, 2001: 74).

BOX 7.5 What children think about standardized testing: A Canadian schoolchild's contribution

I am 12 and I go to a Canadian elementary school. I am in grade seven. I live with my parents who take me to school most of the time. In school we have many subjects, about nine a day. We have two breaks and one recess. School goes for about eight hours. Most nights we have little homework unless we have a project or assignment. Every two years students have to do standardized testing. Standardized testing makes most of the students worried, nervous and stressed. I feel that standardized testing is inaccurate because if someone didn't do well in one area that doesn't mean that they are incapable in other things and just because that person doesn't excel in a certain academic area that shouldn't affect the government's view of that student's knowledge. If a person does not do well in some areas this makes the person feel like they won't be successful and that also makes the person feel dumb and worthless.

While teachers report on the stress of trying to fulfil the requirements of national curricula, less is known about how children experience standardized testing, although research shows that children experience school as something *done to* them, and it would follow that they experience testing in the same way. The emphasis in schools is on preparing the child to be an adult citizen who contributes to the modern-day, industrialized, capitalist society, and part of preparing children for that is the production of the standardized child via testing (Devine, 2002: 312). However, as the above vignette shows, children themselves assume that their individual performance is what is being tested.

What do children think about school?

Despite the importance of school in children's everyday lives, children have been asked for their views on school only rarely (but more work has been done in England in ascertaining children's voices, see Robinson (2014), for example, who has usefully reviewed much of the research in this area). One notable study is that of Sherman (1997) who talked to five-year-old Scottish children about 'why we go to school.' According to the children, school was necessary for their futures as working adults. They also felt that they had no choice about whether or not they went to school, and that they were subject to adult direction and control in this matter. However, the excerpt below demonstrates that some children do enjoy and appreciate school.

BOX 7.6 Henry

Every day at school is fun because I get to see my friends, even though I don't always get to play the games I like to play. But the one thing they could improve at school would be doing more PE (physical education) lessons because I love doing sport. The lessons are taught excellently and I normally learn something new every day in all my lessons. The teachers are very kind and encouraging making school very enjoyable. My least favourite thing about school is getting homework because it gets me all worried and worked up!

Asking children what they liked or enjoyed most about school, Alderson (2000a) found that the three most frequent replies were sports, some lessons, and 'seeing my friends.' As mentioned earlier in this chapter, friendship is important to children in the school context. Perhaps a more telling example of what children want from school can be found in a Swedish study in which children were asked to describe their dream school. The predominant themes that emerged were that such a school would be a place of 'friendship, freedom and fun.' Kostenius (2011: 519), the study's author, writes that a dream school would be a 'school where the children are enjoying themselves, and belonging to a "we" where they feel free to speak their mind. Their dream school is a place where they are able to be involved and influence aspects of school which concern them.' Interestingly, children did not often mention learning when describing their dream school. Rather, their dream schools were places where they would be valued as human beings. It is sad that this is a dream, and not reality, for children.

Conclusion: Power and control – resistance and agency in school

Much of this chapter has detailed the ways in which children in school are subject to power and control, and the way that time is structured in school. Children have little voice in school – one of the main institutions of childhood. For example an article which reviewed three studies exploring the voices of children and young people in relation to discipline in school in the United Kingdom concluded that 'young people continue to have less say in education than in many other public arenas, and that even when research gathers and values their views, education policy still shows little genuine interest in acting on those views' (McCluskey, 2014: 100), echoing Lansdown et al.'s (2014) assertion that children's voices should be listened to in school. Children's agency and competence in all aspects of their everyday lives, including school, is also an important consideration. While children may indeed be controlled, they are still able to exercise agency and resistance to school rules and norms. Employing Klocker's discussion of thin and thick agency, we have seen that in the school context children's agency is thinned in that children have only a few opportunities to exert their agency within the restrictive atmosphere of the school (2007: 85). However, Klocker's argument also helps us to see even the smallest acts of resistance or the choices that children make as agentic. The examples and discussions presented in this chapter detail the ways in which children experience school. The following chapter explores children at work and here we will again see the themes of power and control, agency, and resistance.

Exercise and reflection points

1. Thinking of Klocker's (2007) discussion of thin and thick agency (see Chapter 2 for reminder) and reflecting back on your experience of being a schoolchild, do you feel that you were subject to control at school which thinned your agency? If so, in which situations did that happen? How did that make you feel? What aspects of being a schoolchild thickened your agency? What kinds of actions and choices help to thicken children's agency at school? Prepare a list of points for discussion, for example as follows:

I felt that my agency was 'thinned' when....	I felt that my agency was 'thickened' when...

   From the list, think of a set of strategies that teachers could use in order to make school more of a *children's place* rather than an adult-oriented place for children.
2. Malala has suggested that money saved from spending on arms would enable every child to get free education. Do you think this is likely? Why, or why not? Is the abolition of child work the answer? Can you think of any strategies which might contribute to achieving universal education?

Further reading

Devine, D. (2003) *Children, power and schooling: How childhood is structured in the primary school,* Staffs: Trentham Books Ltd.

Qvortrup, J., Corsaro, W. A., and Honig, M. (2011) *The Palgrave handbook of childhood studies,* New York: Palgrave Macmillan.

Qvortrup, J. (2001) 'School work, paid work and the changing obligations of childhood' in Mizen, P., Pole, C. and Bolton, A. (ed.) *Hidden hands: International perspectives on children's work and labour,* New York: Routledge Falmer.

Sherman, A. (1997) 'Five-year-olds' perceptions of why we go to school,' *Children and Society,* vol. 11, pp. 117–127.

Simpson, B. (2000) 'Regulation and resistance: Children's embodiment during the primary-secondary school transition' in Prout, A. (ed.) *The body, childhood and society,* Hants: Macmillan Press Ltd.

CHAPTER 8

Children at Work

Keywords: Thin and thick agency, child work, child labour

Still concerned with the examination of constructions of childhood, and the way that childhood is experienced by children, this chapter turns to the topic of work. It is often said, particularly in the West, that play is what children *do*. In other words, play characterizes childhood. However children throughout the world also work, whether within the family, for pay, or as a form of slavery. When childhood is romanticized and constructed as a time of play and innocence, as it is in the West, the realities of many children's lives worldwide are ignored and, as we shall see, the meaning that work has for children is also ignored. In this chapter we look at constructions of childhood as they relate to the debates about work and continue the exploration of structure in children's everyday lives and the demonstration of children's competence and agency.

A common theme woven through the discussion of child work is that of the lost childhood. The idea of the lost childhood turns on the belief that there is one superior, universal ideal of childhood (e.g. the universal child of the UNCRC, the Western discourse of the romantic child) and that child workers are missing out on this 'best' childhood. Much of the discussion about child work is framed within a child protectionist stance in which the idea of children in work contradicts what it means to be a child. Further, child work is seen to be a problem only for children in the developing world, obscuring the fact that children throughout the entire world work.

We have seen in earlier chapters that children were removed from the world of work to the institutions of home and school – 'the useful labour of the nineteenth century child was replaced by educational work for the useless child' (Zelizer, 2010: 13). Children today are perceived as passive receptacles being filled with learning in school and with appropriate cultural socialization in the home. However, as Qvortrup has shown, a consideration of the active role that children take on in relation to learning might result in children's role in the education process being given more importance in society. The 'useless' schoolchild might then again be seen as useful (2001: 94). Children's work at school is part of their overall ability to be successful in the labour market, and children's engagement with learning displays competence and capacity (Qvortrup, 2001).

Child work and child labour

In spite of the use of the phrase *child work* up until this point to refer to all children's work, a distinction is usually made between *child work* and *child labour*, with the former used to describe children's work in the developed world, and the latter used to describe children's work in the developing world. This distinction highlights the fact that children working is considered problematic only for children in the developing world and obscures the fact that children throughout the entire world – the developing *and* developed world – work. The distinction that is made between children's work in the developing and developed world maps the issue onto global divisions, and later in the chapter examples will be presented to illustrate this.

The conventions and recommendations on child work and labour of the International Labour Organization (ILO) and the United Nations Convention on the Rights of the Child (UNCRC) are the most significant international agreements that govern child work and labour. Both documents argue that 'light' work from the age of 12 can be beneficial to children, that is to say, work which does not interfere with education or the moral, social, and physical development of the child (Minimum Age, 1976 [Convention #138]; UNCRC Article 32; see also Invernizzi, 2005). In this context, light work (and this is what we are generally thinking of when we think about child work) is commonly understood to be the kind of work that children in the developed world might engage in – babysitting, yard work, and so on. Such activities are said to 'contribute to children's development and to the welfare of their families; they provide them with skills and experience, and help to prepare them to be productive members of society during their adult life' (ILO, 2006). What is clear from this excerpt is that the ILO document reflects dominant constructions of childhood: childhood as a time for development into future adulthood. Recently the ILO has issued a statement regarding new legislation in Bolivia which has made it legal in that country for children between 10 and 14 to work if they are in self-employment, and allows children aged 12 to 14 to work for others as long as they are enrolled in school, and as long as they have parental permission. This legislation is clearly in contravention of the ILO convention #138 and as such the ILO is concerned that this goes against the aim of eliminating child labour (http://www.ilo.org/ipec/news/WCMS_250366/lang--en/index.htm).

Child labour, however, is defined by the ILO as follows: children below the age of 12 working in *any* economic activity, children aged 12 to 14 years engaged in 'harmful' work, and children of any age engaged in the worst forms of work, which ILO Convention #182 defines as enslavement (forced recruitment, prostitution, trafficked children, or children forced into illegal activities), work which exposes children to hazardous materials, excessively long hours of work, or heavy work (ILO, Worst forms of child labour, 1999). The definitions employed by the ILO and the UNCRC, as some authors have pointed out (White, 1999 for example), demonstrate a lack of understanding of local geographies and cultures. Both the ILO and the UNCRC, as already mentioned, are heavily influenced by, and contribute to, Westernized constructions of childhood, and exporting those constructions to other contexts and cultures (Monaghan, 2012). In reality, as comforting as it might be for those of us in the West to think that child work and labour is a problem 'somewhere else,' there is no neat geographical split between developed and developing worlds when looking at child work and child labour as some of the examples in this chapter highlight.

Working children

There are a variety of statistics relating to the extent of child work. Wells (2009: 100) notes that one in four African children aged 5 to 14 work, and one in five Asian/Pacific children of the same age work, compared to one in 20 in Latin America and the Caribbean. Following the description of child work contained within the ILO, this section describes examples from research focusing on 'light' work. There is a small amount of academic work which focuses on Canadian childhoods, particularly in relation to child work. Covell and Howe (1999) carried out a study that provides data on Canadian children's work and their perspectives on it. They studied children aged 12 to 17 in two Canadian provinces with high unemployment. They found that between 41 per cent and 53 per cent of students worked part time, mainly in the informal sector (e.g. babysitting, yard work, and so on). Most respondents reported that they worked in order to have money to buy the things that they liked, while some students worked in order to contribute to the family income (1999: 231–233). Hansen et al. (2001) remark that child work is something that parents are keen to encourage, because young people are seen to develop positive general skills such as time management, money management, self-reliance, and so on (see also Howieson et al., 2006, for a similar discussion of child work in Scotland, UK).

Aitken and colleagues (2006) explored the state-initiated Paidimeta programme in Tijuana, Mexico, implemented to regulate children's work as supermarket packers. The programme was aimed at children aged 8 to 14, and was intended to teach children, as the future workforce, a good work ethic. The young supermarket packers were not paid for their work but were 'volunteers,' although they could accept tips from customers whose bags they packed. Legally children aged 14 and over in Mexico have to be paid for their work, so the companies employing the 'volunteers' let them go when they reached that age. Though seemingly unhelpful, ineffective, and exploitative, the study demonstrated the children's sense of dignity and responsibility from their work. Children appreciated the opportunity to earn money in the form of tips most of which went to help out their families (Aitken et al., 2006: 378). It is interesting to note that although the conventions on work stipulate that no children under 12 should work, the Paidimeta programme – a government programme – was aimed at children aged eight and older. This serves as just one example of the ambiguity around children and work.

Child agricultural work in North America

While there are no accurate figures, between 300,000 and 800,000 children work in agriculture in the USA. These figures may include children working unpaid on their parents' farms or children working as migrant workers. There are no figures available for children under 12 years old (likely because work under this age is illegal under the ILO/UNCRC so employers keep no records), but it is likely that there are significant numbers of child agricultural workers of, or below, this age. Many of these children are economic migrants from Mexico who make the choice to work in the United States so that they are able to send money home to their families (Carpena-Mendez, 2007). Writing about the history of the introduction of age limits on child work in North America, Zelizer (2010) comments that farming jobs were traditionally seen as good work, compared to industrial jobs (likely drawing on notions of childhood as close to nature), and thus child work on farms has been consistently exempted from regulation. Eventually, however, child work was divided into two categories: farm work at home without pay was allowed (as long as it did not interfere with schooling) but farm work for pay was seen by the authorities as child labour and therefore banned. Again, this reveals an ambiguity about child work and labour – while it might make those of us in the developed world comfortable to see child labour as happening 'somewhere else,' the reality is that it also happens in our own backyard. I am here problematizing the notion, discussed above, that we can see work and labour neatly mapped onto global divisions. What we can also see is that romantic discourses of idyllic childhoods in which children are close to nature are preserved through policies that legitimize unpaid work on the family farm (Zelizer, 2010: 6).

We now turn to a contemporary example of child agricultural work within the family. In a study undertaken by the author that explored adults' experiences of growing up in Canadian Mennonite communities, the subject of work appeared in many of the interviews. Some of the interviewees' families had frequently migrated between Mennonite colonies in Mexico and Southwestern Ontario for seasonal work while others had settled in Ontario after a period of migration. Work and responsibility are the dominant characteristics of childhood in Low German-speaking Mennonite families, unlike the play and freedom from responsibility that is found in Westernized conceptions of childhood. It should be noted, however, that the childhoods described to me by Mennonite adults were experienced within a Western culture. Within the same Western context, then, we have radically different conceptions of childhood (that is, non-Mennonite Canadian versus Mennonite conceptions) based – in this case – on Mennonite culture, faith, and tradition. The Mennonite adults interviewed, when reflecting on their childhoods, described a daily experience made up of work and brief episodes of play; work was central in their daily lives. Most of the interviewees in this study described working 10 to 12 hours a day, either on their family farm or as seasonal migrant workers picking tomatoes in Southwestern Ontario. There appeared to be little sense of agency or choice expressed in these recollections, but a sense of duty and responsibility was clear – and yet these are the very characteristics that are considered to be outside contemporary conceptualizations of childhood.

All of the interviewees talked about the early age at which they began work in either the home or on the farm, showing the centrality of work in the lives of Low German-speaking Mennonite children. We can see that there are very few opportunities for play (work must be done first), and working such long hours would leave very little time to play in any event, although one interviewee (Male, interviewee F) did describe brief episodes of play among the straw bales. This interviewee, starting at the age of eleven, was working longer hours than many adult males outside of this Mennonite community would. He was also part of the family's migrant work in Canada from the age of five. The kind of work carried out by this young man could not be classified as 'light work' according to the ILO, but rather fits with a characterization of child labour (that is, any work carried out under the age of 12). This is a contradiction in a 'developed' country like Canada where very young children are employed in harvesting the food that other children their age, enjoying the more romanticized, protected, experience of childhood, eat. The reality of many children's everyday lives is that they are not spent in play and education, but in the local production and harvesting of the food that we eat.

Gender divisions in children's work

To continue with the example of the study of Mennonite childhoods, work within Low German-speaking Mennonite families was clearly gendered in nature. Girls' work was carried out inside the home, or in the vegetable garden, while boys worked on the farms. Work was also – for the girls at least – dependent on birth order. The eldest girl in a family would take on many of the responsibilities, but her sisters would also take these on as they grew older.

BOX 8.1 Agatha

Gender divisions in children's work in a Mennonite family, contributed by Agatha:

I am the ninth child in a family of ten. There was no question in our family but that the children worked to sustain the family though my experience was different from my older brothers and sisters. My oldest brother spent much of his summers as a teenager working with my father who was in construction. I also heard the story of how my older siblings hoed beets for a local farmer when they were children. My father, even though he had made all the arrangements, pulled my siblings from the field because he felt that they were expected to work too hard and too long hours for the little amount of money that they earned. As teenagers some of my older siblings returned to the beet fields to earn spending money for themselves.

Unlike my older siblings, I got my first job only after I finished high school. But that didn't mean I didn't work when I was a child, especially in summer. The vegetable garden required the most work. The jobs I hated were picking stones, hoeing and weeding, and canning tomatoes. I loved shelling peas and husking corn. I remember the wheelbarrows full of corn my mother picked that us kids had to husk. When we finished one barrowful, one of us would bring the husks to the pasture for our horse – a real treat for him – and then we'd start on the next barrow.

But I also had lots of time to play in summer, and the garden was a wonderful playroom. We blew bubbles through the greens of onions, we used the cornrows to hide in when we played "no bears out tonight," we ate carrots, kohlrabi and rhubarb to our hearts' content, we carved the cucumbers that my mother had forgotten to pick and that had grown too large to eat into cradles. In my family the work was divided quite clearly along gender lines. My brothers would often accompany my father to construction jobs, especially in summer. The work my sisters and I did was more the domestic side of things. Cleaning, cooking and yard work – though my brothers did help mow the grass. There were seven daughters, and there was a very definite ranking of work in our household, especially the Saturday cleaning. The oldest girls cleaned the kitchen and dining room, the middle girls cleaned the bedrooms, and the youngest – that was me – had to do all the grunge work: empty and wash the garbage cans, sweep and wipe the basement stairs, and clean the porch and bathroom.

I prepared my first meal as an older child. I was the only girl at home and my father and brother were working in the shop. I knew I had to make lunch. So I cooked macaroni. I didn't know that you had to first bring the water to a boil and then add the macaroni – so that day the three of us had a gooey mess for lunch.

Most of the people I spoke with when doing this research had many stories of work and responsibility in the home, from a very young age. Another interviewee described how she worked alongside her mother in caring for the family, preparing and cooking food, and so on. She started cooking for the family at age seven. Interviewee 'B' was the eldest girl in her family of 16 siblings, and together with her next-eldest sister carried out many of the household tasks. They were responsible for laundry, cooking and serving the food to the family. Interviewee 'B' also described how the entire family worked together in the harvest. However, the eldest girls in the family began work much earlier in the day, making sure all the children were up and dressed, and feeding them breakfast. At lunchtime, they would run home from picking in the fields to put the midday meal on the table so that everyone could eat – but this meant that they had little time to get their own meals, or to rest. Similarly, children's working responsibilities in the Howa tribe in Sudan also indicate gendered role expectations. While boys attend school, work in agriculture, and play agriculture-focused games together, girls fetch water, take care of siblings, and are not expected to attend school (Katz, 2004: 8–10). However, as Wells (2009) has pointed out, household work is often excluded from definitions of 'work' and thus the work of girls may be hidden in statistics.

Child domestic work

Regulations about domestic work were added to the ILO Convention in 2013 as Convention #189 and became binding international law. This allows an estimated 10.5 million child domestic workers worldwide to be included in the conventions and to have their rights protected under the Convention. Child domestic work is defined by the ILO as employment in a third-party household (that is, not the home of the child's family) where the child provides services for that household. The definition excludes children carrying out similar work in their own homes and 'in reasonable conditions, and under the supervision of those close to them.' Such work is, according to the convention, 'an integral part of family life and of growing up, [and] therefore something positive' (http://www.ilo.org/).

Chapter 2 introduced the work of Klocker (2007), who discussed the concepts of thin and thick agency in her study of child domestic workers. Jensen (2014) has also studied child domestic workers, in this case children employed by middle-class families in Bangladesh. There are approximately 148,000 child domestic workers in Dhaka, Bangladesh, most of whom began working between the ages of 8 and 11. According to ILO Convention #182, these children are engaged in the worst form of child labour. However, many of the children Jensen spoke to felt that they were materially better off as child domestic workers than they had been with their families – their housing and food were significantly better in employment than in their own family – even though most of them slept on the floor, and were not allowed to sit on furniture or to eat with the family that they worked for. Like Klocker (2007), Jensen found that the children's agency was very thin, but that most of them were able to demonstrate agency even if it was only to go up to the roof of their apartment building to meet with other child domestic workers and escape the surveillance and control of their employers.

While there is often an assumption that child workers and labourers are forced to work by parents, Bessel (2011), who carried out a significant amount of research with child workers in Indonesia, found that children made clear choices to work. She gathered information from children who worked in factories and on the streets, and from children who scavenged for a living. Some of these children were expected by their families to work, but the main impetus for children working was poverty. Even within the structural constraints these children lived with, she reported children were making a choice about whether to work or not, and enjoyed many benefits of working, even in the most dangerous industries. For example, 12–16-year-old girls who left villages to work in factories were glad they could contribute money to their families, but also liked that they could keep back a proportion of their earnings to spend on themselves. Also, they had greater choices over their own lives, especially when it came to marriage. This was partly because the status of the girl within the family had increased as she contributed to the family income, but also because in the city they had a wider selection of young men to choose a husband from (Bessel, 2011: 566). Child labour reformers who do not take into account the context, experience, and reality of working children's lives, but who try to impose Western standards of childhood on those children, fail to see the agency and competence of child workers.

The work that children do is not just physical labour, as Seymour (2005, 2011) usefully reminds us. Reporting on a study that explored the raising of children in families where the home and the family business were in the same location (hotels, bed and breakfasts), she showed how children contributed not only their physical labour, but also their emotional labour to the family business. They did emotion work in many ways, such as presenting a positive self to the guests – which may or may not be the 'real' self, presented away from the scrutiny of the guests.

In helping to entertain the hotel's guests, children's emotional labour was appreciated by parents as 'good for business' (Seymour, 2005: 97). Children's presence in family-run hotels and guesthouses contributed to the familial ambience and the guests welcomed this. This is not simply appreciated but came to be expected by guests and parents alike as the following comment by a mother, talking about her son demonstrates: 'He brings all the bags down... and that gives him some pocket money, you know. The little old ladies like to see the kids with us so we just more or less got him to do that. He was a bit reluctant at first, but I think he's found out. People give him tips you see and he likes that' (Seymour, 2005: 102). Seymour contended that children's compliance with the demands of carrying out emotional labour for the family business was often done in order for personal gain in the form of tips and treats. Thus children's labour in this example was less about passive exploitation than about mutual advantage.

Numerous examples in this chapter have not only demonstrated the agency that children exercise in their daily lives in relation to the work that they do, but also that work can lead to other, equally important changes and life events such as marital choice. The following section details children's views on work, and again explores child agency, particularly in the creation of working children's organizations.

Children's views on work and working children's organizations

Mizen et al. (2001: 38–50), in their study of 70 British working children, found that work for the participants had several benefits. First, for some young people, work was an antidote to boredom and a chance to interact with others. It also provided them with a sense of independence from parents. The young people also valued the money they earned because it allowed them to purchase things they wanted and spend money on entertainment, games, sports, and so on. The young people appreciated that the money they earned relieved some of the financial burden their parents carried, and the choices they made to take paid work reflected both a need to work and a desire to work.

In her study of Northern Ireland children, Leonard (2004) interviewed more than 500 15-year-old children to find out their views on their right to work. She noted the tension between protecting children and encouraging them to make choices for themselves – a tension which, as we have already seen, is present in the UNCRC. Under UK legislation, children need the permission of their parents to take paid employment. When asked about this, 58 per cent of the children agreed that adults should have a voice in their employment, while 32 per cent thought that they alone should decide what jobs they took (Leonard, 2004: 51). Children also thought that they should be seen as competent and trustworthy, able to decide how many hours to work, and when to work.

In her research, Leonard shows that the children took paid work in order to gain adult status and independence from parents. To do this, however, they often employed strategies to manage parental objections to their work. For example, some of the children in Leonard's study did not tell their parents what kind of work they were doing if it was dangerous. Others negotiated parents' approval by convincing them that their education would not suffer because of their work.

Under current UK legislation, working children have no protection in terms of minimum wage nor in terms of health and safety. As Leonard discovered, the laws put into place to protect children *from* work were actually harming children under the legal age limit who *were* working. Children felt that the protections extended to adult workers should be extended to them if they were doing the same work as adults (Leonard, 2004).

Banning child work?

There are many children throughout the world engaged in labour and in the worst forms of child labour, and their plight ought not to be dismissed. Many NGOs and other bodies are keen to eradicate child labour. Often in these well-intentioned efforts, geography and local culture are not taken into account adequately, nor is the meaning of child work and labour for children, as Aitken et al. (2006) have pointed out. An illustrative example of the damage inflicted by ill-conceived attempts to ban child labour is the Child Labor Deterrence Act introduced by the American senator, Tom Harkin. This bill, if it had been implemented, would have imposed a US boycott on the importation of any goods produced by companies using child labour. Even though never implemented, the effects of the proposed Act were devastating for child workers. In Bangladesh, children previously employed in the garment industry were dismissed when fear of the proposed boycott set in. Many of those children had to take more poorly paid jobs instead. Although it is the aim of those who wish to eliminate child labour for children to attend school rather than work, children in this example did not do so but instead continued to look for further employment (White, 1996). Paid employment – for example in the garment industry – often offers better conditions for child workers than working in the household or on the family farm.

Khanam and Ross (2011), who carried out a study in Bangladesh, contend that child-labour bans are rarely of little use. The majority of the children in their study worked in the informal sector, such as within the family or in agriculture, and so any ban would bypass them. Further, more than a quarter of the children reported not going to school simply because they didn't like it. The assumption underlying child labour bans is that once removed from work children will attend school. But as this example shows, that is not the case. The child labour issue is clearly more complex than simply removing children from paid employment. Khanam and Ross made several policy change suggestions that would take into account their findings. Rather than merely banning child labour, they suggested improving schooling to make it more attractive to children and introducing a system of educational subsidies that would make school attendance more appealing than working.

In 2010, participants at a global ILO child labour conference in The Hague, Holland, created a document entitled 'Roadmap for achieving the elimination of the worst forms of child labour by 2016' with the intention of 'accelerat[ing] progress towards the elimination of the worst forms of child labour by 2016, while affirming the overarching goal of the effective abolition of child labour.' The roadmap is based on the premise that eliminating the worst forms of child labour is best achieved by working towards eliminating *all* child labour. The document sets out the action that governments can/ should take in order to abolish child labour, and is supported by 97 countries. Among the most important recommendations are:

- each supporting country should develop legislation against child labour
- free, compulsory education should be available to all children
- social protections should be put in place to support families taking children out of the work force.

(Road map, 2010)

While it is unarguable that the worst forms of child labour (slavery, trafficking, prostitution, etc.) need urgent attention and legislation to deal with them, banning all child labour as a strategy to eradicate the worst forms may prove problematic. As will be shown in the following section, children who work do not necessarily want to stop working.

Child workers – whether in the developed or developing world – frequently do not want to be 'protected' from work. Rather, what they want is the right to work, to be treated fairly, and to get an education at the same time. As Leibel (2004) shows, working children's movements are not new but

---

BOX 8.2 The Kundapur Declaration

1. We want recognition of our problems, our initiatives, proposals and our process of organisation.
2. We are against the boycott of products made by children.
3. We want respect and security for ourselves and the work that we do.
4. We want an education system whose methodology and content are adapted to our reality.
5. We want professional training adapted to our reality and capabilities.
6. We want access to good health care for working children.
7. We want to be consulted in all decisions concerning us, at local, national or international levels.
8. We want the root causes of our situation, primarily poverty, to be addressed and tackled.
9. We want more activities in rural areas and decentralisation in decision making, so that children will no longer be forced to migrate.
10. We are against exploitation at work but we are for work with dignity with hours adapted so that we have time for education and leisure.

(http://www.concernedforworkingchildren.org/empowering-children/childrens-unions/the-kundapur-declaration/)

---

can be traced back to the 1830s, and demonstrate children's efforts to gain respect and fair pay and safe working conditions. Perhaps the best known working children's organization is the International Movement of Working Children. At a conference held in Kundapur, India in 1996, 29 working children from different countries met and developed their own set of demands. The Kundapur Declaration (2012) makes very clear that children want to be valued and have their work recognized.

These are not excessive demands. Ill-conceived movements to ban child labour and to boycott products manufactured by children ignore the reality of working children's lives. Children have economic responsibilities in support of themselves and their families. The notion that childhood is about play and innocence and not work and responsibility is a romanticized, Westernized construction of childhood, and as has been shown throughout this textbook, is frequently not the reality of children's lives. Working children often suffer more from attempts to ban their work than they might suffer from working, as illustrated in the above example of the negative effects the Harkin Bill had on child garment workers in Bangladesh. Child work does not have to be synonymous with exploitation (Leibel, 2004), although it could be argued that movements against it and laws which prohibit it create exploitation when children have no rights.

Conclusion

This chapter has explored children's work. While play is properly thought to be the province of childhood, the chapter has shown that, for many children, work takes precedence over play. Taking seriously what children say about their everyday lives allows us to see those realities. In the light of all the scholarship that has been done in the last 15 years that places children's perspectives and experiences at the centre of research, why is it that policy directed at working children seems to ignore this academic work? Bessel (2011) contends that policymakers and decision makers continue to hold generational and universalistic ideas about what childhood should be. In a similar vein, Wells (2009) argues that it is people's conception of childhood that contributes to this – if we see working children only as victims of 'lost childhoods,' we make it impossible for them to organize in order to speak out in favour of better conditions. As the discussion of children's rights and citizenship in Chapter 4 demonstrated, protectionist policies can effectively silence children. Childhood is kept in the walled garden of innocence and children's competencies, agency, and everyday realities are not acknowledged.

Exercise and reflection points

1. Do you think it is helpful to make a distinction between child work and child labour? Why, or why not?
2. Can you think of any examples of working children in your community? Why do these children work? Who benefits from children's work in your examples?
3. Prepare two reasoned arguments for discussion – one in favour of banning child work, and one against. Which argument do you think carries the most weight? Which one might thicken children's agency? Which one might thin children's agency?

Further reading

Liebel, M. (2004) *A will of their own: Cross cultural perspectives on working children,* London: Zed Books.

Mizen, P., Pole, C. and Bolton, A. (2001) *Hidden hands: International perspectives on children's work and labour,* New York: Routledge Falmer.

Zelizer, V. A. (2010) 'From child labour to child work: Redefining the economic world of children' in Sternheimer, K. (ed.) *Childhood in American society: A reader,* Boston: Pearson Education Inc.

CHAPTER 9

Children at Leisure

Keywords: Leisure, play, disappearance of childhood, media, technology, child as future, control

Do children have 'leisure'? Leisure is commonly seen to be something that is in opposition to work (that is, something that adults possess or do) while 'play' is the term applied to what children do. As such, the term leisure connotes an elitist view, while 'play' has been seen as mere distraction. The term play has many definitions and connotations – something simple, something 'childish,' something with no real purpose or aim. Play is therefore something that has been mapped onto age categories. However, adults also play; thus I would argue that play is not an exclusively child-like activity. Also, in view of the fact that millions of children work, and if we take the view that what children do in school is work, we can therefore talk about children as engaging in leisure. Talking about children's leisure, rather than simply focusing on play, allows us to recognize children's engagement in work (whether that work consists of schoolwork or other) and allows us to broaden the investigation into all forms of leisure: play, media use, technology, and so on.

There is another advantage to looking at leisure in childhood: that a focus merely on play reinforces the difference between adulthood and childhood, positioning one against the other, and allowing us as adults to police and control this aspect of childhood. While there may be a view that play is a trivial activity, in public and academic discussions there are a plethora of concerns about what children do in their leisure time: that children do not play 'properly' anymore; that children no longer know how to 'play'; that electronic media has destroyed 'real' childhood; that children have 'lost' their imaginations. The themes dominating academic work on children and play reflect either a focus on the role of play in the successful development of children, or on play as anticipatory socialization. According to these perspectives, play serves an important purpose either developmentally or socially. For example, it is thought that playing with toys helps teach children the roles and skills they may need as adults. In this way, play reinforces acceptable social identities. Because play is thought to be so important for future adulthood, adults are concerned about what children do in play. Such concerns are yet another example of what has been argued throughout this textbook, that children are seen as passive, and as *not-yet* and are rooted in a romantic developmental perspective of childhood where adults must 'do something' to prevent the disappearance of childhood. In this chapter, the focus is on the *meaning* that leisure activities (including play) have for children.

Has children's play disappeared?

One of the concerns about children and leisure is that children's traditional play has disappeared – that the songs, games, and rhymes of childhood are no longer a part of children's play. All too often one hears the refrain 'they don't play like they used to.' As far back as the early 1900s commentators were concerned that children no longer knew how to play. This manifested itself as a concern that children's play needed to be supervised and controlled. In the early part of the 20th century, in the United States, the growing mass media (mainly cinema) was of major concern. It was feared that not only would traditional play be affected if children spent time in the cinema, but the parent–child relationship would also be damaged because the attractions of commercial leisure were eroding parental control. Parenting magazines exhorted parents to bring children and young people back into the home, to take children's play seriously and introduce play spaces in the home so that not only could children engage in wholesome play, but they could also be supervised (Jacobson, 1997).

Expressing the view that the play aspect of the culture of childhood is lost has become something of a tradition in and of itself. In the 1940s, when Peter and Iona Opie set out on their life's work to collect the games, songs, and rhymes of childhood play and childhood playground culture in Britain, they were told that they were 50 years too late, that children no longer knew those games (Roberts, 1980). However, they went on to collect and publish thousands of examples of these traditional games in many volumes. It is evident that the fear that childhood traditional play was lost was prevalent when they began their collection in the mid-20th century, but the Opies found conclusively that it was not, that it was still a part of children's play (Opie and Opie, 1959).

Following up on this work, Marsh and Bishop (2014) have carried out secondary data analysis on the data which the Opies collected, and report on that and other research projects they carried out. Looking at continuity and change in children's play, and aiming to challenge the 'disappearance of childhood' thesis (Postman, 1984, see below) they largely found continuities with the findings of the Opies in contemporary British children's play and games, especially in relation to the physical play that children engaged in.

They noted that the mass media was influencing children's play (for example, children drawing on TV shows to structure their play) but note that this has always been present in children's play (Marsh and Bishop, 2014: 75).

Parents monitor and control children's play and leisure, particularly in North America where children's play is overwhelmingly adult-managed; parents push their children to take part in extracurricular schoolwork or organized sports (for example, Little League), with a focus firmly on the child's future employment opportunities (Hart, 1992). The close involvement of adults in children's play societies reflects the assumed importance of play for future development (Montgomery, 2009). In other cultures, however, play is often entirely free of adult management or involvement. Among the Beng in West Africa, children's play spaces stretch to encompass the entire village, and some children are independent from their parents all day, only returning home at meal times. Beng parents are unconcerned about this because they assume another adult or older child in the village will be keeping an eye on their children (Gottleib, 2004). Another, albeit dated, study of play from the discipline of anthropology shows how children's play is of societal importance, rather than the trivialized activity it is taken to be in the West. Rather than seeing childhood play as either preparation for adulthood or as amusement, this chapter contends that instead we need to explore the meanings which play has for children themselves.

Studying the Waso Boorana of Kenya, Aguilar (1994) demonstrated through his ethnographic observation of children aged three to six that the play of children in this culture provided continuity in generational processes and demonstrated the performance of identity. The Waso Boorana were a seminomadic people whose lives were focused on their cattle. Small boys herded lambs in the same way that their fathers herded sheep, and small girls carries 'babies' (bricks or stones) on their backs. This was not, he argued, simply imitative play, but was about performing a gendered identity as members of the group. In one popular game, children incorporated the ritualized greeting with which members of this culture greeted each other in the mornings. Acting out the roles of the adult elders in the greeting ritual, Aguilar argued, ensured that generational processes would not fade away over time. Children's play among the Waso Boorana showed children's 'ways of interacting socially and their ways of asserting and contesting particular identities' (Aguilar, 1994: 30). In other words, children's play demonstrates that children are social actors.

In her study of British schoolchildren, James (1993) also demonstrated the ways in which children's play was about the performance of identity. Status in children's peer groups was gained by having expertise in the game – knowing *how* to play, and knowing the rules of the game. It was participation in the game which counted according to James (1993: 172): 'Playing a game not only permits a child to develop a familiarity with its rules and with the form of play; participation is itself a sign of a child's active engagement with the wider and more complex games of social identity which are played out through performance: the games of status and of gender.' Play is not only about the performance of social identity, but is also transformative, in that everyday objects become something else during play – the bike becomes a fire engine and the dolls turn into babies (James, 1993: 173). Other studies have confirmed the transformative aspect of play. For example, two studies of children's play in Australian primary schools conducted 40 years apart show continuity in the ways in which children, sometimes unseen by adults in school, designate and come to know which spaces of the playground have meaning. A fallen tree had for generations been known to children – but not the adults around them – as a spaceship. Bars and poles in the playground were meeting places or places to swing (Factor, 2004).

As James, Jenks and Prout (1998) have written, childhood is not untouched by the adult world. As the examples above have shown, children's play is shaped by the society in which they live, the cultural norms of that society, and often by adult control over the times and spaces of play. Strandell's (1997) study of children's play in Finland confirmed that play was not a separate child's world but children used play (or more particularly, playfulness) to intrude on adult-imposed order. She described how children used play talk – playing with words and language to subvert adult control and to claim the space for their own – to amuse themselves in situations which were not play, but were more organized periods such as lunchtime. Strandell (1997: 460) provided an excerpt from her research diary describing how the children, after being told to thank the dinner ladies, begin to call 'thanks ladies' one at a time until they are chastised. The children had a great deal of fun in this simple episode of play-talk.

The examples presented here do not show children's play as trivial, nor as separate from adult life. Neither can it be said that children only play. Children all over the world work as we have seen in Chapter 8, and while for some this may intrude on or diminish their opportunities for play, for others play and work are less separate. Punch (2000) studied children's spatial mobility in a small village in rural Bolivia. While adults imposed spatial and temporal boundaries around what children could do and where they could go, she described how children actively negotiated autonomy and agency within these constraints. Play was incorporated into their busy daily lives in ways that adults did not see or know about. Fetching water became an excuse to meet friends and play in the stream; bringing animals in from the hills became an opportunity for play because children could explain their late return home by claiming that the animals took extra time to round up.

While children's play might be constrained and structured by adults, we can see that children demonstrate agency in and through play, while at the same time adhering to the constraints placed on them by adults.

Spaces of play

Childhood research carried out from the discipline of geography has contributed greatly to the academic study of play by providing a spatial analysis of it. This allows us to consider a further dimension of children's everyday experience. Tandy (1999) explored generational change in children's outdoor and indoor play in Australia. Taking as their starting point that children no longer play outdoors because they are inside using technology and electronic media, Tandy had children complete a questionnaire about where they played. Parents were also given a survey, which asked for their recollections of their childhood play spaces. Parents remembered playing outdoors much more than did their children and appreciated the freedom it gave them, but they said that they would not let their children play outside because they feared for their children's safety. Children said that *if they could choose* they would like to play outside. Only about a quarter of the children were allowed to play in their neighbourhood without adult supervision compared to over 80 per cent of parents who played outdoors when they were children. Playing in the home, contended Tandy (1999: 162), 'appears to be the consigned place of play when there is no real choice.'

Looking at children's use of outdoor space in a medium-sized city in Ontario, Canada, Loebach (2013) found that children were outside for different amounts of time depending on which neighbourhood they lived in. In newer subdivisions, children in this study did not play outside even if their parents allowed them to because there was nothing for them do outside. In what she described as 'residential islands' there were no spaces provided for children's use. In contrast, in an older, working-class neighbourhood of the city, children had much more of a sense of belonging and were proud to point out their play spaces. From this study, it is clear that children's requirements of space need to be considered when residential areas are planned if the aim is to have children play outside more.

In South Africa, Benwell (2013) describes how the public facilities for children's play (play parks, etc.) were poorly maintained and therefore not attractive to children or their parents. Children usually played in their own gardens, whether in swimming pools or on jungle gyms, but were lonely because there were no other children to play with in their own gardens as there would be in public parks. In contrast, children living in gated communities had more advantages in terms of outdoor play. Children and parents felt safe outdoors, and the publicly provided play equipment was in good condition which made it appealing to children.

Children in a low-income neighbourhood in Montreal, Canada were found to be outdoors more than children in other neighbourhoods of the city, echoing Loebach's (2013) findings (see above). Children were on the street and sidewalk more than anywhere else in the neighbourhood, although children were observed using the public park too. There was a clear gender difference in park use – girls using the park were more likely than boys to be accompanied by adults. Boys were more likely to use bigger spaces (football fields, etc.) in the park for their play, while girls used the smaller spaces (Castonguay and Jutras, 2010). These findings are similar to those from a study undertaken in Amsterdam, the Netherlands. Karsten (2003) noted that girls were more likely to be chaperoned in public play parks, and that there were gender differences in the spaces used by girls and by boys. Girls tended to play games like hopscotch, or used the swings while boys tended to play soccer in large groups, dominating the bigger spaces. Karsten also noted that the gendered use of the space intersected ethnicity, with Turkish and Moroccan girls very rarely seen in the playground once they reached the age of ten.

The geography of childhood perspective is of value in analysing children's social worlds. We can see from this short review that there are aspects to children's play which constrain them: gender, ethnicity, age, parental fears about safety, and the public provision of spaces, or lack thereof, for children. However, children must be included in the planning and design of spaces, including subdivisions and play spaces. The work of Rasmussen (2004) is illustrative here. In the context of the institutionalization of childhood within the home and the school, she drew a distinction between places for children and children's places. *Places for children* were those designed by adults for children such as a school or playground. In contrast, *children's places* were those that children chose and made meaningful for and by themselves. A children's place could be a corner of a playground, a tree, a crawl space under a house; it could be within a 'place for children' but was marked out as having particular meaning for the children. Children's places were often marginal spaces that adults either ignored or weren't interested in. What distinguished a children's place, stated Rasmussen, was that while both adults and children could point out places for children, only children could point out children's places.

Children, leisure and technology

Children's engagement with electronic media often garners the most concern and objection from adults, and it is to this topic that we now turn. First, it is feared that children spend too much *time* with electronic media; and second, children are believed to be particularly vulnerable to the *effects* of electronic media. This results in the assumption that 'something needs to be done' about children's engagement with electronic media. David Buckingham (2000) has highlighted the fact that the anxiety and concern about children results in measures taken that are, in fact, not about children at all. When does such anxiety arise? What are the concerns about children and electronic media? What measures are taken to address these concerns? What are the measures actually about? This section addresses these issues through a focus on children's engagement with media, in particular, screen-based media.

An overarching concern here is that children, as future adults, are at risk. It is feared that children will be inadequately socialized or that engagement with the media will damage normal development. Further, these concerns imply that childhood itself is at risk. Rather than looking at any effects, which might or might not develop, of children's engagement with media, what I argue here is that focussing on the meaning that media hold for children provides more insight into the everyday social lives of children and young people, revealing children's competencies.

Discussions of children and media have two broad and contradictory bases: 1) media is a good thing, in that it has the potential to empower children; and 2) childhood itself is threatened when children engage media. Some commentators write as if childhood can no longer exist because children are so engaged with media that they are no longer acting as children. Most famously Neil Postman (1982: 80) argued that the dividing line between childhood and adulthood was being eroded because of the accessibility of TV and other leisure technologies which gave children easy access to adult content:

> The new media environment that is emerging provides everyone, simultaneously, with the same information....[E]lectronic media finds it impossible to withhold any secrets. Without secrets, of course, there can be no such thing as childhood.

Childhood, according to Postman (1982: 149), was on a 'journey to oblivion' because children were exposed to everything; no 'mysteries' remained for adults to reveal to children at the appropriate time. According to Postman, childhood could not exist without adult *control*. Television made impossible a separation – a boundary – between childhood and adulthood. The introduction of television, he argued, meant the death of childhood. It can be argued, however, that far from disappearing, the category *childhood* is instead expanding, both in its boundaries and dimensions. In part this is due to the increasing adult control that children experience over many aspects of their everyday life.

Those who draw on the death-of-childhood thesis put forward by Postman are, Moran (2002) argues, drawing on a notion of a golden age of romanticized or remembered childhood. Cassell and Cramer (2008) counter the existence of a golden age by providing a historical context for the contemporary moral panic about the safety of girls online by comparing it to similar concerns that existed a century early when the telephone was introduced in domestic space. Parents at that time feared that the new technology of the telephone would allow predatory males access to their daughters. Such concerns, whether contemporary or from an earlier time, result in adults imposing controls on children's use of technology. That these controls are put in place under the guise of care does not lessen the impact that they have on children and on childhood. Here we have a dual representation of children: on one hand, children's use of media is celebrated while, on the other, the essential nature of childhood (the romantic view that childhood is a time of innocence and purity) is tainted by contact with the media. In particular, advertising and marketing to children is blamed for many social issues, such as eating disorders and obesity (see Chapter 10), and family conflict (Buckingham, 2011). In the 1950s, a British women's magazine carried the following cry:

and what might our children become? They might become a generation who couldn't read a book, or play games out of doors, or amuse themselves with carpentry or trains or butterflies, or the hundreds of hobbies [with] which children can potter so happily. (in Oswell, 1999)

The concern with the child as future (Jenks 1996) is clearly expressed in this quotation – 'what might our children *become*?' Equally evident is the assumption that the 'golden age' of childhood was over – childhood itself was no more. This particular expression of concern was brought on by the introduction of TV in Britain, but it is a concern which could also be found in many concerns about childhood today.

Media effects?

When scholars first began studying the effect of media on audiences, they developed the hypodermic model of media effects. Like an injection, the media message would be incorporated into the very self – humans would be directly affected by what they saw on screen. In later models, a more nuanced view is evident; the incorporation of the media message into people's lives was mediated, for example through person-to-person interaction (Valkenburg et al., 2016). However, any sense that media can be mediated disappears when it comes to concerns about children's use of media. Often those most concerned about it assume a hypodermic effect; they see a direct link between what children see and what they do. Such assumptions are especially prevalent in relation to the effect of screen violence on children's behaviour (see below). To counter some of the concerns expressed by adult commentators about children's use of media, researchers have used audience reception research to look at how children incorporate media into their everyday lives (e.g. Buckingham 1994).

We now turn to exploring the ownership and the use of computer and video games in children's everyday lives as another example that counters adult concerns about the effects of media on children.

Significant attention has been paid in the academic world and in popular discussion to the violence within video games and the possible effects on children – an assumption that seeing violence on screen results in violent acts by the child. Sociologists who study the effect of video games fear that they are having adverse effects on children's ability to socialize (Hadley and Nenga, 2004). There is, then, an assumption that media is harmful to children, and that children are simply passive and uncritical in their consumption of them. There has been significantly less study of the *meanings* which video game play holds for children, or why children like to play them.

An older study, but one that is still drawn on in the 21st century, and one that is evident in everyday 'common sense' discussions held that children's use of electronic media caused social isolation in children (Selnow, 1984); sitting alone in front of a computer screen is seen as potentially damaging

---

BOX 9.1   Example: Play and the incorporation of media by Taiwanese kindergarten and first-grade children

According to Hadley and Nenga (2004), the main values of Confucianism – to be a good peer, to be a good student, and to be a good family member – had been incorporated into the school system in Taiwan, and children further incorporated these values into their make-believe play that drew heavily on TV shows. In planning play, children drew on media characters (for example, Hello Kitty) to include everyone, thus reflecting the value of being a good peer. The children also demonstrated resistance through play – while hitting and kicking violates the value of harmony and being a good peer, children assumed TV characters in order to be able to 'legitimately' use the fighting elements found in the show, and in this way not disrupt harmony and friendship.

to children's social relationships. However, it is not aloneness per se that is worrisome, but the context in which it is experienced. Stutz (1991: 10) characterizes children sitting alone in front of a screen as damaging, but eulogizes 'aloneness' in another setting:

> What is actually happening when the child goes fishing? He is either alone or with only one or two other people. He is silent and usually quite still. He is in a quiet environment... he is gazing into the water; he concentrates intently; he is being challenged by the fish. He is pitting his skills against natural forces. He is in a state of equilibrium between tension and relaxation and his mind is being freed for dreaming. This is surely a wholesome state.

When children are alone with electronic media then it is cause for alarm, but when they are alone with nature, childhood in its 'natural state' blossoms. Paraphrasing Stutz's idyll shows that we could see playing computer games in the same 'idyllic' way: '(S)he is silent and usually still...(s)he concentrates intently; (s)he is being challenged by the game. (S)he is pitting his/her skills against the game....

We can point out other inconsistencies in Stutz's assessment. She bases her view of fishing as wholesome partly on her finding that boys who fish do not kill the fish, but throw them back. However, she fails to note that children who play violent video games do not kill their friends (aka opponents), yet the one activity (fishing) is described as wholesome, while the other (playing video games), the subject of concern. Jenks (1996) demonstrates that the idea of the child being part of nature – a wholesome being – is related to what he terms the Apollonian (or Romantic) child, a pure, innocent child. When children enjoy playing violent video games, we are not able to idolize their purity or honour their innocence because what they are doing is not 'childlike.' Thus, the binary opposition adult/child that sustains the Apollonian child, is shattered – children are doing something that is adult-like.

Studies of children's use of computers and video games, as opposed to studies that focus on social isolation or effects, demonstrate ownership and use of them are important for friendship and peer relations for boys, but not for girls (McNamee 1998a). In South Korea, home entertainment systems are not as common as in the West. Instead, video gamers go to PC 'bangs' or rooms. Boys frequently go to bangs with friends to play games, while girls use them much less than boys. When they do use them they mainly use them to browse the Internet (Stewart and Choi, 2003).

Looking at computer and video game use in Sweden, Aarsand (2007) explored how a digital generation gap was produced in and through social interaction. Using video recordings of activity and talk around computer terminals in homes, he found that children used their superior knowledge of digital media as a strategy to negotiate, to resist control, and to 'keep adults on the edge of their activities' (2007: 250). Interestingly, adults drew on their own incompetence as a strategy to engage the child. Asking a child to explain, or demonstrate the game, enabled talk and participation for the adults. Here we have an example of a power and dependency shift, where children marginalized adults by playing computer and video games.

Increasingly parental fear of children's outdoors safety keeps children in the home (see Holt et al., 2015, for example). In North America, daily life for children is focused on school and extracurricular activities, sometimes to the extent that there is no time left in the day for any other outdoor leisure. This has consequences for the daily experiences of children as spatial boundaries around childhood draw ever tighter. Indeed one research study argues that children's outdoor play areas should be in clear lines of sight of parents and other community members (Holt et al., 2015). While this may reassure parents, it extends the ways in which adults subject children to an ever-increasing gaze. It has been argued that playing with video games 'may provide children with the adventures that they are no longer allowed to have, in spaces which they do not inhabit in any real sense' (McNamee, 2000: 485). Video game play provides an extra dimension, an 'other space' within which children can contest the boundaries that control them. In a similar vein of thought, Jansz (2005: 221) noted that 'in the safe, private laboratory of the video game, the adolescent can freely experiment with emotions and identities, which may help him to cope with the insecurities of adolescent life.' These important aspects of children's video game play come to light when the perspective of the child is taken seriously, and are missed when the focus is purely on effects. In the following section we explore children, childhood, and the Internet, and again discuss concern about and control of children's relation to media.

Children and the Internet

Adults have conflicting views of children and the Internet, which can be mapped onto conceptions of childhood as either a time of competence or as a time of vulnerability. On the one hand, the Internet can be a place of power and autonomy for children; on the other there is a fear that children are at risk, from sexual predators, for example. What is interesting in regard to children's use of the Internet is the way that the view of children as incompetent users has shifted to a concern that children are more at risk because of their computer competency, which exceeds that of adults. It is feared that their competency will put them at risk online because they are alone in virtual space (Valentine and Holloway, 2001). The remedy for this aloneness is, of course, increased parental surveillance and control, necessary because children are presumed to be innocent and in need of protection. The question is, when does care become control?

The issue of cyber bulling has become a predominant concern recently. Although it has been reported to be an increasing problem with several very sad examples of young people committing suicide because of it (Cheung 2012), Mishna et al. (2009) found in their study that many children tended not to report Internet bullying because they did not want their parents to protect them by removing their access to their phones or other media. This shows that children value access to technology more than being protected. Others have noted that the Internet offers children privacy, power, and autonomy (Wyness, 2011), which they do not have in their everyday lives, and it seems that children are unwilling to forgo these in favour of increased parental vigilance. Bond (2013) has also noted that the ways in which children manage risk through their use of mobile phones – for example, blocking people from contacting them – demonstrates clearly the ways in which children are competent social actors.

Those who take a more celebratory view of children's Internet use see it as empowerment for children. Cockburn (2005a: 331–2) noted that children formed a 'community of interest' via the Internet. He argued that the Internet provided an opportunity for collective political action through discussion groups. Further, the Internet could be a mechanism for children to participate in the democratic decision-making process. This may be an overly optimistic view because most children, rather than using the Internet for political action, use it for chatting and socializing with friends. A recent study of teen social media use in the US found that 80 per cent of teenagers are on Facebook, 63 per cent of teenagers exchange texts daily and yet only 35 per cent engage in face-to-face interaction with friends outside of school. The report states 'while the teens we interviewed preferred socializing in person, they often found this difficult due to parental restrictions, overscheduled lives, and limited transportation options' (Marwick and boyd, 2012: 3). Studies of children and young people's use of Internet demonstrate how children use instant messages, text, and chat, at a time when their lives are increasingly restricted, to stay connected and to *avoid* social isolation (see also Stern, 2007 who discussed girls' use of the Internet as identity play). Looking at children's use of mobile phones, Bond (2010) noted the central position that it has in children's daily lives and friendship relations. There was also some anxiety and risk associated with it, however. For example, children were aware that text can be misinterpreted, and that even a delay in responding to a text can prove offensive. Thus, the children in Bond's study reported spending a lot of time carefully writing texts in order to minimize being misinterpreted. At the same time, news headlines frequently report the dangers of mobile phone use and bullying, and of course this can happen, as Bond (2010) notes, but largely 'the children use mobile phones to form friendships, and to communicate with text, pictures and mobile content to reinforce the emotional ties with their friendships' (2010: 525). McNamee (1998a) found that – for boys at least – computer games served a similar function.

An extremely large, Europe-wide study has recently been undertaken in relation to children online. Focusing on opportunities and risks as well as implications for policy, this study involved children in 33 countries and has produced many publications. While there is not space here to survey all of those publications, the reader is directed to look at some of the work that has been produced from this research (see http://www.lse.ac.uk/media@lse/research/EUKidsOnline/Home.aspx). One valuable thread to come out of this more recent spate of research has been the shift from looking at effects to *affordances* that the Internet offers to young people. That is to say, 'social networking sites frame but do not determine. It remains open to young people to select a more or less complex representation of themselves linked to a more or less wide network of others' (Livingstone, 2008: 403). Such an approach is in keeping with the views expressed in this chapter that we need to look not at what the media does to children but what children do with the media.

So much has been written and said about children's use of media. From causing social isolation, to children suffering from the negative effects of violent video games, to being blamed for obesity in children, screen-based media is demonized. However, and contradictorily, alongside these moral panics, global movements strive to provide a computer for every child. Since the 1990s, many countries (for example the United States, Canada, the United Kingdom, Australia, Brazil, Malaysia, and Norway; see Odera, 2011 for details) have developed educational policies based on the importance of information and communications technology (ICT) for the contemporary generation and the need to foster computer skills in school. With a global scope in mind, the organization, One Laptop Per Child (n.d.), is working 'to provide [every] child with a rugged, low-cost, low-power, connected laptop [so that] children [can be] engaged in their own education and learn, share and create together. [With computers], they become connected to each other, to the world and to a brighter future.' In this kind of discourse, children's use of screen-based media is hailed as progress, and is celebrated as empowerment. When a child uses technology for education, it is a 'good' thing. When used merely for entertainment it is a problem. Why this difference when the object of discussion (the computer) is the same? It could be argued that when children use computers as entertainment they are not subject to adult control. As an illustration, in my own study one parent said of her daughters, 'if they were that interested in playing them I would restrict them... but because they're not, I don't have that problem' (McNamee, 1998a). Children who are not subject to adult control are always the focus of concern.

Conclusion

In this chapter, we have noted that the concern – sometimes panic – about children and play has a historical component. Since the early 1900s, adults have been concerned that children's proper play is on the brink of disappearing, taking childhood with it. The extent of the concern is related to the perceived importance of play for successful development and socialization, and to the modern conception of childhood as firmly rooted in romantic developmentalism. Children, it is thought, should be protected from the adult world at all times, and particularly when they play. We have also seen how the space of childhood play is constrained and controlled by adults.

Keeping children safe within the walled garden of childhood innocence ensures that the boundary around childhood innocence is maintained, but also ensures that it can be policed. If children are doing something that is other than 'appropriate' childhood activity (for example, enjoying violent video games instead of going fishing), we can no longer see childhood as a time of innocence and purity.

Exercise and reflection points

1. Thinking about some of the places and spaces that you liked to play in as a child, were these *children's places* or *places for children?* What might have been the differences between these two types of space and the ways that you experienced them?
2. Reflect on your engagement with media as a child. Why did you like it? Were there any instances where your engagement with it was controlled by adults? How did this make you feel?
3. Article 38 of the UNCRC states that: *1. States Parties recognize the right of the child to rest and leisure, to engage in play and recreational activities appropriate to the age of the child and to participate freely in cultural life and the arts. 2. States Parties shall respect and promote the right of the child to participate fully in cultural and artistic life and shall encourage the provision of appropriate and equal opportunities for cultural, artistic, recreational and leisure activity.*
   In the light of the discussion in this chapter, deconstruct Article 38. What does it mean? What image of the child is held here? What kind of leisure is the article focused on? What is being excluded?

Further reading

Bond, E. (2014) *Childhood, mobile technologies and everyday experiences: changing technologies = changing childhoods?* London: Palgrave Macmillan.

Marsh, J. and Bishop, J.C. (2014) *Changing Play: Play, media and commercial culture from the 1950s to the present day* Berkshire: OU Press.

McNamee, S. (2000) 'Foucault's heterotopia and children's everyday lives' *Childhood: A journal of global child research*, vol. 7(4), pp. 479–492.

Opie, P. and Opie, A. (1959) *The lore and language of schoolchildren*, Oxford: Oxford University Press.

Walkerdine, V. (2007) *Children, gender, video games: Towards a relational approach to multimedia*, London: Palgrave Macmillan.

CHAPTER 10

Children and Health

Keywords: Embodiment, agency, competence, difference and normality, medical model, social model, child obesity

We have by now become well aware of the importance of seeing childhood as a social construction through the many examples provided in this textbook. In this chapter, we will look at childhood health and illness as a social construction (reminder: social construction theory holds that there is no objective, external 'reality' but rather it is constructed through interaction). You may wonder how health can be socially constructed – isn't it something that we feel physically, that is, something that is embodied? The answer on both fronts is yes: 'health' can be socially constructed and yes, it is an embodied experience – that is to say, 'the daily lived experience for humans of both having a body and being a body' (Lupton, 2003). We experience illness in our bodies and minds, and yet these experiences are socially, historically, and culturally constructed.

The model that dominates understandings of health and illness is a biomedical model based on 'objective' scientific discourse. However, if we look cross culturally and historically, we see radically different ways in which health and illness are experienced. Among the Beng of West Africa, for example, infant death is attributed to spirit, witchcraft, and poverty. It may be that the spirit of the child was not ready to be born alive, or it may wish to die soon after birth if it is dissatisfied with its surroundings or the care that parents provide. Alternately, the correct sacrifice to the Earth spirit may not have been made, thereby causing the death of the newborn (Gottleib, 2004). These explanations are a world away from the biological Westernized model, and yet for the Beng, they hold as much importance as our reliance on medicine does for us. As Christensen (2000) notes, when childhood is conceptualized as a period of vulnerability and dependence, as it is in the West, cultural context and alternative constructions of childhood and vulnerability are ignored (see the discussion of HIV/AIDS and childhood below). This chapter begins with an overview of the development of institutionalized child health care in the West, before looking at children's competence in health, their agency and their experiences of illness, factors which can be overlooked if only the biomedical model is used to understand health and illness. We look at cultural context, children and disability and the latest concern about child health in the developed world, childhood obesity. Throughout we note that the focus on the child in health is related to the notion of childhood as futurity. Thus, it is argued, maintaining and addressing child health is not simply for the benefit of 'the child,' but for future society – children are, in a real sense, the future adults of society. State investment in child health, therefore, can be seen as an approach which sees children as future capital for the state to draw on.

A history of institutionalized child health care

In the United States during the industrialization of the 19th century, when increasing large numbers of people moved to the large cities and towns in order to find employment, concern about the health of poor children grew. Philanthropists noted the impoverished and crowded conditions they lived in, their unsafe workplace environments, and the high risk of infection they faced (Sloane, 2008). Spearheaded by middle-and upper-class women, paediatric wards and children's hospitals were established. The first children's hospital opened in Philadelphia in 1855. Five years later there were more than 30 children's hospitals in North America. These early children's hospitals were not primarily designed as places for medical care, although medical care was provided. The hospitals and children's wards were designed to be 'happy homes' and were 'intended as places of comfort and cure as well as moral and spiritual education for the "little sufferers" and their parents' (Sloane, 2008: 42). The promoters of institutionalized child health hoped that in these new health facilities societal reform and improvement of children's health would go hand in hand. Providing the sick, poverty-stricken child with a glimpse of what a 'happy home' could be like, surrounded by adults who were teaching children how to be a 'better' kind of child, the early wards and hospitals for children were designed to mould society through their focus on the child as malleable and as future. The business of institutionalized child health was, then, about curing children *and* curing society. The future health of the family and the state was seen to be dependent on the care of children: 'the idea that the physical health of children was a state investment became widely accepted. [This] meant a shift in the perception of children from family "chattels" or parental possessions to "social capital"' (Cusins-Lewer and Gatley, 2008: 86).

Similar movements to 'correct' childhood (and hence ensure a better society in the future) through health provision were developing throughout the industrializing world in the late 19th century and early 20th century. In New Zealand, 'healthy spaces' for children – green spaces for playgrounds and kindergartens – were developed to ensure that New Zealand children did not have to live in the kind of conditions that the poor of the United Kingdom lived in. Also popular in the early 20th century were open-air schools. Developed first in Germany, the open-air school blended health care and education. Children, especially poor children, with or at risk from TB were well fed, took exercise, and were able to breathe cleaner air and take appropriate rest (Châtelet, 2008). These schools became sites for the medical monitoring of childhood, and paved the way for the child study movement (see Chapter 2) which brought the medical profession into schools. The marriage of medicine and education in preventative medicine also had its roots in open-air schools (Armstrong, 1983). Beginning in the early 20th century, it was the medical profession and not mothers who were seen to be the experts in caring for children (James and Hockey, 2007).

The discourses of childhood (see Chapter 1), and in particular the discourse of age, are threaded through institutional settings such as children's hospitals. When Great Ormond Street, a famous children's hospital in the United Kingdom, first opened, only children between the ages of two and ten were admitted. Babies under two were treated with their mothers, while children older than ten were treated in adult wards. It is likely that children aged over ten were seen as 'too adult' in their habits and morals and thus put younger children at risk of 'infection' from their bad habits. Gradually the age range of children admitted to children's hospitals has increased, and in the United Kingdom, children to the age of 16 are admitted (James and Curtis, 2012). James and Curtis argue that this increasing age range reflects a gradual expansion of the category 'child,' thus demonstrating the socially constructed nature of childhood.

How does this wide age range affect the experience of children and young people today who are hospitalized? Children's wards tend to be brightly coloured with child-friendly images such as cartoon characters painted on walls and stuck on windows. Younger children may appreciate this, but older children and young people probably consider this too childish. While the intention in designing hospital space is to create a comfortable and familiar setting for children, older children are excluded. Older children also experience the rules in children's hospitals (e.g. lights out by 10 p.m., curtains must not be drawn around the bed) as restrictive. Used to more autonomy at home, they experience stays in hospital as confining.

Children's agency and competence in health

We cannot talk about children and health without reference to the work of Myra Bluebond-Langner (1978) and her groundbreaking study of children with leukaemia. Bluebond-Langner carried out an ethnographic study of children in a paediatric oncology ward focussing on communication and social order, that is, how the taken-for-granted expectation that children will outlive their parents becomes disrupted when children suffer from a fatal illness. She found that the children were aware of their prognosis even though hospital staff and parents had never told them. Bluebond-Langner's work is a powerful critique of developmental psychology and traditional socialization theory. She demonstrated children's competence and agency in matters of death and dying, a matter children had previously been thought incapable of understanding. Developmental theory held that until children were older (that is, approaching adulthood) they had no concept of death, and therefore could not comprehend their own impending death. Based on this assumption, medical staff and parents of her study did not inform children of their prognosis, leaving the child isolated.

Both children and adults engaged in what Bluebond-Langner terms a practice of mutual pretence, where all parties acted as if the child was not dying. Children used mutual pretence to protect their parents and other adults from the fact that they were aware of their prognosis, while adults kept silent to protect the child.

How, then, did children come to know about their illness and prognosis if the adults around them did not tell them? Using the ethnographic technique of participant observation Bluebond-Langner was able to see the children in real-life action, rather than in experimental or observational conditions. She observed children eavesdropping when they could, and keeping each other informed as to what various drugs did and why they were prescribed them. In using such strategies, children demonstrated that they were active in socializing themselves and each other into their roles as dying children.

As has been noted, beliefs about childhood, and about children's competencies, influence adults' decisions whether or not to inform children about their health (Alderson, 1992). If we see children as developing, as not-yet adults, and thus as not-yet competent, we are likely to withhold difficult information from them because we feel that they cannot deal with it. But Bluebond-Langner eloquently demonstrated that children as young as three could and did understand their own illness and prognosis. Based on her findings, she produced a stage model of children's understanding of death, but it was not based on age as psychological models are. Rather, her model of the development of children's understanding was grounded in children's own experiences of their illness, irrespective of the age of the child. Her work has provided a valuable stimulus to the social study of childhood, illustrating children's competence and agency.

Christensen (1993), who explored children helping other children who were sick or injured, provides another example that demonstrates children as competent agents in regard to health. She distinguished between a child's intention to help and motive for helping. A child may intend to help the sick or injured children but may or may not do so. However, regardless of the outcome, the motive to help was present. Christensen gives the example of a boy who had a headache at an after-school centre, and was waiting to be collected by his parent. He told Christensen about a girl who turned down the music and told the other children to be quiet because he had a headache. Although the boy said the music hadn't bothered him, and that her help didn't *actually* help him, he perceived her action as help because he knew she had intended to help him.

Children have traditionally been seen, by virtue of their age and perceived incompetence, to have unreliable ideas about their sickness. In a somewhat old, but useful, analysis Prout (1986) carried out an ethnographic study of children's sickness and school absences. Talking to teachers and other school staff about children's sickness, he found that children's claims to be sick were often dismissed by adults in school. In particular, school staff drew on their assumptions about and prejudices of the child's family (in particular the notion of the over-indulgent mother was often invoked) to decide whether children were really ill. Unless children were visibly ill, or were ones who did not often claim to be sick, teachers made them 'wait and see.' If the teacher felt the child really was sick, they were sent to see the school secretary who made a further assessment of the child's illness before calling a parent to come and collect the child. In some cases, the secretary would send the child back to class, thus ignoring the child's claim of feeling ill. Girls were more often considered to be 'little actresses' in their sickness claims than were boys. Here we have an example of children's ability to decide for themselves whether they are ill or not being constrained by adult perceptions of 'real' illness, in which gender and assumptions about good parenting play a part.

Difference and normality: Childhood and disability

There are three main models of disability: the medical model, the social model, and a more recent approach which attempts to move the field on. While the medical model sees impairment or disability as grounded in the individual pathology, and which requires medical intervention to treat, the social model holds that individuals are disabled through the inability of society to remove barriers to equal access – for example – and to promote inclusive policies. The argument held that disability in society was a result of discrimination and oppression. The social model is largely based on a social constructionist perspective and was an important shift in theorizing disability. More recently, however, it has been argued that the social model ignores the reality of the physical experience of impairment or disability. That is to say, that even if discrimination was removed, the individual would still have a physical impairment which might impact on their equality of access to employment, for example (Shakespeare, 2006).

It has been pointed out that while the social study of childhood and disability studies have both become influential fields since the early 1990s, it is seldom that the two coincide. Further, it has been claimed that research into the lives of disabled children is marginalized in work carried out in the social study of childhood (Watson, 2012). Moreover, Tisdall (2012) has convincingly argued that the development of both childhood studies and disability studies have positioned themselves in opposition to existing more dominant paradigms and it is now time for both disability studies and childhood studies to widen their fields of enquiry. She comments that research with disabled children can only be of benefit to both fields (2012: 189).

In this section we discuss childhood and disability, difference and normality from the perspective of the child. Disabled children have been seen as 'different' and as particularly vulnerable and thus in need of care and protection. This affects a disabled child in two ways, argues Priestly (1998). 1) The biomedical focus on intervention means that the child is subject to greater surveillance and monitoring, and 2) the vulnerability of the impaired child prompts adults to increase care of them and control over their lives. Children, however, said that they suffered most from having no privacy and autonomy because they were always with an adult carer. The disabled child's ability to form friendships and to interact with other children was also impacted because of the constant presence of adults.

Children's identity as disabled was fluid and contextual, at times emphasized and at other times down played (Priestly, 1998; Holt, 2004). Examples of this fluidity can be found when looking at children with disabilities in the school environment. In many educational systems, inclusion or 'mainstreaming' has become common practice, rather than placing children into 'special' schools for children with particular needs. However, within mainstream schools, children with particular 'needs' are separated out, not into separate schools, but into ability groups, or classroom space is divided so that those with 'special needs' are seated together. While this makes it easier for teaching staff, it also emphasizes that the disabled children are different, which leaves them more vulnerable to stigmatization (Holt, 2004; Priestly 1998).

In light of the medical and social models of disability defined above, it has been argued that both relate more to adult experiences of disability than to children's. Proposing a 'new paradigm' of what it means to be a disabled child, Watson (2012) argues that without a new, relational, approach, the lives of children with disabilities will only ever be partially understood. The new approach would allow disabled children to participate in the research itself, identifying areas of research which are important to them. Such an approach would assume that disabled children are not a homogenous group and would allow for variety in experiences, which intersect with issues of class, gender, geography, ethnicity, and so on. It would take seriously changes throughout childhood and the fluidity of identity and experience. It would explore how different conditions disable in different ways. And finally, it would challenge oppression and exclusion (Watson, 2012: 199–200). Such an approach is long overdue and the potential benefits to children and to the study and understanding of childhood are great.

BOX 10.1 Rosie

When describing my childhood some would say that it was anything but 'normal.' To them I say, my childhood was not normal, it was unique and I would not have changed a thing. I grew up as a triplet, and one of my sisters, Claire, had cerebral palsy. Her condition was one she was born with and it left her in a wheelchair with little sight, and almost no verbal skills but a lot of spark. My childhood was a balancing act, for as much as my parents strived to give my sister and me a traditional childhood; there was also the more visible need to care for Claire. My roles varied depending on which sister I was with. When interacting with Claire my role in the house was almost a caregiver. My task was simple, every morning I went into her room and checked to see if she was awake and if she was I would read her a story. Beyond that I would sometimes take on small voluntary roles, feeding, dressing, cleaning, etc. When my other sister, Elaine, and I were together traditional childhood roles occurred. Together we played all games imaginable, it was carefree. In terms of my parents, they struggled too with the roles they should inflict on us. It was no question that raising my sister was difficult and as a result Elaine and I often got asked to help out around the house with Claire. However at the same time they didn't want my sister's disability to hold Elaine and I back. Overall, whether or not my childhood was 'normal' or not, I think my childhood was very fulfilling. Growing up in my unique situation I learned about struggle, care and acceptance. My sister Claire brought a certain joy to my life and taught me many things that I believe I only found out about because of my childhood experience. I am extremely grateful for my childhood experiences and without those experiences I would not have become who I am today.

Children, as we have noted throughout this textbook, are commonly envisioned as vulnerable and in need of care and protection. The disabled child is thus doubly seen to need care and protection. However, studies which have looked at children's experiences of disability in the sibling relationship reveal that disabled children and their siblings do not highlight difference in their discussions (e.g. Stalker and Connors 2004), and do not identify themselves as dependent. In a study which looked at the oldest siblings with disabilities, Seredity and Burgman (2012) found that as older siblings, the disabled children showed concern, protection and caregiving for their younger siblings. In all, the sibling relationships of children with and without disabilities was not too different.

Constructions of the child as different or as normal or, as James (1993) discusses, as 'differently normal' vary according to context. For example, when medical professionals classify a child as different because of a chronic illness or impairment, parents' narratives about their child might downplay difference and emphasize normality. In contrast, when trying to get the child's condition recognized or diagnosed by the medical profession then parents tend to play up difference and show how the child does not meet definitions of 'normal.' Examples of this can be seen in the different ways that families deal with asthmatic children. Once the diagnosis has been made, some families work very hard to ensure that the condition and the treatment of it does not exaggerate the child's difference in the family and in the wider social context (James, 1993).

Health cross-culturally

James (1998) has pointed out how images of sick and suffering children – often children in developing countries – which are intended to provoke compassion in the (adult) viewer, reinforce and in fact intensify the discourses of childhood which describe it as a time of innocence and vulnerability (see also Holland, 2004). The suffering child's body, captured on film and shown repeatedly around the world, both positions suffering children as 'other' and also positions the viewer as responsible for saving that child (Holland, 2004; see discussion below). An illustration of this can be found in the contemporary attention being paid to AIDS orphans in sub-Saharan Africa. Fassin (2008) notes that until the late 1990s children were largely absent from any discussion of AIDS, but that they have quite rapidly become the centre of attention. The discussion of children with AIDS or children who are orphaned by AIDS draws heavily on the discourse of childhood as a time of innocence and vulnerability. This discourse positions children as needing adult care and attention, and positions adults firstly as responsible for children's care, and yet contradictorily, guilty of transmitting the disease.

It was estimated that by 2015 there could be as many as two million AIDS orphans. These projected figures were causing alarm in the parts of Africa where AIDS is rampant. Fassin (2008), however, provides a more tempered view. First, he has deconstructed these figures: most orphaned children are actually orphans because of violence, not because of AIDS. Also, it is a very common practice in Africa to raise children outside of the natal family; traditionally they are sent to villages to be raised by grandparents and other kin – therefore children are already being raised apart from parental control. The important point to note from Fassin's work is the way in which representations and images of children are central to the discourse of childhood innocence and vulnerability. However, he also points out that residents of a suburban area of one city objected to the establishment of an orphanage, arguing that it would devalue their properties. Clearly, not everyone is moved by images and representations of the tragic child.

Children are also making their own decisions about their health care in Africa. One study found that children were making the choice to move away from their homes into orphanages. Even when children were living with relatives or guardians, a move to an orphanage was seen as advantageous in that good food and medical treatment would be more readily available to the sick child. Interviews carried out with children and their relatives revealed that children were healthier and happier after moving to an orphanage. In addition, connections with family members were easily maintained, so that the children could still take part in family celebrations (Johnson and Vindrola-Padros, 2013). Again, studies such as this contribute to our understanding of children as agents and experts on their own lives, rather than as passive victims.

In a globalized world, contends Robson (2004), we need to understand more about how children and young people are impacted by global processes, for example, how the privatization of health care and poverty caused by neoliberalism – people cannot afford good nutrition and medical services thus they get sick more often – impacts the AIDS pandemic in sub-Saharan Africa. As parents become less able to care for families, children as young carers or as heads of households fill the gap, acting as agents, 'a creative and active response by them and their households' (Robson, 2004: 239). However, at the same time as they are displaying their capacity for agency and for care, notes Robson, they are also bearing the brunt of global economic practices.

Children, health, and the obesity 'epidemic'

What is interesting about the recent 'obesity epidemic' is the extent to which children's media consumption (particularly screen-based advertising media) and obesity brought on by consumption of junk food have been linked. Children's engagement with screen-based media drives much of the moral panic, or concern, about childhood obesity and overweight children. However, in one study, researchers established an association between being overweight and video game use, but no association with TV watching. Of interest here is the finding that overweight children under eight years old spent only a 'moderate' amount of time playing video games, while children with low weight spent either a little or a lot of time playing (Vandewater, Shim and Caplovitz, 2004). Such findings counter some of the assumptions about the causes of childhood obesity.

As Buckingham (2011: 6) has noted, children's media consumption is currently considered an urgent social problem, and advertising and marketing to children are blamed for a wide range of problems, to the point where 'the debate often seems to be about the wholesale destruction of childhood itself.' The choices that children have of how to spend their leisure time and what to eat are faulted in this debate with little regard being paid to the *lack* of choice children often have in these areas. There is no consensus on the 'causes' of obesity. The reasons vary: how children spent their leisure time, (too much screen time); media advertising 'junk' to children; the unhealthy meals served in school cafeterias; and the lack of physical education classes in schools. Each of these problems has solutions proposed, which will be addressed in this section. However, it is significant that the first three receive the most attention while little is paid to the last.

It is not only the obese child's body that is of concern, however. Researchers have argued that media exposure can at one and the same time 'make' children fat, and it can also make them over-thin. Herbozo and colleagues (2004) carried out a study on children and body image focused on thinness rather than being overweight. They drew on 'effects' research (a way of looking at media which assumes that it directly affects children in some way or another, but which ignores social context of media reception), concluding that children were unable to distinguish between the real and the imaginary in screen-based media (see also Horgan et al., 2012). According to them, the majority of messages about the desirability of thinness came from mass media. Children, they contended, internalized these sociocultural ideas about body shape and displayed a prejudice against children who are not thin (Herbozo et al., 2004, 22–23).

What is problematic about this study is the research method. University students analysed children's books and videos for body image messages which they thought would impact children. From this, the authors draw conclusions about the messages transmitted to children by media. Does the fact that university students (some of them graduate students) can identify body-image messages in children's media lead automatically to the argument that such media affects children? Might a study exploring children's own understandings and interpretations of the books and videos be a more useful starting point? Assumptions based on a psychological model of childhood which does not take into account children's competencies can only reveal part of the story. Children's use of the media, in Herbozo et al.'s study, is blamed for both the 'obesity epidemic' and the fear that young girls will succumb to eating disorders because of representations of thinness.

For those subscribing to and contributing to moral panic, children are incompetent in their consumption of media, incompetent in their consumption of food, and also incompetent in how they make choices about their leisure activities. However, in contemporary society children's leisure opportunities are constrained by parental fears of stranger danger. Children are increasingly being kept indoors and out of public space, which may contribute to a decrease in physical activity and heighten the chances of weight increase. We might want to consider how much of what children do in their leisure time is therefore about their choices (Loebach, 2013).

One group of researchers advocated a return to previous constructions of childhood. Tremblay and colleagues (2005) compared fitness levels of 8–13-year-olds in Ontario and Saskatchewan in two groups: Old Order Mennonite children and non-Mennonite children. They found that Old Order Mennonite children had a significantly lower body mass index (BMI) than non-Mennonite children. According to the researchers, this is because Mennonite children worked on the family farm and around the home, and did not engage in screen-based leisure as Canadian children did. They contended that a back-to-basics lifestyle could help promote fitness and reduce obesity in non-Mennonite children. Ironically, this is the very kind of childhood (i.e. working alongside adults, responsibility rather than play) that was rejected in favour of the current romanticized perception of childhood (see Chapter 1).

Advertising bans

The food industry has come under attack because of the way it markets junk food to children (Linn and Novosat, 2008). Horgan et al. (2012: 456) are not subtle in their criticism of marketing: 'if unhealthy foods are the wares of a toxic food environment, marketing is the peddler.' Measures are being taken to address such marketing – everything from bans to the self-regulation of food manufacturers – but there has been little consolidated effort. In the United Kingdom, direct TV advertising of foods high in fat and sugar to children under 16 has been banned since 2006. In Canada, the food industry has pre-empted an advertising ban by regulating itself. It now markets 'healthy' products (e.g. apples in children's meals in fast food restaurants). Sixteen of the largest candy, fast-food, and soft-drink companies pledged either to not advertise directly to children under 12, or to market only their healthier products to them.

In the United Kingdom, policy related to food in school has become about students' spatial movements. When school meal services, directed by state policy intended to counter obesity, began introducing healthy meals, the number of pupils eating school lunches dropped. Children instead were bringing packed lunches or eating at the many nearby food outlets. (On average, every secondary school in the United Kingdom has 24 fast food outlets in close proximity to it.) Schools were then encouraged to impose a stay-on-site policy, whereby children were not allowed to leave the school grounds at all at lunchtimes, thus symbolically or physically locking in children (Pike and Colquhoun, 2012: 437). In this example, children are controlled in both their spatial movements and in being able to make choices about the food they eat.

In British Columbia, Canada, following a ban on junk food in schools, some enterprising students began selling candy from their lockers. In the first week they made 200 dollars. They donated the profits to a local children's hospital, and were hailed as heroes. This is an illuminating example of both resistance and enterprise, and displays the obvious tension between control over children's food and how resistance to control is seen – even by the health professionals – as heroic!

As noted above, one of the measures taken in addressing the obesity 'epidemic' is to blame children for their food consumption and to try and encourage healthy eating. However, as Brembeck and Johansson (2010: 807) state, 'children's eating takes place in arenas and on terms that are defined by adults.' Adults purchase and prepare food for children, and adults determine when and where food can be eaten. Any resistance to this control that children might display will probably be at times when, and in spaces where, they can escape the adult gaze. As we can see in several examples in this textbook, however, those times and spaces are rare in children's everyday lives.

Children and mental health: The example of ADHD

Earlier in this chapter we discussed conceptions of 'normal' and 'different' in relation to children and health. As we also discussed in Chapter 2, developmental psychology largely framed childhood in terms of normal and abnormal development and thus the child who fell outside of the 'normal' range of parameters was thought to need intervention. Here we turn to exploring how children diagnosed with attention deficit hyperactivity disorder (ADHD) are positioned as different and needing treatment. ADHD comprises a range of symptoms which vary in their severity and which include inattention, impulsivity, and over-activity (Brady, 2014). Healy contends that ADHD is the 'most visible symbol of the bio-medicalisation of childhood disorders' (Healy 2006). Children's behaviour is treated medically with the use of drugs (amphetamines) to modify the child's social behaviour. While undoubtedly some children with ADHD benefit from taking drugs that control their symptoms, some researchers have pointed out that using drugs to treat ADHD can also be a means of social control, where medical definitions of normality and difference are applied to deviant behaviour (Rafalovich, 2013).

Schools play an important role in dealing with ADHD. Teachers are often the ones to advise a referral of a child suspected of having the disorder to doctors. It has also been pointed out that pharmaceutical companies manufacturing the drugs used to treat ADHD conduct education campaigns for teachers in which they advise teachers how to identify ADHD in children and when to refer children (Oswell, 2013: 184).

Twenty years ago at a time when the teaching and medical professions refused to consider the behaviour of a child a medical condition, parents of children with ADHD fought to have a diagnosis identified and appropriate treatment developed for their children. The consequence of identifying the disorder has meant, though, that the diagnosis and treatment of ADHD has almost become an epidemic, especially in the West. However, the United Kingdom has lower rates of diagnosis than Canada and the United States. This has been attributed to the different stances taken in relation to childhood in the United Kingdom and North America. Disciplining, or controlling, children, rather than medicating them is the focus in the UK. In North America, medicating children is the focus; 90 per cent of the world's Ritalin is prescribed in North America (Rafalovich, 2013). This is an important point, and demonstrates that childhood is culturally specific. It is also temporally specific. Currently it is believed that ADHD is caused by malformed structures within the brain and thus the appropriate treatment is medication. Previously, ADHD was believed to have environmental causes, for example, food additives were blamed for the behaviour (Rafalovich, 2013). Between 1994 and 2005, treating ADHD with medication has risen 274 per cent worldwide, and this is often attributed to the increasing dominance of biomedicine (Prosser, 2013). It cannot be ignored that for many parents and their children, a brain-based explanation for their child's behaviour comes as a relief. Such a diagnosis means that the fault 'is neither the child's nor the parents' (Singh, 2012).

As yet little research has been carried out which explores children's experiences of having ADHD. In one valuable study (Brady, 2014) that solicited children's thoughts on their diagnosis, researchers demonstrated how children took responsibility for their own wellbeing, including the managing of their medication. Showing how children made active choices in relation to their health, Brady described a boy who took his medication if he needed to focus (while doing maths homework) but preferred not to take his tablets if he needed to think creatively (when doing art work). LeFrançois and Coppock (2014) argue that what is needed is a deconstruction of the biomedical essentialization of children's worlds to show mental health as socially constructed. This will involve researchers looking more closely at the discourses and experiences of children suffering from various forms of mental health including ADHD.

Conclusion

In this chapter, we have looked at health as a social construction. We began by looking at the development of institutionalized child health provision in the West and noted that such provision was based on a perceived need to improve the future stock of the nation, as well as a desire to alleviate suffering. The example of obesity demonstrates that this view is still prevalent in discourses about children's healthy or unhealthy bodies. The discussion of children and death drew on Myra Bluebond-Langner's (1979) ethnographic research and demonstrated clearly that children possess agency and competence in health. Like many of the examples provided throughout this text, the ones in this chapter affirm that the social study of childhood, which takes the perspective of the child seriously, is a necessary shift if we are to understand children's experiences and to continue to deconstruct discourses of childhood which serve to frame those experiences in unhelpful ways.

Exercise and reflection points

1. What approach, if any, should be taken in relation to child obesity and overweight children? Draft the approach that you think (a) the government should take; (b) the medical profession should take, and (c) the educational system should take. How might these approaches benefit from listening to children?
2. This chapter has discussed competence and agency in children's experiences of health and illness. Think of comparative or similar examples in your own experience, or the experience of someone you know. Reflect on how these experiences made you/someone else feel at the time. What would have made a difference in how you felt?
3. What do you think might be the effect of implementing Westernized understandings of health and illness in other cultures?

Further reading

Bluebond-Langner, M. (1978) *The private worlds of dying children*, Princeton: Princeton University Press.

Brembeck, H. and Johansson, B. (2010) 'Foodscapes and children's bodies,' *Culture Unbound*, vol. 2, pp. 797–818.

Fassin, D. (2008) 'AIDS orphans, raped babies, and suffering children: The moral construction of childhood in post apartheid South Africa' in Comacchia, C., Golden, J. and Weisz, G. (ed.) *Healing the world's children: Interdisciplinary perspectives on children's health in the twentieth century*, Montreal and Kingston: McGill-Queen's University Press.

James, A. (1998) 'Children, health and illness' in Field, D. and Taylor, S. (ed.) *Sociological perspectives on health, illness, and health care*, Oxford: Blackwell Science.

CHAPTER 11

Globalization and Diversity in Childhood

Keywords: globalization, diversity, cultural relativism, universalism, 'lost' childhoods, child soldiers

How *should* we see children? What are the implications for children in seeing them from a particular perspective? This book has throughout problematized the concept of childhood and it was noted that seeing childhood as socially, historically, and culturally constructed has been the focus of the social study of childhood. This new perspective has also allowed researchers to demonstrate the many ways in which children are agentic and competent, thereby reframing what can be said about childhood. By looking at childhood from the perspective of the child, rather than the adult, we can see the meaning and the experience of childhood for children. At a time when concern for children is high, as evidenced by the 1989 UNCRC which set out a range of global rights for children, this chapter focuses on issues highlighted earlier in relation to Westernized conceptions of childhood, and asks, 'Can we talk about childhood, or should we talk about childhoods?' This chapter, then, brings together a range of examples from research in order to show how seeing childhood as culturally constructed allows a multiplicity of childhoods to emerge, and also enables us to deconstruct and critique global, Westernized policies that affect children, such as the UNCRC. In order to begin this discussion, we first ask, 'What is globalization and how does it affect the lives of children?'

Globalization

Globalization refers to the phenomenon that the world economy is on its way to becoming a single integrated system (Prout, 2005). Wyness (2011: 61) describes it as 'a series of objective processes that bring political, cultural and economic systems together.' In other words, there is a sameness throughout the world of all these systems. How, you might ask, does the merging of world economies relate to and affect childhoods? Rizinni and

Bush (2002: 371) provide a useful working definition of globalization as it affects children:

> Globalization is a process that opens nation-states and societies to many influences that originate beyond their borders. These changes are likely to decrease the primacy of national economic, political and social institutions thereby affecting the everyday context in which children grow up and interact with the rest of society.

Childhood, and children's experience of it, cannot be divorced from wider structural forces. World economies affect everyone, and children may be disproportionally affected by the globalizing process and yet this does not involve hearing from children themselves about the effects of globalization (Fass, 2003).

The effects of globalization on children and childhoods

Effects on poverty and work

When children are aware that they are poor relative to other children – relative poverty – they feel social exclusion most keenly. In a globalized world, children living in poverty often realize they are poor in relation to other children worldwide through global media. They then notice the effects of poverty on their daily lives. While globalized world markets may help decrease poverty in some areas of the world, as a whole, the number of people living in poverty increased by 100 million in the 1990s (Rizzini and Bush, 2002: 371). Half of all the children in the world live in poverty; one in three of the world's children have no adequate shelter, while one in five have no access to clean water. At the same time, the rich of the world are getting richer and the gap between rich and poor within nations is widening (Shah, 2013).

Global solutions to child poverty are not simple. The United Nations is currently attempting to deal with it through the Millennium Development Goals (MDG) (2015). Commissioned in 2002 by the Secretary-General of the United Nations, the MDG were developed to tackle poverty, hunger, and disease. Eight areas were targeted: the end of poverty and hunger, universal education, gender equality, child health, maternal health, the control of HIV/AIDS, environmental sustainability, and global partnership. In partnership with bodies such as the World Bank, UNICEF, the World Health Organization, the International Monetary Fund, and others, the project aimed to halve the number of people in the world who existed on less than $1 per day. While the UN claimed that this goal would be met by the 2015 deadline, this proved not to be the case. More recently the UN has introduced the Sustainable

Development Goals (SDG) under the 'Transforming our world: the 2030 agenda for sustainable development' document (see https://sustainabledevelopment.un.org/sdgs), which lists 17 goals to be accomplished by the year 2030. The goals include eliminating poverty and hunger, reducing inequalities and tackling environmental concerns among others. For example, one of the aims of Goal 4 'To ensure inclusive and equitable quality education and promote lifelong learning opportunities for all' is to ensure that by 2030 all children – both boys and girls – complete primary and secondary education (https://sustainabledevelopment.un.org/sdg4). One can hope that the SDGs are more effective; however, efforts to deal with poverty have been impacted by the global economic crisis of the past few years, meaning that more jobs have been lost and thus more workers and their families are living in extreme poverty.

The rights of children as outlined in Article 27 of the UNCRC are still not ensured and it would appear that even beyond the 2015 date of the MDG many of the world's children will still have an inadequate standard of living and suffer from poor nutrition and inadequate housing. This will leave many children with fewer choices about whether or not to work, although, as has been noted, even where there is little choice, children can and do exert agency (Klocker 2007).

Fass (2003) has pointed out that one of the effects of globalization is that children are becoming more visible in the cash economy. This visibility has resulted in increased calls from Western observers to do something about child labour. (As we saw in our discussion of work, poorly thought-out approaches in response to demands to do something can have devastating consequences

BOX 11.1 Article 27 of the UNCRC

1. States Parties recognize the right of every child to a standard of living adequate for the child's physical, mental, spiritual, moral, and social development.
2. The parent(s) or others responsible for the child have the primary responsibility to secure, within their abilities and financial capacities, the conditions of living necessary for the child's development.
3. States Parties, in accordance with national conditions and within their means, shall take appropriate measures to assist parents and others responsible for the child to implement this right and shall in case of need provide material assistance and support programmes, particularly with regard to nutrition, clothing and housing.

for children as in the case of the child garment workers in Bangladesh (see also White, 1996).) According to Atiken et al. (2006: 382), children are the most flexible producers and consumers in the globalized world, because they both produce the goods through their labour and purchase them, suggesting 'children are the pivotal artefacts of contemporary globalization.' However, the argument that children provide the globalized economy with a cheap, disposable workforce has been countered by Cigno et al. (2002), who found no evidence that globalization in and of itself raised the incidence of child labour. The more salient factor was the educational background of the workforce in any particular country. If a country had an uneducated workforce, the higher wages globalization created reduced the incentive to put a child in school. Instead, parents encouraged their children to work. In contrast, in countries that had a well-educated workforce, the promise of higher wages encouraged parents to send their children to school. The effects of globalization are therefore, they claim, ambiguous (Cigno et al., 2002). This is an interesting argument, but one that leaves the issue of child labour and child poverty in a globalized economy as still – or even more – relevant *particularly* in countries with a poorly educated workforce.

In this section I draw on the work of White (1996), who discussed four aspects of globalization as it related to children: lifestyle, adult ideas about childhood, the enforcement of standards, and the globalization of ideas about children's rights. Using his four points, I will introduce the work of other analysts in order to further illuminate the issues.

Lifestyle

White (1996) argued that children produced many of the global products aimed at child consumers: toys, clothing, and other items of children's culture. He contended that in a global world, the issue has shifted from having *enough* food or clothing to children wanting certain *kinds* of things, whether that was Nike shoes or McDonald's food (see also Ruddick, 2003). This was *one* of the reasons that children chose to enter the labour market. By working they could earn enough money to buy the very products that they were often making. Some scholars have argued that in globalization, children's culture has become homogenized (Prout, 2005) in that the same products are available everywhere. However, as Cross and Smith (2005) have pointed out, the globalization of toys and commercial culture for children is not a new phenomenon, but originated at the turn of the 20th century.

One study of the globalization of children's culture and lifestyle explored how globalization became embedded in young people's lives through their use of the media. Lemish et al. (1998) carried out research with children and youth in Denmark, France, and Israel. In face of fears that children would lose their local cultural heritage and become Westernized because of the widespread availability of Western media forms, the authors found that while there were differences in the three countries studied, there were also similar interests, activities, and media preferences in all three. According to the authors, two processes were at work: (i) the children in this study adopted a global perspective on social life (drawn from their engagement with media); but (ii) they did this *alongside* their own cultural values. The fear of children becoming Westernized, then, is not supported by this study. However, because children tend to be seen as future, and because Western societies are so heavily invested in ensuring the continuation of society in the future, any inkling that childhood is on a different path causes alarm. What might our future society look like if children would not adopt 'our' cultural values and beliefs?

Ideas about childhood

Globalization, White (1996) argued, involved homogenization of ideas about what a proper childhood should be (ideas which are premised on Westernized notions of childhood), for example, children should be at school and not at work. As we have seen in discussions earlier in this textbook, however, children have always worked in some form or another. Further, in the Global South children often have to go to work in order to be able to afford to go to school. Education is not free in many parts of the world. Woodhead (1999), in a study of over 300 children in several settings (Bangladesh, Ethiopia, the Philippines, and Central America), asked children about the work that they did. Children said that while they would prefer to go to school, working was a necessity for them. Woodhead noted that describing the childhoods of work children as 'lost' hurt working children, who were proud of the work that they did and the contribution that they made. What was needed, argued Woodhead, was to listen to children and take their perspectives into account. Working children are aware of the opinions that the rest of the world holds about them, and are insulted when they are described as victims or as deprived. The globalization of ideas about childhood that draw on Westernized conceptions can never work because childhood as a concept is socially and culturally constructed, and children's lives are not the same throughout the world. Boyden (1997) provides a telling example: in parts of the United Kingdom it is illegal to leave children under 14 years of age in charge of younger children; in Peru a significant number of children between the ages of 6 and 14 are heads of households. Global policies which impose standards on children which are heavily influenced by Western notions of what childhood should be discriminate against other forms of childhood. A 'real' childhood is taken to be the Westernized version (that is, ideas and discourses about childhood as carefree, safe and happy) and thus currently practice and theory tends to give that a priority. Childhood experience which falls outside of this conception is therefore seen as not being a proper childhood. Nonetheless, the Westernized version of childhood provides the basis for both international and national social policy *irrespective* of children's realities. It is important, therefore, to take account of cultural specificity and difference.

The enforcement of standards

The globalization of the enforcement of standards for children, which White (1996) refers to, involves the implementation of boycotts against companies employing child labour. However, as he noted, these boycotts were only effective in terms of goods produced by children for the export market, but were ineffective in addressing most common forms of work that children do – unpaid work for parents – that is not subject to any global standards. While there is an assumption that work within the family is not as damaging to children as paid work, in fact many children prefer paid labour rather than unpaid work in the family. In paid work, they too can take part in the globalization of consumption (White 1996; see also Finn et al., 2010).

The globalization of children's rights

Lastly, White discussed the globalization of children's rights. Here he noted that there was a disjunction between organizations such as the International Labour Organization (ILO) seeking to abolish child labour and non-governmental organizations (NGOs) working on the ground that are seeking to empower working children and to recognize their right to work. Global policies governing childhood, Boyden (1997: 222) reminds us, have been created without input from the very people they are aimed at: 'the global construction of childhood is one in which children have played no part whatsoever: children definitely did not participate in the drafting of the Convention; nor have they been consulted as to the most effective manner of implementation' (see also Aitken et al., 2007). Boyden has also noted that there is little available evidence that children are better off because of the Convention, as the focus has been on whether or not countries are meeting their obligations under it, not measuring how – or indeed whether – children's lives have improved, and thus research is urgently needed in this area. To a large extent this has been addressed by the publication of the booklet 18 Candles, which contains comments and reflections on the Convention written in 2007 (18 years after the Convention was introduced) by the 18 members of the Committee on the Rights of the Child (Connors et al. 2007 available online at http://www.ohchr.org/Documents/Publications/crc18.pdf).

Childhood diversity

Several examples have been provided throughout this textbook of childhood in different cultures as represented in research, and in this section other examples of childhood diversity are explored. By discussing *childhoods* rather than *childhood* we can draw attention to social divisions such as ethnicity, class, gender, and so on (James et al., 1998). Global processes shape children and young people's home lives and, at the same time, structure their wider experiences. Exploring aspects of globalization and the effect on child carers in Zimbabwe, Robson (2004) explains how, as a result of global economics affecting national policies, children's experiences are affected. In line with neoliberal policies, Zimbabwe, like many other countries, decreased social spending on public health care. This, at the time of a global pandemic of HIV/AIDS, seriously affected people's lives. As poverty increased, so did the rate of prostitution, because women had fewer and fewer options of how to support themselves. In such an environment, the risk of contracting HIV increased because poverty made it more difficult for women to acquire condoms and treatment of STDs. Poor households could not afford nutritious diets and medical care, and thus when parents become sick, their care often fell to children. Yet, their role as carer was invisible because such work has not been recognized as work in globalized notions of exploited child labour, even though children bear the brunt of global economic restructuring. This should not be taken to mean that children are not acting as agents and should be pitied or seen as victims; in caring for their parents or other family members, they are making a rational, and active response to the effects of global economic poverty (Robson, 2004).

A further example of childhood diversity is street children. The term *street children* can refer to children who work on the streets but live at home, or children who live and work on the street, or it may encompass children who live on the streets but return home for the weekend, thus illustrating diversity within the term itself, as well as in the varied experiences of children who use the street (Glauser, 1997).

Bordonaro (2012) notes that there are many factors that cause children to live on the street. To live on the street is a choice for many poor children who are attracted to the money that can be made from begging and the relative abundance of food available in cities. However, for many other children the street is an escape from violence and corporal punishment in the home. Bordonaro, who studied boys on the street, found that one of the main reasons why the boys remained on the street was the freedom and autonomy it offered them. Turning to the street is a solution for many children and young people, not a problem (Bordonaro, 2012).

Girls also live on the streets but their experiences are different than boy street children. In Indonesia the discourse of femininity emphasizes the subordination of girls and women to boys and men, and thus the presence of girls on the street challenges cultural conceptions of gender. Girls cannot go out where they please, they cannot leave the house without permission, they cannot smoke or drink. In the face of these gendered understandings of femininity, street girls are subject to discrimination from both other (male) street children and from adults. Girls living on the street are characterized (by adults and by street boys) as *rendan*, a term that is more comparable in meaning to prostitute than street child. Thus, girls living on the streets remain trapped in traditional cultural constructions of gender in relation to what is, and is not, appropriate. However, street girls employ a range of strategies

---

BOX 11.2 Childhood in Rwanda

As Kelia walks out of the school gates in Musanze, Rwanda, her struggles and stress disappear for 40 minutes as she races her classmates home. Dodging through cornfields, sprinting across dirt patches, stepping from rock to rock, Kelia enters a world where, for a brief moment, she gets to choose what happens, and how. The children of the Ruhengeri district are one of the first generations to arise from the 1994 genocide, where almost one million Rwandans – mostly Tutsis – were murdered. Kelia and her generation live in a country that has experienced hurt, pain, devastation, and fear. Not only are the living conditions in this developing country challenging, but there are also pressures on the children of Rwanda, as the future generation, to build up a country that will know success and accomplishment. However, in spite of all the weight they carry, Rwandan children are the ones who recognize joy and who choose to dance when they don't want to walk. The stereotypes of African children are many, and yes, their life is a lot harder than most children's, but the words that best describe Rwandan children include: joyful, determined, and wise.

Contributed by 'Maria,' a student who worked with Rwandan children

to resist this kind of discrimination and to survive on the streets. Through adopting a masculine style of dress and bodily presentation they reject stereotypical notions of femininity, argues Beazley (2002). In addition, they use scarification and substance abuse to further demonstrate that they belong to the group of street girls. The girls use different spaces of the city than do the boys, and create a network of contacts to provide them with support, protection, and material goods. Thus, even within a group such as street children, there is no homogeneity but diversity and difference, as well as examples of competence, agency, and resistance.

Child soldiers

The final example of childhood diversity I want to explore is that of child soldiers. The children in this group might well have childhoods that are the least like a Westernized concept of childhood as a time of play and innocence. Child soldiers in the Lord's Resistance Army (LRA) in Northern Uganda have recently received considerable attention. This has largely been due to Invisible Children, an organization dedicated to raising the visibility of child soldiers in Uganda and advocating on their behalf. While child soldiers in the LRA are not the only child soldiers in the world, the research that Cheney (2005) has done provides analysis of child soldiers that can move us beyond simplistic notions of children as mere victims towards seeing the complexities of childhood and this plays out in children's lives. In particular, what we can see in the discussion about child soldiers are notions of childhood innocence versus 'lost' childhoods. The LRA began as a resistance movement against the Ugandan government, with a stated aim of freeing the Acholi of Northern Uganda. In order to continue its war against the government, thousands of children – mostly quite young children – were abducted to serve in the LRA. Mainly children were taken, it is believed, because children were easier to control and to indoctrinate with the aims of the LRA. Once abducted, children were quickly brutalized into the lifestyle of the LRA and forced to kill and to capture other children. Abducted girls became the 'wives' of commanders in the LRA, often bearing children to them and frequently becoming infected with HIV (Cheney, 2005).

Child soldiers are both victims of and perpetrators of violence – they have acted against the state and are seen by some as heroes of the rebellion yet as children they were forced into the army. Holding to a world view in which children should be saved, but rebels should not, how does the Ugandan army distinguish between children and combatants, asks Cheney (2005: 35), when children are the combatants? Children's charities have advocated for the child soldiers, asking that they be treated as children. However, Cheney (2005: 36) writes:

> UNICEF operates on a western essentialist model of childhood that idealizes children as innocent and harmless. This notion fails to account for circumstances in which the child may be the aggressor. It pigeonholes children as only innocent victims of war and not as potential perpetrators, because under this construction children and violence cannot possibly be commensurate.

The Ugandan army's response to organizations like UNICEF has been to argue that constructions of childhood, as promoted in the UNCRC or by UNICEF, do not apply in this case because the child soldiers do not fit into the category *child* at all.

In her research in a reception centre which rehabilitated former child soldiers, Verma (2012) found that the child soldiers offered various versions of their experiences depending on who their audience was. They tailored their experiences to fit the expected discourse of child as victim when talking to staff (Cheney, 2005). In their stories of returning, the children provided narratives that coincided with the model that the NGOs used in providing rehabilitation: child soldiers have lost their childhood of innocence and play, and it can only be restored through therapeutic help. Yet amongst themselves, the children recalled their experiences in a different light. When no adults were present, they presented themselves as neither child nor victim, but often recounted their experiences with a sense of pride and even on occasion nostalgia. Also, some of the returning or escaped children had acquired positions of status in the rebel army which they had to lose in the process of being 'turned' into children (Verma, 2012: 450). As Verma demonstrated, the complexity of experience of the former soldiers was missed when the official version of child soldiers as victims predominated.

It should also be noted that historically armed forces have always included children among their ranks. For example, Roman children would join the army to escape poverty and labour. In the American Revolution, many soldiers were under 16. In the First and Second World Wars, children lied about their age so that they could join up and fight. Why, Stearns (2005) asks, have we stopped admiring children's capacity to contribute during times of war and instead see it as a violation of childhood? Similar points are made by Rosen (2007), whose article clearly articulates the contrast between the adoption of a global definition of childhood in global approaches to children and the reality of local childhoods in which children may choose – for a variety of reasons – to be child soldiers. Should we see them as innocent victims or moral agents?

An example: The case of Omar Khadr

Omar Khadr, a Canadian citizen, was found in a compound in Afghanistan in 2002 following a gun battle with US soldiers. He was 15 years old. He had been shot, but was detained after it was claimed that he threw a grenade which killed a US soldier. He was interrogated and later transferred to Guantanamo, remaining in prison until his late 20s when he was released and returned to Canada where he lives with his lawyer and family. There have been disputes as to whether he was the person who threw the grenade or not. What is interesting in this example is perhaps – for our purposes – less about what happened in that compound in Afghanistan, but in terms of the question about who is a child, and the status of child soldiers in law. Article 38 of the UNCRC bars States Parties from recruiting any person into their national armed forces who is below the age of 15 – and yet the Convention holds that any person under the age of 18 is a child. Under the 'optional protocol' attached to the convention, Article 3 states any recruits under 18 should receive 'special protection' due to their status as a child. This means that national armies *can* recruit children over the age of 15 – however Article 4 of the special protocol explicitly prohibits armed groups who are not the national armed forces (i.e. rebel groups) from recruiting children under the age of 18. Clearly there are several tensions here, and the tensions do not appear to be resolved. As Rosen (2009) points out, children recruited into national armed forces aged between 15 and 18 are considered to be no different than the adult soldiers. However, if they commit war crimes they are not to be subject to prosecution because of their age. Rosen concludes that:

> International human rights law increasingly defines all persons under age eighteen as vulnerable children in need of protection. However, these bodies of law fail to grapple with the problem of child soldiers who commit terrible war crimes. The silence of international law on this issue is deafening, but the record of harsh responses of national courts to war crimes committed by child soldiers shows a pressing need for the development of an international approach. (Rosen 2009: 16)

Here we can see that the universalizing discourses of childhood drawing on a Westernized conception of what childhood is, or should be, fails to reflect the diversity of children's experiences. Failure to recognize diversity fails children in two ways. First, children whose childhoods do not fit Western concepts of childhood are deemed deficient; second, these children are marginalized, or to use Aitken's (2001) term, they are 'unchildlike' children. A childhood is only a 'lost' childhood when seen from a universal perspective, and when attention is not paid to child*hoods* in all their diversity.

Conclusion: Childhood diversity, the problem of universalism and cultural relativism

Given the discussion above, we have to consider issues of universalism versus cultural relativism. Do we look at childhood from the general, or from the particular? From the global perspective or the local experience? Of course this dichotomy between the two options is over-simplified and may be unhelpful, as Ansell (2010) notes, but it is useful to distinguish between the two in order to aid understanding of the issues.

Universalism in terms of childhood can be seen in the dominant discourses and global policies for children, the 1989 UNCRC being one example. In them, the assumption is made that childhood is an age-bound, developmental process, and positions children as different from, and inferior to, adults. Children are in need of protection and although they increasingly have rights to participation, these are largely granted (or withheld) at the discretion of adults. The cultural relativist position challenges the assumption that age separates childhood from adulthood, and that children are vulnerable and lack agency (Rivard, 2010). The relativist position is, of course, largely the position taken by those working in the social study of childhood, notwithstanding the approach taken by Qvortrup, for example (see Chapter 2), which does provide a basis for analysing childhood as a permanent structure in society.

There are dangers in both the universal and the relativist approaches to childhood, as White (1999) has pointed out. While a universal approach to childhood fails to take diversity into account, cultural relativism tends to see all cultures and cultural practices as equally valid and therefore neutral in all its aspects. Take, for example, the cultural practice of female genital mutilation. Is it sufficient to say that because it is a cultural matter nothing needs be done to address it (Jones, 2005)? White (1999: 137) proposes a more useful and productive approach and suggests that a relativist position be used to demonstrate,

> respect for the ways of life of others, a tool of learning and understanding, a useful corrective to pseudo-universalist notions, a way of shaking up and questioning supposed universalist ideas, a way of opening our eyes to the variety of human ideology and practice, but not a basis for legitimizing whatever we may see when we do this.

In this sense, the relativist position becomes a critical tool with which to unravel universalism, and acknowledge that all cultures (and all childhoods) are different, but at the same time it becomes a tool to highlight injustice within that culture (Ruddick, 2003: 335). A relativistic approach can then assist in a critique of universalizing processes which ignore difference and diversity.

Exercise and reflection points

1. Are child soldiers innocent victims or moral agents? Discuss in your class.
2. What is a child? How might universal definitions of childhood help or hinder our understanding? What might be the problems of taking a relative position on childhood? What are the benefits of looking at childhood from a relativistic standpoint?

Further reading

Rizinni, I. and Bush, M. (2002) 'Globalization and children,' *Childhood: A journal of global child research*, vol. 9(4), pp. 371–374.

Twum-Danso Imoh, A. and Ame, R. (2012) *Childhoods at the intersection of the local and the global*, London: Palgrave Macmillan.

Rosen, D.M. (2007) 'Child soldiers, international humanitarian law, and the globalization of childhood,' *American Anthropologist*, vol. 109(2), pp 296–306.

White, B. (1996) 'Globalization and the child labour problem,' *Journal of International Development*, vol. 8(6), pp. 829–839.

White, B. (1999) 'Defining the intolerable: Child work, global standards and cultural relativism,' *Childhood: A journal of global child research*, vol. 6(1), pp. 133–144.

Final Thoughts

This text has offered the 'new' paradigm as a framework for seeing children, childhood and the child. It has been argued that earlier perspectives which took a quasi-scientific view on childhood cannot adequately tell us everything that there is to know, that is to say, children's own perspectives, agency and competence are frequently not visible to us from such studies. Partly, this has been due to the research methods employed, which have tended to see the child as the object of research rather than as an active subject, and which have lacked a consideration of the child in interaction with the world. However, the various disciplines are increasingly incorporating elements of the social study of childhood in their analyses, and the social study of childhood is now – at last – beginning to move into the mainstream of social analysis. There is still some way to go, but with the contributions from social geography, education, children's cultures, social history, and from scholars exploring the literature of childhood the field is expanding and consolidating. At the time of writing, it does feel very much as if the social study of childhood has come of age, and scholars are now looking for further theoretical developments to carry the study into its adulthood.

There has been some divergence or division within childhood studies between those who focus on theories of structure and commonality and those who focus on theories of action and difference. James (2010) in his discussion of the current state of affairs in childhood studies – or perhaps, where it should be – introduces the notion of 'warp and weft' to resolve this apparent split. The analogy of weaving cloth that he uses brings together different strands, or threads, within the discipline and, in the manner of weaving cloth, the warp and weft of the cloth make individual strands stronger.

He points out that the empirical value of weaving structure and diversity together is that we can chart how children's experiences are framed at a macro level by commonalities that make them different from adults before exploring children's agency and diversity, or childhood as structure. In this way we can see children as not simply constrained by, but also as enabled by structure. Taking the two strands (structure and diversity) together, says James, '[...] will ensure the continued academic rigour and theoretical development of childhood studies, without the need for creating and sustaining false dichotomies, or sacrificing the potential political power that comes from the recognition of childhood as a single social category, which must be distinguished from adulthood' (James, 2010: 497). Thus there are several strands of thought which move the field of childhood studies beyond the early, and very necessary, focus on the child as actor worthy of study in his or her own right to a more nuanced understanding of childhood in society.

In many countries throughout the world children's rights are beginning to be taken seriously, although, as has been pointed at several points throughout in this text, that journey is far from over. The various NGOs working with children and on childhood are attempting to tackle issues of poverty and the worst forms of child labour and are raising children's voices. Again, there remains much work to be done. It is for the students reading this textbook to carry the mission further as they graduate and move into their chosen fields of work. I hope that you take these theories and understandings of children, childhood, and the child with you as you continue to develop the field.

References

Aarsand, P.A. (2007) 'Computer and video games in family life: The digital divide as a resource in intergenerational interactions', *Childhood: A Journal of Global Child Research*, vol. 14, no. 2, pp. 235–256.

Abebe, T. (2009) 'Multiple methods, complex dilemmas: Negotiating socio-ethical spaces in participatory research with disadvantaged children', *Children's Geographies*, vol. 7, no. 4, pp. 451–465.

Adams, N., Carr, J., Collins, J., Johnson, G. and Matejic, P. (2012) 'Households below average income: An analysis of the income distribution 1994/5–2010/11', *Department for Work and Pensions* (online) available: https://www.gov.uk/government/uploads/system/uploads/attachment_data/file/200720/ful (accessed June 2014).

Aguilar, M.I. (1994) 'Portraying society through children: Play among the Waso Boorana of Kenya', *Anthropos*, vol. 89, pp. 29–38.

Aitken, S. (2001) 'Global crisis of childhood: Rights, justice and the unchildlike child', *Area,*, vol. 33, no. 2, pp. 119–127.

Aitken, S., Lopez Estrada, S., Jennings, J. and Aguirre, L.M. (2006) 'Reproducing life and labour: Global processes and working children in Tijuana, Mexico', *Childhood: A Journal of Global Child Research*, vol. 13, no. 3, pp. 365–387.

Aitken, S., Lund, R. and Kjørholt, A.T. (2007) 'Why children? Why now?' *Children's Geographies*, vol. 5, no. 1–2, pp. 3–14.

African Charter on the Rights and Welfare of the Child http://pages.au.int/acerwc/documents/african-charter-rights-and-welfare-child-acrwc.

Alanen, L. (1988) 'Rethinking Childhood', *Acta Sociologica*, vol. 31, no. 1, pp. 53–67.

Alanen, L. and Mayall, B. (ed.) (2001) *Conceptualizing child-adult relations*, London: Routledge Falmer.

Albanese, P. (2009) *Children in Canada today*, Oxford: Oxford University Press.

Alderson, P. (1992) 'In the genes or in the stars? Children's competence to consent', *Journal of Medical Ethics*, vol. 18, pp. 119–124.

Alderson, P. (2000b) 'UN Convention on the Rights of the Child: Some common criticisms and suggested responses', *Child Abuse Review*, vol. 9, pp. 439–443.

Alderson, P. (2000c) 'Children as researchers: The effects of participation rights on research methodology', in Christensen, P. and James, A. (ed.) *Research with children: perspectives and practices*, London: Falmer.

Alderson, P. (2001) 'Research by children', *International Journal of Social Research Methodology*, vol. 4, no. 2, pp. 139–153.

Alderson, P. (2007) 'Competent children? Minors' consent to healthcare treatment and research', *Social Science and Medicine*, vol. 65, pp. 2272–2283.

Amit-Talai, V. (1995) 'The waltz of sociability: Intimacy, dislocation and friendship in a Quebec high school', in Amit-Talai, V. and Wulff, H. (ed.) *Youth cultures: A cross cultural perspective*, London: Routledge.

Ansell, N. (2010) 'The discursive construction of childhood and youth in AIDS interventions in Lesotho's education sector: Beyond global-local dichotomies', *Environment and Planning D: Society and Space*, vol. 28, no. 5, pp. 791–810.

Ariés, P. (1962) *Centuries of childhood: A social history of family life*, New York: Knopf.

Armstrong, D. (1983) *Political Anatomy of the Body: Medical Knowledge in Britain in the Twentieth Century*, Cambridge: Cambridge University Press.

Bacon, K. (2010) *Twins in society: Parents, bodies, space and talk*, New York: Palgrave Macmillan.

Bacon, K. (2012) '"Beings in their own right"? Exploring children and young people's sibling and twin relationships in the minority world', *Children's Geographies*, vol. 10, no. 3, pp. 307–319.

Bacon, K. and Frankel, S. (2014) 'Rethinking children's citizenship: negotiating structure, shaping meanings', *International Journal of Children's Rights*, vol. 22, no. 1, pp. 21–42.

Bacon, K., Frankel, S. and Faulks, K. (2013) 'Building the "Big Society": Exploring representations of children and citizenship in the national citizen service', *International Journal of Children's Rights*, vol. 21, no. 3, pp. 488–509.

Bala, N. (2004) 'Child welfare in Canada: An introduction', in Bala, N., Zapf, M.K., Williams, J., Vogl, R. and Hornick J.P. (ed.) *Canadian child welfare law: Children, families and the state*, Toronto: Thompson Educational Publishing Inc.

Barrat, D. (1986) *Media Sociology*, London: Tavistock Publications Ltd.

Barrett, M. and McIntosh, M. (1982) *The anti-social family*, London: Verso.

Barker, J. and Weller, S. (2003) '"Is it fun?" Developing children centred research methods', *International Journal of Sociology and Social Policy*, vol. 23, no. 1/2, pp. 33–58.

Barter, C. and Renold, E. (2000) '"I wanna tell you a story": Exploring the application of vignettes in qualitative research with children and young people', *International Journal of Social Research Methodology*, vol. 3, no. 4, pp. 307–323.

Beazley, H. (2002) 'Vagrants wearing make-up: Negotiating spaces on the streets of Yogyakarta, Indonesia', *Urban Studies*, vol. 39, no. 9, pp. 1665–1683.

Beazley, H., Bessel, S., Ennew, J. and Waterson, R. (2009) 'The right to be properly researched: Research with children in a messy, real world', *Children's Geographies*, vol. 7, no. 4, pp. 365–378.

Bendelow, G. and Mayall, B. (2002) 'Children's emotional learning in primary schools', *European Journal of Psychotherapy*, vol. 5, no. 3, pp. 291–304.

Benwell, M.C. (2013) 'Challenging minority world privilege: Children's outdoor mobilities in post-apartheid South Africa', *Mobilities*, vol. 4, no. 1, pp. 77–101.

Bessel, S. (2011) 'Influencing international child labour policy: The potential and limits of children-centred research', *Children and Youth Services Review*, vol. 33, no. 4, pp. 564–568.

Birnbaum, R. and Saini, M. (2013) 'A scoping review of qualitative studies about children experiencing parental separation', *Childhood: A journal of global child research*, vol. 20, no. 2, pp. 260–282. doi: 10.1177/090756821245418.

Bluebond-Langner, M. (1978) *The private worlds of dying children*, Princeton: Princeton University Press.

Bluebond-Langner, M. (2008) '"I'm an anthropologist": Adolescents studying children and each other', *Anthropology News*, vol. 49, no. 4, April, pp. 14–15.

Bond, E. (2010) 'Managing mobile relationships: children's perceptions of the impact of the mobile phone on relationships in their everyday lives', *Childhood: a global journal of child research*, vol. 17, no. 4, pp. 514–529.

Bond, E. (2013) 'Mobile phones, risk and responsibility: understanding children's perceptions' *Cyberpsychology: Journal of Psychosocial Research on Cyberspace*, vol. 7, no. 1 doi: 10.5817/CP2013-1-3.

Bond, E. (2014) *Childhood, mobile technologies and everyday experiences: changing technologies = changing childhoods?* London: Palgrave Macmillan.

Böök M.L. and Perälä-Littunen, S. (2008) '"Children need their parents more than a pizza in the fridge!" Parental responsibility in a Finnish newspaper', *Childhood: A Journal of Global Child Research*, vol. 15, no. 1, pp. 74–88.

Bordonaro, L.I. (2012) 'Agency does not mean freedom: Cape Verdean street children and the politics of children's agency', *Children's Geographies*, vol. 10, no. 4, pp. 413–426.

Boyden, J. (1997) 'Childhood and the policy makers: A comparative perspective on the globalization of childhood', in James, A. and Prout, A. (ed.) *Constructing and reconstructing childhood: Contemporary issues in the sociological study of childhood*, London: Falmer Press.

Bradley, C. (2013) 'Images of childhood in classical antiquity', in Fass, P. (Ed.) *The Routledge history of childhood in the Western world*, pp. 17–38.

Brady, G. (2014) 'Children and ADHD: Seeking control within the constraints of diagnosis', *Children and Society*, vol. 28, pp. 218–230.

Brannen, J. and Heptinstall, E. (2001) 'Family life: What the children think', *Young Minds Magazine*, vol. 54, no. 1, pp. 22–24.

Brembeck, H. and Johansson, B. (2010) 'Foodscapes and children's bodies', *Culture Unbound*, vol. 2, pp. 797–818.

Browne, N. and George, R. (1999) '"Are you in or are you out?" An exploration of girl friendship groups in the primary phase of schooling', *International Journal of Inclusive Education*, vol. 4, no. 4, pp. 289–300.

Brym, R.J., Lie, J. and Nelson, A., (2005) *Sociology: your compass for a new world*, Toronto: Nelson.

Buckingham, D. (1994) 'Television and the definition of childhood', in Mayall, B. (ed.) *Children's childhoods: observed and experienced*, London: Falmer Press.

Buckingham, D. (2000) *After the death of childhood: Growing up in the age of electronic media*, Cambridge: Polity Press.

Buckingham, D. (2011) *The material child: Growing up in consumer culture*, Cambridge: Polity Press.

Burman, E. (1994) *Deconstructing developmental psychology*, London: Routledge.

Cahill, C. and Hart, R. (2007) 'Re-thinking the boundaries of civic participation by children and youth in North America', *Children, Youth and Environments*, vol. 17, no. 2, pp. 213–225.

Caputo, V. (2007) '"She's from a 'good family'": Performing childhood and motherhood in a Canadian private school setting', *Childhood: A Journal of Global Child Research*, vol. 14, no. 3, pp. 173–192.

Carpena-Mendez, F. (2007) '"Our lives are like a sock inside-out": Children's work and youth identity in neoliberal rural Mexico', in Panelli, R., Punch, S. and Robson, E. (ed.) *Global perspectives on rural childhood and youth: young rural lives*, New York: Taylor and Francis Group.

Cassell, J. and Cramer, M. (2008) 'High tech or high risk: Moral panics about girls online', in McPherson, T. (ed.) *Digital youth, innovation and the unexpected*, The John D. and Catherine T. MacArthur Foundation Series on Digital Media and Learning, Cambridge MA: The MIT Press, pp. 53–76.

Castonguay, G. and Jutras, S. (2010) 'Children's use of the outdoor environment in a low-income Montreal neighbourhood', *Children, Youth and Environments*, vol. 20, no. 1 pp. 200–230. Retrieved [August 2013] from http://www.colorado.edu/journals/cye.

Centre for Social Justice (2007) (online) available: www.socialjustice.org [June 2014].

Châtelet, A. (2008) 'A breath of fresh air: Open air schools in Europe', in Gutman, M. and de Coninck-Smith, N. (eds). *Designing modern childhoods: history, space and the material culture of children*, New Brunswick, NJ: Rutgers University Press.

Chen, E.S.L. and Rao, N. (2011) 'Gender socialization in Chinese kindergartens: Teachers' contributions', *Sex Roles*, vol. 64, pp. 103–116.

Cheney, K.E. (2005) "Our children have only known war': Children's experiences and the uses of childhood in Northern Uganda', *Children's Geographies*, vol. 3, no. 1, pp. 23–45.

Cheung, A. (2012) 'Tackling cyber-bullying from a children's rights perspective', in Freeman, M. (ed.) *Law and childhood studies: Current legal issues, vol. 14*, Oxford: Oxford University Press.

Christensen, P.H. (1993) 'The social construction of help among Danish schoolchildren: The intentional act and the actual content', *Sociology of Health and Illness*, vol. 15, no. 4, pp. 488–502.

Christensen, P. (2000) 'Childhood and the cultural construction of vulnerable bodies', in Prout, A. (ed.) *The body, childhood and society*, Basingstoke: Macmillan Press Ltd.

Christensen, P. (2002) 'Why more "quality time" is not on the top of children's lists: The "qualities of time" for children', *Children and Society*, vol. 16, no. 2, pp. 72–88.

Christensen, P. (2004) 'Children's participation in ethnographic research: Issues of power and representation', *Children and Society*, vol. 18, no. 2, pp. 165–176.

Christensen, P. and James, A. (ed.) (2000) *Research with children: Perspectives and practices*, London: Falmer.

Christensen, P. and James, A. (2001) 'What are schools for? The temporal experience of children's learning in Northern England', in Alanen, L. and Mayall, B. (ed.) *Conceptualizing child-adult relations*, London: Routledge Falmer.

Christensen, P., James, A. and Jenks, C. (2001) '"All we needed to do was blow the whistle": Children's embodiment of time', in Cunningham-Burley, S. (ed.) *Exploring the body*, London: Macmillan.

Christensen, P. and Prout, A. (2002) 'Working with ethical symmetry in social research with children', *Childhood: A Journal of Global Child Research*, vol. 9, no. 4, pp. 477–497.

Cigno, A., Roasti, F.C. and Guarcello, L. (2002) 'Does globalization increase child labour?', *World Development*, vol. 30, no. 9, pp. 1579–1589.

Clark, A. (2004) 'The Mosaic approach and research with young children', in Lewis, V., Kellet, M., Robinson, C., Fraser, S. and Ding, S. (ed.) *The reality of research with children and young people*, London: Sage/Open University Press.

Coad, J. and Evans, R. (2008) 'Reflections on practical approaches to involving children and young people in the data analysis process', *Children and Society*, vol. 22, pp. 41–52.

Cockburn, T. (2005a) 'New information technologies and the development of a children's "community of interest"', *Community Development Journal*, vol. 40, no. 3, pp. 329–342.

Cockburn, T. (2005b) 'Children's Participation in Social Policy: Inclusion, chimera or authenticity?', *Social Policy and Society*, vol. 4, no. 2, pp. 109–119.

Cocks, A.J. (2006) 'The ethical maze: Finding an inclusive path towards gaining children's agreement to research participation', *Childhood: A Journal of Global Child Research*, vol. 13, no. 2, pp. 247–266.

Cohen, S. (1980, 2002) *Folk devils and moral panics: The creation of the Mods and Rockers*, Oxford: M Robertson.

Connors, J., Zermatten, J. and Panayotidis, A. (2007) '18 Candles: The Convention on the Rights of the Child reaches majority', *Swiss Agency for Development and Cooperation*, Switzerland.

Cook, T. and Hess, E. (2007) 'What the camera sees and from whose perspective: Fun methodologies for engaging children in enlightening adults', *Childhood: A Journal of Global Child Research*, vol. 14, no. 1, pp. 29–45.

Corsaro, W.A. (2005) *The sociology of childhood*, 2nd edition, California: Sage.

Covell, K. and Howe, B. (1999) 'Working adolescents in economically depressed areas of Canada', *Canadian Journal of Behavioural Science*, vol. 31, no. 4, pp. 229–239.

Craig, G., McNamee, S. and Wilkinson, M. (2004) *The 'Children's' Fund? Views on the children's fund from Children's Society Projects*, London: The Children's Society.

Craig, G., McNamee, S., Wilkinson, M., James, A., et al. (2005) 'Report No. 1: Evaluating the application process for the Local Network Fund for Children and Young People – Getting the Money': National Evaluation of the Local Network Fund, *Department for Education and Skills*, Research report 683. Hull: DfES Publications.

Cross, G.S. and Smith, G. (2005) 'Japan, the US and the globalization of children's consumer culture', *Journal of Social History*, vol. 38, no. 4, pp. 873–890.

Cunningham, H. (2005) *Children and childhood in western society since 1500*, UK: Pearson Education Ltd.

Cunningham, S. and Lavalette, M. (2004) '"Active citizens" or "irresponsible truants"? School student strikes against the war', *Critical Social Policy*, vol. 24, no. 2, pp. 255–269.

Cusins-Lewer, A. and Gatley, J. (2008) 'The "Myers Park Experiment" in Auckland, New Zealand 1913-1916' in Gutman, M. and de Coninck-Smith, N. (eds). *Designing modern childhoods: History, space and the material culture of children*, New Brunswick, NJ: Rutgers University Press.

Czymoniewicz-Klippel, M.T. (2009) '"Improper" participatory child research: Morally bad, or not? Reflections from the "Reconstructing Cambodian Childhoods" study', *Childhoods Today*, vol. 3, no. 2. (online) available: www.childhoodstoday.org (accessed March 2013).

David, M., Edwards, R. and Alldred, P. (2001) 'Children and school based research: "Informed consent" or "educated consent"?', *British Educational Research Journal*, vol. 27, no. 3, pp. 347–365.

Davis, J.M. (1998) 'Understanding the meanings of children: A reflexive process', *Children and Society*, vol. 12, pp. 325–335.

Day Sclater, S. and Piper, C. (2001) 'Social exclusion and the welfare of the child', *Journal of Law and Society*, vol. 28, no. 3, pp. 409–429.

Del Casino, V.J. (2009) *Social geography: A critical introduction*, Chichester: John Wiley and Sons Ltd.

Denzin, N.E. (2010, 2nd Edition) *Childhood Socialization*, New Jersey: Transaction Publishers.

Dermott, E. and Seymour, J. (ed.) (2012) *Displaying families: A new concept for the sociology of family life*, Hants: Palgrave Macmillan.

Devine, D. (2002) 'Children's citizenship and the structuring of adult-child relations in the primary school', *Childhood: A Journal of Global Child Research*, vol. 9, no. 3, pp. 303–319.

Devine, D. (2003) *Children, power and schooling: How childhood is structured in the primary school*, UK: Trentham Books Ltd.

Dixon, J. (2008) 'Young people leaving care: Health, well-being and outcomes', *Child and Family Social Work*, vol. 13, pp. 207–217.

Donzelot, J. (1979) *The policing of families*, New York: Pantheon Books.

Dorfman, L. and Schiraldi, V. (2001) *Off balance: Youth, race and crime in the news*, (online) available: http://www.justicepolicy.org/uploads/justicepolicy/documents/off_balance.pdf (accessed August 2012).

Dorrer, N., McIntosh, I., Punch, S., and Edmund, R. (2010), 'Children and food practices in residential care: Ambivalence in the "institutional" home', *Children's Geographies*, vol. 8, no. 3, pp. 247–259.

Dowdeswell, T.L. (2013) "Tirelessly working to dispense her own wisdom": A history of Mennonite mothers and scientific motherhood', in Fast, K. and Epp Butler, R. (eds). *Mothering Mennonite*, Toronto: Demeter Press.

Earls, F. (2011) 'Children from rights to citizenship', *The Annals of the American Academy of Political and Social Science*, vol. 633, pp. 6–16.

Edwards, R., Hadfield, L., Lucey, H. and Mauthner, M. (2006) *Sibling identity and relationships: Sisters and brothers*, London: Routledge.

Erenriech, B. and English, D. (1978) *For her own good: two centuries of the experts' advice to women*, Toronto: Random House.

Factor, J. (2004) 'Tree stumps, manhole covers and rubbish tins: the invisible play-lines of a primary school playground', *Childhood: A Journal of Global Child Research*, vol. 11, no. 2, pp. 142–154.

Factory Act, 1833 UK. Downloaded from http://www.nationalarchives.gov.uk/education/resources/1833-factory-act/ (accessed November 2015).

Fass, P. (2003) 'Children and globalization', *Journal of Social History*, vol. 36, no. 4, pp. 963–977.

Fass, P. S. (ed.) (2013) *The Routledge history of childhood in the western world*, London and New York: Routledge.

Fassin, D. (2008) 'AIDS orphans, raped babies, and suffering children: The moral construction of childhood in post apartheid South Africa', in Comacchia, C., Golden, J. and Weisz, G. (ed.) *Healing the world's children: interdisciplinary perspectives on children's health in the twentieth century*, Montreal and Kingston: McGill-Queen's University Press.

Fine, G.A. and Sandstrom, K.L. (1988) *Knowing children: Participant observation with minors*, California: Sage Publications.

Finn, J.L., Nybell, L.M. and Shook, J. (2010) 'The meaning and making of childhood in the era of globalization: Challenges for social work', *Child and Youth Services Review*, vol. 32, pp. 246–254.

Fortin, J. (2008) 'Children as rights holders: Awareness and scepticism', in Invernizzi, A. and Williams, J. (ed.) *Children and citizenship*, London: Sage.

Foster, S., Villanueva, K., Wood, L., Christian, H. and Giles-Conti, B. (2014) 'The impact of parents' fear of strangers and perceptions of informal social control on children's independent mobility', *Health and Place*, vol. 26, pp. 60–68.

Freeman, M. (2007) *Article 3: The best interests of the child. A commentary on the United Nations Convention on the Rights of the Child* Boston: Martinus Nijhoff Publishers.

Freeman, M. (2011) 'Culture, childhood and rights', *The Family in Law*, vol. 5, no. 15, pp. 15–33.

Gil'adi, A. (1992) *Children of Islam* (online) available: http://www.palgraveconnect.com/pc/doifinder/10.1057/9780230378476 (accessed 14 April 2015).

Glauser, B. (1997) 'Street children: Deconstructing a construct', in James, A. and Prout, A. (ed.) *Constructing and reconstructing childhood: Contemporary issues in the sociological study of childhood*, London: Falmer Press.

Global Initiative to End All Corporal Punishment of Children (n.d.) (online) available: www.endcorporalpunishment.org (accessed June 2014).

Gnaerig, B. and MacCormack, C.F. (1999) 'The challenges of globalization: Save the Children', *Nonprofit and Voluntary Sector Quarterly*, vol. 28, no. 4, pp. 140–146.

Goldson, B. (2001) 'The demonization of children: From the symbolic to the institutional', in Foley, P., Roche, J. and Tucker, S. (ed.) *Children in society: Contemporary theory, policy and practice*, Milton Keynes: Palgrave in association with the Open University.

Goode, E. and Ben-Yehuda, N. (2009) *Moral panics: The social construction of deviance*, Boston: Wiley-Blackwell.

Gottlieb, A. (2004) *The afterlife is where we come from: The culture of infancy in West Africa*, Chicago: University of Chicago Press.

Greene, S. and Hogan, D. (2005) *Researching children's experiences: Approaches and methods*, London: Sage Publications.

Grover, S. (2004) 'Why won't they listen to us? On giving power and voice to children participating in social research', *Childhood: A Journal of Global Child Research*, vol. 11, no. 1, pp. 81–93.

Hadfield, L., Edwards, R. and Mauthner, M. (2006) 'Brothers and sisters: A source of support for children in school?', *Education 3–13: International Journal of Primary, Elementary and Early Years Education*, vol. 34, no. 1, pp. 65–72.

Hadley, K.G. and Nenga, S.K. (2004) 'From Snow White to Digimon: Using popular media to confront Confucian values in Taiwanese peer cultures', *Childhood: A Journal of Global Child Research*, vol. 11, no. 4, pp. 515–536.

Halden, G. (2003) 'Children's views of family, home and house', in Christensen, P. and O'Brien, M. (ed.) *Children in the city: Home, neighbourhood and community*, London: Routledge Falmer.

Hansen, D.M., Mortimer, J.T. and Kruger, H. (2001) 'Adolescent part-time employment in the United States and Germany: Diverse outcomes, contexts and pathways', in Mizen, P., Pole, C. and Bolton, A. (ed.) *Hidden hands: International perspectives on children's work and labour*, New York: Routledge Falmer.

Hanson, K. (2012) 'Schools of thought in children's rights', in Liebel, M. (ed.) *Children's rights from below: Cross cultural perspectives*, London: Palgrave Macmillan.

Hart, R.A. (1992) 'Participation: From tokenism to citizenship.' *Innocenti Essays No. 4*, UNICEF, (online) available: www.unicef–irc.org/publications/pdf/childrens_partici pation.pdf (accessed June 2013).

Hattenstone, S. (2000) 'They were punished enough by what they did', *The Guardian*, 30 October, (online) available: www.guardian.co.uk/uk/2000/oct/30/bulger.simon hattenstone/print (accessed 2 November 2012).

Healy, D. (2006) 'Framing ADHD children: A critical examination of the history, discourse, and everyday experience of attention deficit/hyperactivity disorder', *Social History of Medicine*, vol. 19, no. 1, pp. 177– 178.

Hemrica, J. and Heyting, F. (2004) 'Tacit notions of childhood: An analysis of discourse about child participation in decision-making regarding arrangements in case of parental divorce', *Childhood: A Journal of Global Child Research*, vol. 11, no. 4, pp. 449–468.

Henaghan, M. (2012) 'Why judges need to know and understand childhood studies', in Freeman, M. (ed.) *Law and childhood studies: Current legal issues*,14, Oxford: Oxford University Press.

Hendrick, H. (1997) 'Constructions and reconstructions of British childhood: An interpretative survey, 1800 – present', in James, A. and Prout, A. (ed.) *Constructing and reconstructing childhood: Contemporary issues in the sociological study of childhood*, London: Falmer Press.

Heptinstall, E. (2000) 'Gaining access to looked after children for research purposes: Lessons learned', *British Journal of Social Work*, vol. 30, pp. 867–872.

Herbozo, S., Tantleff-Dunn, S., Gokee-Larose, J. and Thompson, K. (2004) 'Beauty and thinness messages in children's media: A content analysis', *Eating Disorders*, vol. 12, pp. 21–34.

Heydon, R.M. and Iannacci, L. (2008) *Early childhood curricula and the de-pathologizing of childhood*, Toronto: University of Toronto Press.

Heywood, C. (2001) *A history of childhood: Children and childhood in the west from medieval to modern times*, UK: Polity.

Hill, M. (2005) 'Ethical considerations in researching children's experiences', in Greene, S. and Hogan, D. (ed.) *Researching children's experiences: Approaches and methods*, London: Sage.

Hill, M. (2006) 'Children's voices on ways of having a voice: Children's and young people's perspectives on methods used in research and consultation', *Childhood: A Journal of Global Child Research*, vol. 13, no. 1, pp. 69–89.

Hill, M., Laybourn, A. and Stafford, A. (2003) '"Having a say": Children and young people talk about consultation', *Children and Society*, vol. 17, pp. 361–373.

Hobbes, T. (1651) *Leviathan* downloaded from http://www.gutenberg.org/files/3207/3207-h/3207-h.htm (accessed November 2015).

Holland, P. (2004) *Picturing childhood: The myth of the child in popular imagery*, London: Taurus.

Hollos, M. (2002) 'The cultural construction of childhood: Changing conceptions among the Pare of Northern Tanzania', *Childhood: A Journal of Global Child Research*, vol. 9, no. 2, pp. 167–189.

Holloway, S.L. and Valentine, G. (2000) 'Children's geographies and the social studies of childhood', in Holloway, S.L. and Valentine, G. (ed.) *Children's geographies: Playing, living, learning*, London: Routledge.

Holt, L. (2004) 'Childhood disability and ability: (Dis)abelist geographies of mainstream primary schools', *Disability Studies Quarterly*, vol. 24, no. 3 (online) available: http://dsq-sds.org/article/view/506/683, (accessed June 2014).

Holt, N.L., Lee, H. Millar, C.A. and Spence, J.C. (2015) 'Eyes on where children play': A retrospective study of active free play', *Children's Geographies*, vol. 13, no. 1, pp. 73–88.

Horgan, K.B., Choate, M. and Brownell, K.D. (2012) 'Television food advertising: Targeting children in a toxic environment', in Singer, D.G. and Singer, J.L. (ed.) *Handbook of children and the media*, California: Sage.

Howe, B. (2007) 'A question of commitment', in Howe, R.B. and Covell, K. (ed.) *Children's rights in Canada: A question of commitment'*, Waterloo: Wilfred Laurier University Press.

Howieson, C., McKechnie, J. and Semple, S. (2006) 'The nature and implications of the part-time employment of secondary school pupils', *Final report to the Scottish Executive Enterprise and Lifelong Learning Department*, Edinburgh: SEELLD.

Hsiung, P.C. (2005) *A tender voyage: Children and childhood in Late Imperial China*, California: Stanford University Press.

Hunleth, J. (2011) 'Beyond "on" or "with": Questioning power dynamics and knowledge production in "child-oriented" research methodology', *Childhood: A Journal of Global Child Research*, vol. 18, no. 1, pp. 81–93.

International Labour Organisation (1999) 'Worst forms of child labour' Downloaded from http://ilo.org/dyn/normlex/en/f?p=NORMLEXPUB:12100:0::NO::P12100_ILO_CODE:C182 (accessed January 2014).

International Labour Organisation (2006) 'Tackling hazardous child labour in agriculture: Guidance on policy and practice', *International Labour Organization*, (online) available: http://www.ilo.org/safework/info/instr/WCMS_110200/lang—en/index.htm (accessed January 2014).

Invernizzi, A. (2005) 'Perspectives on children's work in the Algarve (Portugal) and their implications for social policy', *Critical Social Policy*, vol. 25, no. 2, pp. 198–222.

Ivec, M., Braithwaite, V. and Harris, N. (2012) '"Resetting the relationship" in indigenous child protection: Public hope and private reality', *Law and Policy*, vol. 34, no. 1, pp. 80–103.

Jacobson, L. (1997) 'Revitalizing the American home: Children's leisure and the revaluation of play, 1920–1940', *Journal of Social History*, vol. 30, no. 3, pp. 581–596.

James, A. (1993) *Childhood identities: Self and social relationships in the experience of the child*, Edinburgh: Edinburgh University Press.

James, A. (1998) 'Children, health and illness', in Field, D. and Taylor, S. (ed.) *Sociological perspectives on health, illness, and health care*, Oxford: Blackwell Science.

James, A. (2004) 'Understanding childhood from an interdisciplinary perspective: problems and potentials', in Pufall, P. and Unsworth, R. (eds.) *Rethinking Childhood*, New Jersey: Rutgers.

James, A. (2007) 'Giving voice to children's voices: Practice and problems, pitfalls and potentials', *American Anthropologist*, vol. 109, no. 2, pp. 261–272.

James, A. (2011) 'To be (come) or not to be (come): Understanding children's citizenship', *The Annals of the American Academy of Political and Social Science*, vol. 633, pp. 167–179.

James, A. (2013) *Socialising children*, London: Palgrave Macmillan.

James, A. and Curtis, P. (2012) 'Constructing the sick child: The cultural politics of children's hospitals', *The Sociological Review*, vol. 60, pp. 754–772.

James, A. and Hockey, J. (2007) *Embodying health identities* Basingstoke: Palgrave Macmillan.

James, A. and James, A.L. (2001) 'Childhood: Toward a theory of continuity and change', *The Annals of the American Academy of Political and Social Science*, vol. 575, no. 1, pp. 25–37.

James A. and James, A.L. (2004) *Constructing childhood: Theory, policy and social practice*, London: Palgrave Macmillan.

James, A. and James, A.L. (2008/2012) *Key concepts in childhood studies*, London: Sage Publications.

James, A. and Jenks, C. (1996) 'Public perceptions of childhood criminality', *British Journal of Sociology*, vol. 47, no. 2, pp. 315–331.

James, A., Jenks, C. and Prout, A. (1998) *Theorizing childhood*, London: Polity.

James, A. and A. Prout (1995) 'Hierarchy, boundary and agency: Towards a theoretical perspective on childhood', *Sociological Studies of Children*, vol. 7, pp. 77–99.

James, A. and Prout, A. (1997) *Constructing and reconstructing childhood: Contemporary issues in the sociological study of childhood*, 2nd edition, London: Falmer Press.

James, A.L., James, A. and McNamee, S. (2004) 'Constructing children's welfare: Putting children and young people first?', *Seen and Heard*, vol. 14, no. 2, pp. 26–35.

James, A.L. (2010) 'Competition or integration? The next step in childhood studies?' *Childhood: a journal of global childhood research*, vol. 17, no. 4, pp. 485–499.

Jansz, J. (2005) 'The emotional appeal of violent video games for adolescent males', *Communication Theory*, vol. 15, no. 3, pp. 219–241.

Jenks, C. (1996) *Childhood*, London: Routledge.

Jenks, C. (2009) 'Constructing childhood socially', in Kehily, M.J. (ed.) *An introduction to childhood studies*, Berkshire: Open University Press.

Jensen, K.B. (2014) 'Space-time geography of female live-in child domestic workers in Dhaka, Bangladesh', *Children's Geographies*, vol. 12, no. 2, pp. 154–169.

Johnson, G.A. and Vindrola-Padros, C. (2013) '"It's for the best": Child movement in search of health in Njabini, Kenya', *Children's Geographies*, vol. 12, no. 2, pp. 219–231. doi: 10.1080/14733285.2013.812307.

Jones, G.A. (2005) 'Children and development: Rights, globalization and poverty', *Progress in Development Studies*, vol. 5, no. 4, pp. 336–342.

Karsten, L. (2003) 'Children's use of public space: The gendered world of the playground' *Childhood: a journal of global child research*, vol. 10, no. 4, pp. 457–473.

Katz, C. (2004) *Growing up global: Economic restructuring and children's everyday lives*, Minneapolis: University of Minneapolis Press.

Kellet, M. (2005) 'Children as active researchers: A new research paradigm for the 21st Century?', *NCRM Methods review papers*, NCRM/003, p. 4, London: ESRC National Centre for Research Methods.

Kellet, M., Forrest, R., Dent, N. and Ward, S. (2004) '"Just teach us the skills please, we'll do the rest": Empowering ten-year-olds as active researchers', *Children and Society*, vol. 18, pp. 329–343.

Khanam, R. and Ross, R. (2011) 'Is child work a deterrent to school attendance and school attainment?', *International Journal of Social Economics*, vol. 38, no. 8, pp. 692–713.

King, P. (1998) 'Thomas Hobbes's Children', in Turner, S.M. and Matthews, G.B. (ed.) *The philosopher's child: Critical essays in the western tradition*, Rochester: University of Rochester Press, (online) available at: http://individual.utoronto.ca/pking/articles/Hobbes_on_Children.pdf (accessed July 2013).

Kjorholt, A. (2011) 'Rethinking young children's rights for participation in diverse cultural contexts', in Kernan, M. and Singer, E. (ed.) *Peer relationships in early childhood education and care*, London and New York: Routledge.

Klocker, N. (2007) 'An example of "thin" agency: Child domestic workers in Tanzania', in Panelli, R., Punch, S. and Robson, E. (ed.) *Global perspectives on rural childhood and youth: Young rural lives*, New York: Routledge.

Komulanen, S. (2007) 'The ambiguity of the child's "voice" in social research', *Childhood: A Journal of Global Child Research*, vol. 14, no. 1, pp. 11–28.

Kostenius, C. (2011) 'Picture this – our dream school! Swedish schoolchildren sharing their visions of school' *Childhood: a journal of global child research*, vol. 18, no. 4, pp. 509–525.

Kraftl, P., Horton, J. and Tucker, F. (eds) (2012) *Critical Geographies of Childhood and Youth: Policy and practice*, Bristol: Policy Press.

Kundapur Declaration, The. (2012) (online) available: http://www.concernedforworkingchildren.org/empowering–children/childrens–unions/the–kundapur–declaration/ (accessed 23 June 2014).

Lancy, D.F. (2008) *The Anthropology of Childhood: Cherubs, Chattels, Changelings*, New York: Cambridge University Press.

Lansdown, G. (2011) *Every Child's Right to be Heard: A resource guide on the UN Committee on the rights of the child General Comment No. 12*, Save the Children Fund, UNICEF.

Lansdown, G., Jimerson, S. and Shahroozi, R. (2014) 'Children's rights and school psychology: children's right to participation', *Journal of School Psychology*, vol. 52, pp. 3–12.

Le François, B.A. and Coppock, V. (2014) 'Psychiatrised children and their rights: Starting the conversation', *Children and Society*, vol. 28, pp. 165–171.

Lee, N. and Motzkau, J. (2011) 'Navigating the bio-politics of childhood', *Childhood: A Journal of Global Child Research*, vol. 18, no. 1, pp. 7–19.

Lemish, D., Drotner, K., Liebes, T., Maigret, E. and Stald, G. (1998) 'Global culture in practice: A look at children and adolescents in Denmark, France and Israel', *European Journal of Communication*, vol. 13, no. 4, pp. 539–556.

Leonard, M. (2004) 'Children's views on children's right to work: Reflections from Belfast', *Childhood: A Journal of Global Child Research*, vol. 11, no. 1, pp. 45–61.

Leonard, M. (2006) 'Segregated schools in segregated societies: Issues of safety and risk', *Childhood: A Journal of Global Child Research*, vol. 13, no. 4, pp. 441–458.

Lewis, A. (2010) 'Silence in the context of "child voice"', *Children and Society*, vol. 24, pp. 14–23.

Lewis, V., Kellet, M., Robinson C., Fraser, S. and Ding, S. (ed.) (2004) *The reality of research with children and young people*, London: Sage / Open University Press.

Liebel, M. (2004) *A will of their own: Cross-cultural perspectives on working children*, London: Zed Books.

Leibel, M. (2012) *Children's rights from below: cross cultural perspectives*, New York: Palgrave Macmillan.

Linn, S. and Novosat, C. (2008) 'Calories for sale: Food marketing to children in the twenty-first century', *The Annals of the American Academy of Political and Social Science*, vol. 615, no. 1, pp. 133–155.

Lister, R. (2007) 'Why citizenship: Where, when and how children?', *Theoretical Inquiries in Law*, vol. 8, no. 2, pp. 693–718.

Livingstone, S. (2008) 'Taking risky opportunities in youthful content creation: teenagers' use of social networking sites for intimacy, privacy and self-expression', *New Media and Society*, vol. 10, no. 3, pp. 393–411.

Locke, J. (1693). 'Some Thoughts Concerning Education.' Downloaded from http://www.bartleby.com/37/1/ (accessed August 2013).

Loebach, J.E. (2013) 'Children's neighbourhood geographies: Examining children's perception and use of their neighbourhood environments for healthy activity' (Doctoral dissertation), Retrieved from University of Western Ontario – Electronic Thesis and Dissertation Repository (Paper 1690) (online) available: http://ir.lib.uwo.ca/etd/1690 (accessed November 2013).

Lupton, D. (2003) 'The social construction of Medicine and the Body', in Albrecht, G.L., Fitzpatrick, R. and Scrimshaw, S.C. (eds.) *The Handbook of Social Studies in Health and Medicine*, London: Sage Publications Ltd.

Madge, N. and Willmott, N. (2007) *Children's views and experiences of parenting*, York: Joseph Rowntree Foundation.

Mandell, N. (1988) 'The least-adult role in studying children', *Journal of Contemporary Ethnography*, vol. 16, pp. 433–467.

Marsh, J. and Bishop, J.C. (2014) *Changing play: play, media and commercial culture from the 1950s to the present day*, Berkshire: Open University Press.

Marwick, A. and boyd, D. (2012) 'Teens text more than adults, but they're still just teens', *The Daily Beast* (May 20), (Online) available: http://www.pewinternet. org/Media–Mentions/2012/Teens–Text–More–Than–Adults–But–Theyre–Still–Just– Teens.aspx (accessed 21 May 2012).

Matthews, H. (2003) 'Coming of age for children's geographies', *Children's Geographies*, vol. 1, no. 1, pp. 3–5.

Maxwell, G. (2009) 'Poverty in Ontario – failed promise and the renewal of hope', *Canadian Council on Social Development*, (online) available: http://www.cdhalton.ca/ pdf/Poverty-in-Ontario-Report.pdf (accessed 23 June 2014).

Mayall, B. (1994) *Children's childhoods: Observed and experienced*, London: Falmer Press.

Mayall, B. (2002) *Towards a sociology for childhood: Thinking from children's lives*, Buckingham: Open University Press.

Mayall, B. (2013) *A history of the sociology of childhood*, London: Institute of Education Press.

McCluskey, G. (2014) 'Youth is present only when its presence is a problem': Voices of young people on discipline in school', *Children and Society*, vol. 28, pp. 93–103.

McNamee, S. (1998a) *Questioning video game use: An exploration of the spatial and gender aspects of children's leisure*, (unpublished doctoral dissertation), Hull: University of Hull.

McNamee, S. (1999) 'I won't let her in my room: Sibling strategies of power and resistance', in Seymour, J. and Bagguley, P. (ed.) *Relating intimacies*, London: Macmillan.

McNamee, S. (2000) 'Foucault's heterotopia and children's everyday lives', *Childhood: A Journal of Global Child Research*, vol. 7, no. 4, pp. 479–492.

McNamee, S., James, A.L. and James, A. (2005) 'Family law and the construction of childhood in England and Wales', in Goddard, J., McNamee, S., James, A.L. and James, A. (ed.) *The politics of childhood: International perspectives, contemporary developments*, Hants: Palgrave Macmillan.

McNamee, S. and Seymour, J. (2013) 'Towards a sociology of 10-12 year olds? Emerging methodological issues in the "new" social studies of childhood', *Childhood: A Journal of Global Child Research*, vol. 20, no. 2, pp. 156–168 doi: 10.1177/0907568212461037.

Measuring child poverty: New league tables of child poverty in the world's rich countries (2012) *Innocenti Report Card 10*, Florence: UNICEF Innocenti Research Centre.

Minimum Age convention: Convention concerning Minimum Age for Admission to Employment (1976) *International Labour Organisation Convention #138*, (online) available: http://www.ilo.org/dyn/normlex/en/f?p=NORMLEXPUB:12100:0::NO:12 100:P12100_INSTRUMENT_ID:312283:NO (accessed December 2013).

Mishna, F., Saini, M and Solomon, S. (2009) 'Ongoing and online: children and youth's perceptions of cyber bulling', *Children and Youth Services Review*, vol. 31, no. 12, pp. 1222–1228.

Mizen, P., Pole, C. and Bolton, A. (2001) 'Why be a school age worker?', in Mizen, P. Pole, C. and Bolton, A. (ed.) *Hidden hands: International perspectives on children's work and labour*, New York: Routledge Falmer.

Monaghan, K. (2012) 'Early child development policy: The colonization of the World's childrearing practices?' in Twum-Danso Imoh, A. and Ame, R. (eds) *Childhoods at the intersection of the local and the global*, Basingstoke: Palgrave Macmillan.

Montandon, C. (2001) 'The negotiation of influence: Children's experience of parental educational practices in Geneva', in Alanen, L. and Mayall, B. (ed.) *Conceptualizing child-adult relations*, London: Routledge Falmer.

Montgomery, H. (2009) *An introduction to childhood: Anthropological perspectives on children's lives*, Sussex: Wiley-Blackwell.

Moore, L. and Kirk, S. (2010) 'A literature review of children's and young people's participation in decisions relating to health care', *Journal of Clinical Nursing*, vol. 19, pp. 2215–2225.

Moran, J. (2002) 'Childhood and nostalgia in contemporary culture', *European Journal of Cultural Studies*, vol. 5, no. 2, pp. 155–173.

Morgan, D. (1996) *Family connections: An introduction to family studies*, Cambridge: Polity.

Morgan, D. (2011a) 'Locating "Family Practices"', *Sociological Research Online*, vol. 16, no. 4, p. 14.

Morgan, D. (2011b) *Rethinking Family Practices*, London: Palgrave.

Naftali, O. (2010) 'Caged golden canaries: Childhood, privacy and subjectivity in contemporary urban China', *Childhood: A Journal of Global Child Research*, vol. 17, no. 3, pp. 297–311.

Narine, S. (2012, April 1) '60s scoop turns horrifying experience into strong advocacy', *Saskatchewan Sage*, p. 3.

NatCen Social Research, Office for Public Management and New Philanthropy Capital. (2013) Evaluation of National Citizen Service: Findings for the evaluation of the 2012 summer and autumn programmes (online) available: http://natcen.ac.uk/media/205475/ncs_evaluation_report_2012_combined.pdf (accessed June 2014).

Nieuwenhuys, O. (2008) 'Editorial: The ethics of children's rights', *Childhood: A Journal of Global Child Research*, vol. 15, no. 4, pp. 4–11.

Oakley, A. (1994) 'Women and children first and last: Parallels and differences between children's and women's studies', in Mayall, B. (ed.) *Children's childhoods: Observed and experienced*, London: Falmer.

Odera, F.Y. (2011) 'Emerging issues in the implementation of computer technology into Kenyan secondary school classrooms', *International Journal of Science and Technology* [Electronic], vol. 1, no. 6, pp. 260–268, (online) available: http://ejournalofsciences.org/archive/vol1no6/vol1no6_12.pdf (accessed June 2014).

Ontario Association of Children's Aid Societies (2006) *Youth leaving care: An OACAS survey of youth and CAS staff*, Toronto: OACAS.

Opie, I and Opie, P. (1959) *The lore and language of school-children*, Oxford: Clarendon Press.

Oswell, D. (1999) 'And what might our children become? Future visions, governance and the child television audience in postwar Britain', *Screen*, vol. 40, no. 1, pp. 66–87.

Oswell, D. (2013) *The agency of children: From family to global human rights*, New York: Cambridge University Press.

Pascoe, C.J. (2007) *Dude, you're a fag: Masculinity and sexuality in high school*, Berkeley: University of California Press.

Payne, R. (2012) '"Extraordinary survivors" or "ordinary lives"? Embracing "everyday agency" in social interventions with child-headed households in Zambia', *Children's Geographies*, vol. 10, no. 4, pp. 399–341.

Percy-Smith, B. and Thomas, N. (Eds.) (2010) *A handbook of children and young people's participation: Perspectives from theory and practice*, London: Routledge.

Pike, J. and Colquhoun, D. (2012) 'Lunchtime lock-in: Territorialisation and UK school meals policy', in Kraftl, P., Horton, J. and Tucker, F. (ed.) *Critical Geographies of Childhood and Youth*, Bristol: The Policy Press.

Postman, N. (1982) *The disappearance of childhood*, New York: Delacorte Press.

Priestly, M. (1998) 'Constructions and creations: Idealism, materialism and disability theory' *Disability and Society*, vol. 13, no. 1, pp. 75–94.

Prosser, B. (2013) 'Attention deficit hyperactivity disorder in Australia: Perspectives from the Sociology of Deviance', *Journal of Sociology*, published online ahead of print doi: 10.1177/14407833.13514643, (accessed 23 June 2014).

Prout, A. (1986) 'Wet children' and 'little actresses': Going sick in primary school', *Sociology of Health and Illness*, vol. 8, no. 2, pp. 113–136.

Prout, A. (2005) *The future of childhood: Towards the interdisciplinary study of children*, London: Routledge Falmer.

Pryor, J. and Emery, R.E. (2004) 'Children of divorce', in Pufall, P. and Unsworth, R. (ed.) *Rethinking Childhood*, NJ: Rutgers.

Punch, S. (2000) 'Children's strategies for creating playspaces: Negotiating independence in rural Bolivia', in Holloway, S.L. and Valentine, G. (ed.) *Children's geographies: Playing, living, learning*, London: Routledge.

Punch, S. (2002a) 'Interviewing strategies with young people: The "secret box", stimulus material and task based activities', *Children and Society*, vol. 16, pp. 45–56.

Punch, S. (2002b) 'Research with children: The same or different from research with adults?', *Childhood: a Journal of Global Child Research*, vol. 9, no. 3, pp. 321–341.

Punch, S. (2005) 'The generationing of power: A comparison of child-parent and sibling relations in Scotland', in Bass, L. (ed.) *Sociological Studies of Children and Youth*, vol. 10, no. 10, pp. 169–188.

Punch, S. (2008) '"You can do nasty things to your brothers and sisters without a reason": Sibling's backstage behaviour', *Children and Society*, vol. 22, no. 5, pp. 333–344.

Punch, S. and McIntosh, I. (2009) '"Barters", "Deals", "Bribes" and "Threats": Exploring sibling interactions', *Childhood: A Journal of Global Child Research*, vol. 16, no. 1, pp. 49–65.

Qvortrup, J. (Ed.) (1994) *Childhood Matters: Social theory, practice and politics*, Aldershot: Avebury.

Qvortrup, J. (2001) 'School work, paid work and the changing obligations of childhood', in Mizen, P., Pole, C. and Bolton, A. (ed.) *Hidden hands: International perspectives on children's work and labour*, New York: Routledge Falmer.

Qvortrup, J., Corsaro, W.A., and Honig, M. (2011) *The Palgrave handbook of childhood studies*, New York: Palgrave Macmillan.

Rafalovich, A. (2013) 'Attention Deficit Hyper-activity Disorder as the medicalization of childhood: Challenges from and for Sociology', *Sociology Compass*, vol. 7, no. 5, pp. 343–354.

Rasmussen, K. (2004) 'Places for children – children's places', *Childhood: A Journal of Global Child Research*, vol. 11, no. 2, pp. 155–173.

Reynold, E. (2002) '"Presumed innocence": (Hetero)sexual, heterosexist and homophobic harassment among primary school girls and boys', *Childhood: A Journal of Global Child Research*, vol. 9, no. 4, pp. 415–434.

Rivard, L. (2010) 'Child soldiers and disarmament, demobilization and reintegration programs: The universalism of children's rights vs. cultural relativism debate', *The Journal of Humanitarian Assistance*, (electronic) available: http://sites.tufts.edu/jha/archives/772 (accessed 23 June 2014).

Rizinni, I. and Bush, M. (2002) 'Globalization and children', *Childhood: A Journal of Global Child Research*, vol. 9, no. 4, pp. 371–374.

Roadmap for achieving the elimination of the worst forms of child labour by 2016 (2010) *Outcome Document, The Hague Global Child Labour Conference 2010*, (online) available: http://www.ilo.org/ipecinfo/product/viewProduct.do?productId=13453 (September 5 2012).

Roberts, A. (1980) *Out to play: The middle years of childhood*, Aberdeen: Aberdeen University Press.

Robinson, C. (2014) 'Children, their voices and their experiences of school: what does the evidence tell us?' *Cambridge Primary Review Trust* UK, (online) available: http://cprtrust.org.uk/wp-content/uploads/2014/12/FINAL-VERSION-Carol-Robinson-Children-their-Voices-and-their-Experiences-of-School.pdf (accessed January 2016).

Robson, E. (2004) 'Hidden child workers: Young carers in Zimbabwe', *Antipode*, vol. 36, no. 2, pp. 227–248.

Robson, E., Bell, S. and Klocker, N (2007) 'Conceptualising agency in the lives and actions of rural young people', in Panelli, R., Punch, S. and Robson, E. (ed.) *Global perspectives on rural childhood and youth: Young rural lives*, New York: Taylor and Francis Group.

Rosen, D. (2007) 'Child soldiers, international humanitarian law, and the globalisation of childhood', *American Anthropologist*, vol. 109, no. 2, pp. 296–306.

Rosen, D. (2009) 'Who is a child? The legal conundrum of child soldiers' *Connecticut Journal of International Law*, downloaded from http://www.lexisnexis.com July 21st 2015.

Rousseau, J. (1979) (trans. A. Bloom) *Emile: On education,* USA: Basic Books.

Ruddick, S. (2003) 'The politics of aging: Globalization and the restructuring of youth and childhood', *Antipode*, vol. 35, no. 2, pp. 334–362.

Rustemier, S. (2004) 'Prevalence of violence against children in the UK: A preliminary summary of research', *Global Initiative to end all corporal punishment of children*, Paper presented at the young people's meeting, UNICEF in July 2004.

Ryan, P.J. (2008) 'How new is the "new" social study of childhood? The myth of a paradigm shift', *Journal of Interdisciplinary History* XXVIII, vol. 4, pp. 553–576.

Ryan, P.J. (2010) 'Discursive tensions on the landscape of modern childhood', *Educare Ventenskapliga Skrifter*, vol. 2, pp. 11–37.

Ryan, P.J. (2011) '"Young rebels flee psychology": Individual intelligence, race and foster children in Cleveland, Ohio between the world wars', *Paedagogica Historica*, vol. 47, no. 6, pp. 767–783.

Selnow, G. (1984) 'Playing videogames: The electronic friend', *Journal of Communication*, vol. 34, no. 2, pp. 148–156.

Seredity, C. and Burgman, I. (2012) 'Being the older sibling: Self perceptions of children with disabilities', *Children and Society*, vol. 26, no. 1, pp. 37–50.

Seymour, J. (2005) 'Entertaining guests or entertaining the guests: Children's emotional labour in hotels, pubs and boarding houses', in Goddard, J., McNamee, S., James, A.L. and James, A. (ed.) *The politics of childhood: International perspectives, contemporary developments*, Hants: Palgrave Macmillan.

Seymour, J. (2007) 'Treating the hotel like a home: The contribution of studying the single location home/workplace', *Sociology*, vol. 41, no. 6, pp. 1097–1114.

Seymour, J. (2011) 'Family hold back': Displaying families in the single-location home/workplace' in Dermott, E. and Seymour, J. (eds.) *Displaying Families: A new concept for the sociology of family life*, Hants: Palgrave Macmillan.

Seymour, J. (2015) 'Approaches to children's spatial agency: Reviewing actors, agents and families' in Hackett, A., Procter, L. and Seymour, J. *Children's Spatialities: Embodiment, Emotion and Agency*, London: Palgrave Macmillan.

Seymour, J. and McNamee, S. (2012) 'Being parented? Children and young people's engagement with parenting activities', in Waldren, J. and Kaminski, I. (ed.) *Learning from the children: Childhood, culture and identity in a changing world*, Oxford: Berghann Books.

Shah, A. (2013) 'Poverty facts and stats', *Global Issues*, (online) available: http://global issues.org/article/26/poverty–facts–and–stats (accessed 20 January 2013).

Shakespeare, T. (2006) *Disability rights and wrongs* New York: Routledge.

Sherman, A. (1997) 'Five-year-olds' perceptions of why we go to school', *Children and Society*, vol. 11, pp. 117–127.

Shier, H. (2001) 'Pathways to participation: Openings, opportunities and obligations', *Children and Society*, vol. 15, pp. 107–117.

Sheir, H. (2010) 'Pathways to participation revisited: Learning from Nicaragua's child coffee workers', in Percy-Smith, B. and Thomas, N. *A handbook of children and young people's participation: Perspectives from theory and practice* London: Routledge.

Shier, H. and Méndez, M.H. (2014) 'How children and young people influence policy-makers: Lessons from Nicaragua', *Children and Society*, vol. 28, pp. 1–14.

Simons, M. (1557) The education of children downloaded from http://www. mennosimons.net/ft056-education.html (accessed November 2015).

Simpson, B. (2000) 'Regulation and resistance: Children's embodiment during the primary-secondary school transition', in Prout, A. (ed.) *The body, childhood and society*, Hants: Macmillan Press Ltd.

Sinclair, R. (2004) 'Participation in practice: Making it meaningful, effective and sustainable', *Children and Society*, vol. 18, pp. 106–118.

Singer, E. and Doornenbal, J. (2006) 'Learning morality in peer conflict: A study of schoolchildren's narratives about being betrayed by a friend', *Childhood: A journal of Global Child Research*, vol. 13, no. 2, pp. 225–245.

Singh, I. (2012) 'Brain talk: Power and negotiation in children's discourse about self, brain and behaviour', *Sociology of Health and Illness*, vol. 35, no. 6, pp. 813–827.

Sinha, V. (2013) 'The structure of aboriginal child welfare in Canada', *The International Indigenous Policy Journal*, vol. 2, no. 4 (Retrieved from: http://ir.lib.uwo.ca/iipj/vol4/iss2/2).

Sloane, D.C. (2008) 'A (better) home away from home: the emergence of children's hospitals in an age of women's reform', in Gutman, M. and de Coninck-Smith, N. (Eds). *Designing modern childhoods: history, space and the material culture of children*, New Brunswick, NJ: Rutgers University Press.

Smart, C. (2007) *Personal life*, Cambridge: Polity.

Smith, R. (2000) 'Whose childhood? The politics of homework', *Children and Society*, vol. 14, pp. 316–325.

Solberg, A. (1997) 'Negotiating childhood: Changing constructions of age for Norwegian children', in James, A. and Prout, A. (ed.) *Constructing and reconstructing childhood: Contemporary issues in the sociological study of childhood*, London: Falmer Press.

South African School's Act, The. (1996) Downloaded from http://www.acts.co.za/south-african-schools-act-1996/ (accessed November 2015).

Spyrou, S. (2011) 'The limits of children's voices: From authenticity to critical, reflexive representation', *Childhood: A Journal of Global Child Research*, vol. 18, no. 2, pp. 151–165.

Stalker, K. and Connors, C. (2004) 'Children's perceptions of their disabled siblings: 'She's different but it's normal for us', *Children and Society*, vol. 18, no. 3, pp. 218–230.

Statement for the ethical practice for the British Sociological Association (2002), (online) available: http://www.britsoc.co.uk/about/equality/statement-of-ethical-practice.aspx (accessed June 2014).

Stearns, P.N. (2005) *Growing up: The history of childhood in a global context*, Waco, TX: Baylor University Press.

Stewart, K. and Choi, H.P. (2003) 'PC-Bang culture: A study of Korean college students' private and public use of computers and the internet', *Trends in Communication*, vol. 11, no. 1, pp. 63–79.

Strandell, H. (1997) 'Doing reality with play: Play as a children's resource in organizing everyday life in daycare centres', *Childhood: A Journal of Global Child Research*, vol. 4, no. 4, pp. 445–464.

Stutz, E. (1991) *What are they doing now? A study of children aged 7–14*, UK: Quaker Peace Service.

Sutherland, N. (1976) *Children in English-Canadian society: Framing the twentieth century consensus*, Toronto: University of Toronto Press.

Tandy, C.A. (1999) 'Children's diminishing play space: A study of inter-generational change in children's use of their neighbourhoods', *Australian Geographical Studies*, vol. 37, no. 2, pp. 154–164.

Tisdall, K. (2012) 'The challenge and challenging of childhood studies? Learning from disability studies and research with disabled children', *Children and Society*, 26 pp 181–191.

Tisdall, K. and Punch, S. (2012) 'Not so 'new'? Looking critically at childhood studies', *Children's Geographies*, vol. 10, no. 3, pp. 249–264.

Thompson, F. (2007) 'Are methodologies for children keeping them in their place?', *Children's Geographies*, vol. 5, no. 3, pp. 207–218.

Thorne, B. (1994) *Gender play: Boys and girls in school*, New Jersey: Rutgers University Press.

Tomanovic, S. (2003) 'Negotiating children's participation and autonomy within families', *The International Journal of Children's Rights*, vol. 11, pp. 51–71.

Tremblay, M., Barnes, J.D., Copeland, J.L. and Esliger, D.W. (2005) 'Conquering childhood activity: Is the answer in the past?' *Medicine and science in sports and exercise* (online) available: wweb.uta.edu/faculty/ricard/classes/KINE-5305/good%20 Outlier%20Explanations.pdf pp. 1187–1194.

Tremlett, A. (2005) '"Gypsy children can't learn": Roma in the Hungarian education system', in Goddard, J., McNamee, S., James, A.L., and James, A. (ed.) *The politics of childhood: International perspectives, contemporary developments*, London: Palgrave.

Tri-Council policy statement: Ethical conduct involving research with humans (2010) (online) available: www.pre.ethics.gc.ca/pdf/eng/tcps2/TCPS_2_FINAL_Web.pdf (accessed June 2014).

Trocmé N., Knoke, D. and Blackstock, C. (2004) 'Pathways to the overrepresentation of Aboriginal children in Canada's child welfare system', *Social Service Review*, December, pp. 577–600.

Turmel, A. (2008) *A historical sociology of childhood: Developmental thinking, categorization and graphic visualization*, Cambridge: Cambridge University Press.

Twum-Danso Imoh, A. and Ame, R. (2012) *Childhoods at the intersection of the local and the global*, London: Palgrave Macmillan.

United Nations Convention on the Rights of the Child (1989), (online) available: http://www.ohchr.org/en/professionalinterest/pages/crc.aspx (accessed 1 April 2014).

United Nations Convention on the Rights of the Child (2009) General Comment No. 12 (online) available: http://www2.ohchr.org/english/bodies/crc/docs/AdvanceVersions/ CRC-C-GC-12.pdf (December 2015).

United Nations Convention on the Rights of the Child (2014) General Comment No. 14 'The right of the child to have his or her best interests taken as a primary consideration. (online) available: http://www2.ohchr.org/English/bodies/crc/docs/GC/ CRC_C_GC_14_ENG.pdf (accessed December 2015).

Uprichard, E. (2008) 'Children as "beings" and "becomings": Children, childhood and temporality', *Children and Society*, vol. 22, pp. 303–313.

Uprichard, E. (2010) 'Questioning research with children: Discrepancy between theory and practice?', *Children and Society*, vol. 24, pp. 3–13.

Valentine, G. (1997a) 'My son's a bit dizzy.' 'My wife's a bit soft.': gender, children and cultures of parenting' *Gender, Place and Culture*, Vol. 4. No. 1. UK: Journals Oxford Ltd. pp. 37–62.

Valentine, G. (1997b) '"Oh yes I can." "Oh no you can't": Children and parents' understandings of kids' competence to negotiate public space safely', *Antipode*, vol. 29, no. 1, pp. 65–89.

Valentine, G. and Holloway, S. (2001) 'On-line dangers? Geographies of parents' fears for children's safety in cyberspace', *Professional Geographer*, vol. 53, no. 1, pp. 71–83.

Valkenburg, P.M., Peter, J., and Walther, J.B. (2016) 'Media effects: theory and research', *Annual Review of Psychology*, vol. 67, pp. 315–338.

Van Krieken, R. (1999) 'The 'stolen generations' and cultural genocide: The forced removal of Australian indigenous children from their families and its implications for the sociology of childhood', *Childhood: A Journal of Global Child Research*, vol. 6, no. 3, pp. 297–311.

Vandewater, E.A., Shim, M. and Caplovitz, A.G. (2004) 'Linking obesity and activity level with children's television and video game use', *Journal of Adolescence*, vol. 27, no. 1, pp. 71–85.

Verma, C.L. (2012) 'Truths out of place: Homecoming, intervention, and story-making in war-torn Northern Uganda', *Children's Geographies*, vol. 10, no. 4, pp. 441–455.

Viviers, A. and Lombard, A. (2012) 'The ethics of children's participation: Fundamental to children's rights realization in Africa', *International Social Work*, vol. 56, no. 1, pp. 7–21.

Volante, L. (2004) 'Teaching to the test: What every educator and policymaker should know', *Canadian Journal of Educational Administration and Policy* [Electronic], vol. 35, (online) available: http://umanitoba.ca/publications/cjeap/articles/volante.html (accessed June 23 2014).

Wade, A. and Smart, C. (2002) *Facing family change: Children's circumstances, strategies and resources*, York: Joseph Rowntree Foundation, (online) available: http://www.jrf.org.uk/sites/files/jrf/1842630849.pdf (accessed April 2014).

Waksler, F.C. (1991) *Studying the social worlds of children: Sociological readings*, London: Falmer Press.

Walkerdine, V. (2007) *Children, gender, video games: Towards a relational approach to multimedia*, London: Palgrave Macmillan.

Walkerdine, V. (2009) 'Developmental psychology and the study of childhood', in Kehily, M.J. (ed.) *An introduction to childhood studies*, 2nd edition, Maidenhead: Open University Press.

Watson, N. (2012) 'Theorising the lives of disabled children: How can disability theory help?' *Children and Society*, vol. 26, no. 3, pp. 192–202.

'We can end poverty: Millennium Development Goals and beyond, 2015' (2014) (online) available: http://www.un.org/millenniumgoals/ (June 2014).

Wells, K. (2009) *Childhood in a global perspective*, Cambridge: Polity Press.

West, A. (2007) 'Power relationships and adult resistance to children's participation', *Children, Youth and Environments*, vol. 17, no. 1, pp. 123–135.

White, B. (1996) 'Globalization and the child labour problem', *Journal of International Development*, vol. 8, no. 6, pp. 829–839.

White, B. (1999) 'Defining the intolerable: Child work, global standards and cultural relativism', *Childhood: A Journal of Global Child Research*, vol. 6, no. 1, pp. 133–144.

Woodhead, M. (1999) 'Combatting child labour: Listen to what the children say', *Childhood: A Journal of Global Child Research*, vol. 6, no. 1, pp. 27–49.

Woodhead, M. (1997) 'Psychology and the cultural construction of children's needs' in James, A. and Prout, A. (eds.) (1997) *Constructing and reconstructing childhood: Contemporary issues in the sociological study of childhood*, London: Falmer Press.

Woodhead, M. (2000) 'Subjects, objects or participants? Dilemmas of psychological research with children' in Christensen, P. and James, A. (eds) *Research with children: perspectives and practices*, London: Falmer.

Woodhead, M. (2009) 'Childhood studies past, present and future', in Kehily, M.J. (Ed.) *An introduction to childhood studies* (2nd ed.), Maidenhead: OU Press.

Wyness, M. (2006) Children, young people and civic participation: Regulation and local diversity. UK: *Educational Review*. Vol. 58. No. 2. pp. 209–218.

Wyness, M. (2011) *Childhood and society: an introduction to the sociology of childhood*, Hants: Palgrave Macmillan.

Wyse, D. (2001) 'Felt tip pens and school councils: Children's participation rights in four English schools', *Children and Society*, vol. 15, pp. 209–218.

Zelizer, V.A. (1994) *Pricing the priceless child: The changing social value of children* Princeton: Princeton University Press.

Zelizer, V. A. (2010) 'From child labour to child work: Redefining the economic world of children', in Sternheimer, K. (ed.) *Childhood in American society: A reader*, Boston: Pearson Education Inc.

Index

abandonment of children   12, 13, 16, 18, 76
Aboriginal children   21, 27, 69, 79, 83, 112–3
abortion   12
abuse   21, 41–2, 54, 58, 60, 80, 83, 84, 85, 90, 91, 98, 113
adult–child relationship   11, 29, 36, 45, 47, 50, 54, 64, 108 (*see also* parent-child relationship)
adult control (*see also* parental control)
   children's resistance to   34, 40, 139
   of children   45, 47, 59, 62, 73, 142
   of children's play   136, 139
   of computer use   148
   of disabled children   156
   of time and space   108, 146
adultism (*see* generation)
advertising to children   143, 159, 160–2
   (*see also* child obesity)
   ban of   161
advocacy, definition   5
Africa   4, 17, 63, 92, 125, 138, 140–1, 151, 158–9 (*see also* African Charter on the Rights and Welfare of the Child)
African American children   28, 83
African Charter on the Rights and Welfare of the Child   3, 4, 63–4, 181
agency   4, 5, 14, 31–5, 37, 54, 57, 58, 59, 61, 68–9, 70–2, 81–2, 84, 85, 90, 91, 92, 104, 106–7, 109–21, 118, 127, 130–2, 135, 139, 151, 153–5,

159, 164, 166, 168, 172, 174, 177, 179 (*see also* resistance of children; thin/thick agency)
agricultural work   20, 94, 113, 126–9
AIDS   92–3, 158–9, 167, 172
anti-bullying campaign   72 (*see also* bullying)
Anti-Poverty Legislation, Ontario (2009)   78
Ariès, Phillippe   14–5, 33
assimilation (*see* residential schools)
Attention Deficit Hyperactivity Disorder (ADHD)   4, 162–4 (*see also* Ritalin use)
Australia, children   20, 83, 112–3, 138, 140, 148

Bangladesh, children   130, 132–4, 169, 170
becomings (*see* children as *becomings* and *beings*)
beings (*see* children as *becomings* and *beings*)
biomedicalism   151–2, 156, 163, 164
blank slates (*see* children as blank slates)
Bluebond-Langner, Myra   31, 45, 52–3, 68–9, 153–4, 164–5
Bolivia, children   124, 139–40
boundaries of childhood   5, 15, 17–9, 34, 47–8, 58, 62, 139, 142, 146, 149
British colonies, sending children to   20, 21 (*see also* agricultural work)
British Sociological Association statement of ethical practice   55–6

Made in the USA
Middletown, DE
12 January 2019